If you have a home computer with Internet access you may:
- request an item to be placed on hold.
- renew an item that is not overdue or on hold.
- view titles and due dates checked out on your card.
- view and/or pay your outstanding fines online ($1 & over).

To view your patron record from your home computer click on Patchogue-Medford Library's homepage: **www.pmlib.org**

Plato's Socrates as Narrator

Plato's Socrates as Narrator

A Philosophical Muse

Anne-Marie Schultz

LEXINGTON BOOKS
Lanham • Boulder • New York • Toronto • Plymouth, UK

Published by Lexington Books
A wholly owned subsidiary of The Rowman & Littlefield Publishing Group, Inc.
4501 Forbes Boulevard, Suite 200, Lanham, Maryland 20706
www.rowman.com

10 Thornbury Road, Plymouth PL6 7PP, United Kingdom

Copyright © 2013 by Lexington Books

All rights reserved. No part of this book may be reproduced in any form or by any electronic or mechanical means, including information storage and retrieval systems, without written permission from the publisher, except by a reviewer who may quote passages in a review.

British Library Cataloguing in Publication Information Available

Library of Congress Cataloging-in-Publication Data Available

ISBN 978-0-7391-8330-4 (cloth : alk. paper)
ISBN 978-0-7391-8331-1 (electronic)

∞™ The paper used in this publication meets the minimum requirements of American National Standard for Information Sciences Permanence of Paper for Printed Library Materials, ANSI/NISO Z39.48-1992.

Printed in the United States of America

Contents

Acknowledgments		vii
1	Plato's Socrates as Narrator: A Philosophical Muse	1
2	Listening to Socrates as Narrator of the *Lysis*: Reassessing Friendship, Intellectualism, and Aporetic Endings	17
3	Chastening Charmides	39
4	Performing Philosophy in the *Protagoras*	73
5	Evaluating Eristic in the *Euthydemus*	101
6	Self-Mastery and Harmony in Plato's *Republic*	141
7	Musing on the *Republic*: Its Homeric, Socratic, and Platonic Narratives	167
Conclusion: Composing a Vision of Philosophy from *Plato's Socrates as Narrator*		191
Selected Bibliography		207
Index		219

Acknowledgments

This book has been a long time coming. The twists and turns of life do not always map neatly onto the expected linearity of an academic career. That is a story in its own right, but I will not tell it here. I had the idea that turned into this book slightly over a decade ago. However, the seed of that idea was planted nearly two decades earlier still. My first acknowledgment of gratitude goes to Chuck Salman. He first taught me to love Plato, the philosophical dramatist. Three others at Trinity University (Larry Kimmel, Willis Salomon, and Victoria Aarons) nurtured my philosophical and rhetorical interests and encouraged me to pursue graduate study.

During my graduate years at Penn State, Stanley Rosen and the late David Lachterman cultivated those seeds and deepened my appreciation of Plato in more ways than I can adequately describe. This book and the one to follow bear the marks of their initial guidance through Plato's world. Carl Vaught, who later became my colleague at Baylor for seven years prior to his death, also influenced my thinking in profound ways. I am deeply grateful for the education I received in the Happy Valley and am proud to be a graduate of the Penn State Philosophy Department.

I would also like to thank The College of Arts and Sciences at Baylor University for funding sabbaticals at various stages of this project. I am blessed to have wonderful colleagues in the Philosophy Department and the Honors College who support all the dimensions of my academic work. I am particularly grateful for the mentorship of Bob Baird, Tom Hanks, and Stuart Rosenbaum and the friendship of Lenore and Henry Wright over the years. Special thanks also to the "writing groupies": Heidi Bostic, Steven Pluachek, Amy Antoninka, Lenore Wright, Paul Carron, and Lisa Shaver. Without them, you would not be reading this book today. Thanks also to the many research assistants who helped at various stages along the way: Jessy Jordan,

Lewis Pearson, Paul Carron, and Taryn Whittington. Thanks also to Leslie Ballard for proofreading the final manuscript. Mary Nichols and Rob Miner also deserve thanks for commenting on chapters of this project. Special thanks as well to my chair, Michael Beaty, and the Dean of the Honors College, Tom Hibbs.

The members of the Ancient Philosophy Society, Society of Ancient Greek Philosophy, and Southwestern Philosophical Society have been receptive audiences for many early iterations of these pages. Marina McCoy, Jill Gordon, and Sara Brill have been particularly supportive both personally and professionally for many years. I'm happy to report that you can finally read the whole book!

My parents, Andrea and Michael Frosolono, and sister, Christina Frosolono Sell, have loved me from the very beginning of things. Thanks to Mom for teaching me to read and Dad for teaching me to write. We are, indeed, a family of readers and writers. My brother-in-law, Kelly Sell, provided an inspirational model of staying committed to a goal in the last stages of this endeavor. Finally, to my husband, Jeff Schultz. I dedicate this book to you. Thank you for kindness, patience, love, and love of philosophy, yoga, and travel. I look forward to many happy years together. My golden retriever, Milo, deserves thanks as well just for being the great dog that he is.

Permissions

Earlier formulations of several chapters have been published previously. An overview of this project first appeared as "Know Thyself: Socrates as Storyteller," in *Philosophy in Dialogue Form: Plato's Many Devices,* ed. Gary Scott (Evanston: Northwestern University Press 2007), 82-109. Thank you to Northwestern University Press for permission to republish here. A small part of the *Charmides* chapter appeared as "Socrates and *Sophrosune*: Narrative and Ethics in Plato's *Charmides*," *Listening: A Journal of Philosophy and Religion*, (2007): 13-23. The *Protagoras* chapter is an expanded and refined version of "Socratic Reason and Emotion: Revisiting the Intellectualist Socrates in Plato's *Protagoras*," in *Socrates: Reason or Unreason as the Foundation of European Identity*, ed. Ann Ward (Cambridge: Cambridge Scholars Press, 2007): 1-29. My thanks to Cambridge Scholars Publishing for their permission to republish these works here. A small section of the *Euthydemus* chapter came out as "The Narrative Frame of Plato's *Euthydemus*," *Southwest Philosophy Review* 24 (2009): 163-172. Some of the reflections about narrative irony appear in "Revisiting the Ironic Socrates: *Eironeia* in Socrates' Narrative Commentary," *Southwest Philosophy Review* 29 (2012): 23-32.

Chapter One

Plato's Socrates as Narrator

A Philosophical Muse

As Plato's *Theaetetus* begins, Euclides tells Terpsion about a conversation between Socrates and Theaetetus. Terpsion is eager to hear Euclides' account of the conversation. Euclides is happy to comply. Indeed, he has written down a version of the story for just such an occasion.

> This is the book, Terpsion. You see, I have written it out like this: I have not made Socrates relate the conversation as he related it to me, but I represent him as speaking directly to the persons with whom he said he had this conversation. (These were, he told me, Theodorus the geometer and Theaetetus.) I wanted, in the written version, to avoid the bother of having the bits of narrative in between the speeches—I mean, when Socrates, whenever he mentions his own part in the discussion, says, "And I maintained," or "I said," or, of the person answering, "He agreed" or "He would not admit this." That is why I have made him talk directly to them and have left out these formulae. (143c)

Terpsion applauds Euclides' rhetorical decision: "Well, that's quite in order, Euclides." Euclides turns to his slave and commands him to read the book to them (143c). Given their casual disregard for the value of these narrative comments, it is odd that Plato wrote many of his dramatic dialogues in this very manner.[1] Plato even depicts Socrates as narrating five dialogues in precisely the bothersome way that Euclides describes. How are we to understand this strange occurrence? How might we explain the apparent inconsistency between these remarks in the *Theaetetus* and Plato's own use of narrative in the dialogues? In this book, I analyze the five Platonic dialogues that Socrates narrates: *Lysis*, *Charmides*, *Protagoras*, *Euthydemus*, and *Repub-*

lic.[2] In these five dialogues, Socrates recounts his philosophical efforts to help lead his auditors toward the philosophical life.

In this way, Socrates acts as a philosophical muse. Like the muses who inspire artistic creation, Socrates is a muse who inspires philosophical thinking.[3] It might initially sound odd to think of Socrates in these terms. However, in the *Cratylus*, Socrates speculates that the Muses derived their very name from their "eager desire to investigate and do philosophy" (406a). Like the beautiful-voiced Kalliope herself, Socrates recounts engaging stories of his own philosophical adventures. There are other thematic affinities between Socrates and the Muses. For example, Hesiod describes the Muses as offspring of Zeus and Memory.[4] They are born out of the sustained erotic interactions of Zeus, the symbol of justice, and Memory, the seat of recollection. Socrates' narratives are also erotic offsprings of memory in which he recounts his sustained inquiries into friendship, temperance, virtue, education, and justice.

If there is a sense in which we should properly regard Socrates as a muse, whose muse is he? I have already suggested that he serves as muse to the auditors of his narrated accounts. Surely, Socrates is Plato's muse as well. He inspires Plato to artistic creation of a very particular sort. Plato created the dramatic dialogue, a mode of writing that is philosophical and artistic. By casting Socrates as the narrator of these five dialogues, Plato places his own literary use of Socrates directly in this musical lineage. Like Hesiod, Plato places his own muse, Socrates, at the beginning and often at the end of his songs.[5]

In recent years, many Plato scholars have explored the literary dimensions of the dialogues with great intellectual rigor and enthusiasm.[6] Most contemporary scholarship commonly acknowledges Plato's expertise as both a philosopher and as a dramatic literary stylist.[7] While several scholars have acknowledged the important status of the narrated dialogues, no comprehensive study of Plato's use of narrative techniques currently exists.[8] Unfortunately, Plato's use of narrative, particularly his use of Socrates as a narrator, is often subsumed into discussions about the dramatic nature of the dialogues more generally rather than studied in its own right.[9] This lack of attention to the importance of Socrates' narrative commentary is unfortunate because these carefully crafted narrative remarks add to the richness and profundity of the Platonic texts on many levels.[10] They are fascinating dimensions to consider in their own right as part of Plato's artistic vision. Beyond that, the portrait of Socrates that emerges in these narrated dialogues challenges two dominant understandings: that of Socrates as an intellectualist and that of philosophy as a strictly rational endeavor.[11] To explain briefly, Socrates is frequently associated with an intellectualist viewpoint, which "seems to identify virtue with knowledge and therefore appears to consider the affective side of our nature irrelevant to our virtue, to what counts as a good life."[12] In contrast to this view, I argue that Socrates' role as narrator of the *Lysis, Charmides, Protagoras, Euthydemus,* and *Republic* shows that the standard view of Socrates as an intellectualist is based on an incomplete assessment of Plato's portrait of Socrates.[13] Indeed, Plato's narrative portrait of Socrates reveals that his emotional self-awareness and his ongoing regard for the emotional states of his interlocutors and auditors play a vital role in his philosophical practices. The intellectualist might grant that Socrates is keenly aware of the emotions of his interlocutors—and also of his own—and argue further that one needs to be aware of the emotions so that one will not let them negatively influence philosophical thinking. Under this view, the interplay between emotions and reason would be necessary because of human limitations, even those limitations of the philosopher, but not necessary to philosophizing as such.

I argue against this view. I regard the emotions, both positive and negative emotions, as a necessary component of the practice of philosophy when broadly understood. Although some emotions like fear, anger, or irritation can impede the clear perception of the truth, the pursuit of truth in the deepest sense demands the emotional aspects of our experience as well.[14] The narrative portrait of Socrates' self-awareness does not show him overcoming the emotions full stop, but rather demonstrates how Socrates integrates emotion into his encounters with other people, into his own self-understanding, and into his quest for understanding the nature of the good. Further, Socrates' narrative philosophical practice gives us good reason to regard the practice of philosophy itself as an ongoing interplay between the pursuit of knowledge and application of experience that we gain from both emotion and reason. This interplay brings us into the domain of wisdom, the domain of the beautiful itself which Diotima describes so eloquently at *Symposium* 212b.[15] Finally, I will show that Socrates' descriptions of the highest levels of philosophical activity, in the *Republic* and elsewhere, are laced with emotional language. Socrates' narrative voice functions as eros itself does, as a force that moves the soul toward communion with the Good.

I. NARRATIVE AND THE DRAMATIC STRUCTURE OF PLATO'S DIALOGUES

Scholars commonly acknowledge that structure of the majority of Plato's dialogues fit one of three basic patterns. There are enacted dialogues and two types of reported dialogues. In an enacted dialogue, like the *Gorgias* or the *Laches,* the audience receives the dramatic action directly. There is no mediation of a narrative voice. Plato writes the majority of his dialogues in this manner. Plato also writes two types of reported dialogues. Either Socrates narrates an account of his actions or one of Socrates' followers narrates an account of Socrates' actions.[16] In these dialogues, the narrative audience receives the dramatic action through the narrator's filter.

Simply put, the textually embedded narrator gives the reader additional information to use when interpreting the dialogues. Borrowing Umberto Eco's terminology, Victorino Tejera suggests that the narrative dimensions of the dialogues function as "self-focusing devices" that allow the text itself to guide its own interpretation.[17] I am not suggesting that Socrates' narrative commentary is the only self-focusing device that Plato employs. Indeed, he uses many such devices. First and foremost, he crafts finely drawn characters that interact with each other in ways that illustrate the philosophical themes of the dialogues. Plato interlaces subtle word play, evocative imagery, literary allusion, and poetical references throughout his dialogues. Plato uses irony, humor, and sarcasm as well. Sometimes clarifying of Plato's meaning, sometimes obfuscating it, all of these rhetorical devices focus the reader's attention on the nuances of the dialogues and the philosophical insights contained within them.

Plato's use of narrative itself, particularly his use of Socrates as a narrator, is often subsumed into discussions about the dramatic nature of the dialogues more generally rather than studied as a powerful philosophically orienting tool in its own right. Furthermore, Socrates' narrative commentary functions in a slightly different manner than many of these devices largely due to the self-reflective remarks that Socrates makes as a narrator about his internal states and the internal states of his interlocutors. Regardless of whether Socrates is an entirely trustworthy narrator or not, the presence of these self-reflective narrative remarks gives us a richer and more complex portrait of Socrates than we have in the dialogues without these narrative comments.

Plato's portrait of Socrates' narrative commentary is the focus of my investigation here. In the *Lysis, Charmides, Protagoras, Euthydemus*, and *Republic*, Plato presents Socrates as telling a story about his philosophical activities rather than giving us a direct dramatic account of these activities. In doing so, Plato offers us a dual depiction of Socrates: Socrates the narrator and Socrates as a character in his own narrative. Both Socrates the narrator and Socrates the character are Platonic creations. Although the historical Socrates probably did tell narratives about his own activities, philosophical and otherwise, my analysis focuses on the Platonic portrayal of Socrates as a narrator in these dialogues and not on what the historical Socrates may or may not have said and done.

Though it is not the focus of my investigation, the Platonic portrayal of Socrates as narrator does have some bearing on the broader issue of why Socrates did not write, whereas Plato did. Suppose, for example, that (Plato's) Socrates did not write on the basis of the criticisms of writing he made in the *Phaedrus*—because he wanted to engage his listener in one-on-one conversation that directly addresses the opinions, ways of thinking, feeling, and desires of the interlocutor. It seems that the same criticism of writing would apply to narration, which is a long speech in which the listener remains more or less silent. He is not an *interlocutor*. Similarly, Socrates' distinction in the *Protagoras* between "long speeches" made by sophists like Protagoras and Hippias and short speeches of philosophy raises a similar concern. In both cases, Plato's Socrates objects to speeches in which the audience does not engage in a conversation. One could argue that Socrates' use of narrative is subject to the same critique that he levels against writing and long speech. However, careful attention to Socrates' narrative commentary will illustrate the opposite. Socrates' narrations are attempts to engage his auditor in philosophy. They should lead the auditor to question the matters under discussion. For example, Crito, the auditor of the *Euthydemus*, plays a major role as Socrates' narrative unfolds. He asks Socrates numerous questions at the beginning of the narrative; he interrupts the narrative to ask questions of Socrates at 290e–293b. He even offers his own narrative in response to Socrates' at the end of the dialogue (304d–305c). It may well be that his interactive stance as auditor to Socrates' narration provides a model that all auditors of Socratic narration should emulate.

There are five basic ways in which Socrates' narrative commentary trains the auditor to become more philosophical. To begin, Socrates' narrative commentary is emotionally oriented. We see this emotional orientation in two primary ways: in the insights he provides about his own state of mind and in the observations he makes about other characters. I will explore each of these in turn. First, Socrates frequently gives the auditor insight into his own inner state of mind. For example, he admits to being aroused by Charmides' beauty (*Charmides* 155d), being afraid of Thrasymachus' outbursts (*Republic* 336c), and being captivated by Protagoras' speech (*Protagoras* 328d–e). Although there is certainly an ironic dimension to many of these self-disclosing remarks, we should not discount the importance of his emotional self-disclosure simply because it contains irony. It has an important pedagogical function. By drawing attention to these emotional moments, Socrates draws the auditor into the practice of philosophy itself, a practice that has a strong emotional component. Obviously, the ironic dimensions of these remarks complicate how we interpret them. I have decided to read these remarks in a relatively straightforward manner in the context of each individual dialogue. In the conclusion, I consider how the ironic dimensions of Socrates' self-disclosing commentary function more globally. I consider Socrates' use of irony on this level as a distinct form of Socratic irony, and I discuss what I believe its pervasive presence reveals and conceals about the nature of philosophical practice itself.

Because Socrates the narrator adds important details about his state of mind, which includes his emotional states along with his thought processes, careful attention to Socrates' narrative remarks offers us a complex portrait of how a philosopher engages in the reflective life. To explain further, in an enacted dialogue like the *Gorgias* or the *Euthyphro*, the audience only sees Socrates as a character in the dialogue. Therefore, the dialogic audience primarily observes Socrates in action. We must infer his inner states from his words and his deeds. This inference may be easy to accomplish in some instances. For example, Socrates' words and actions throughout the *Euthyphro* demonstrate that he believes Euthyphro lacks an adequate understanding of piety. At other times, however, Socrates' motives are more opaque. For example, there is little textual evidence in the opening of the *Gorgias* to explain why he allows Chaerephon to detain both of them in the agora so that they arrive late to the feast of speeches (447a). Nor do the dramatic details of the *Philebus* provide much insight into why Socrates seems so eager to leave the conversation (67b). While these enacted dialogues contain many dramatic clues that help the audience interpret Socrates' motivations and actions, when Socrates the narrator reflects on these situations, the audience's perception of Socrates' internal thoughts and motivations greatly increases.

In addition to these self-disclosing comments, we also see the emotional orientation of Socrates' narrative in its emphasis on character development. Socrates includes many details about the personalities, social interactions, and psychological motivations of central characters in his narrative commentary. For example, Socrates describes the effect of Charmides' entrance into the Palaestra (154b–d), Protagoras' desire to show off in front of the crowd (317b), and how Lysis' shyness initially prevents him from joining Socrates and Ctesippus in conversation (206e–207b). By consistently providing this information in his narrative remarks, Socrates incorporates the emotional dimensions of human experience into his practice of philosophy. In doing so, he provides a self-portrait that counters the prevailing model of the intellectualist Socrates.

In my analysis of the *Republic*, I locate two modes of virtue cultivation at work in the text of Plato's *Republic*: the self-mastery model and the harmony model. Simply put, the self-mastery model of virtue requires that the rational part of the soul (the *logistikon*) rule over the appetites and emotions (the *epithumetikon*) with the help of the spirited part of the soul (the *thumetikon*). In this model, the appetites and emotions, associated with the *epithumetikon*, hinder our ability to be virtuous. The *logistikon* must, therefore, master these strong and largely negative forces and work to diminish their influence in our lives as much as possible. The *thumetikon* aids the *logistikon* in this regulative task, serving as its ally in mastering the *epithumetikon* (441e). The self-mastery model prioritizes reason as the means by which we become good and dismisses the role of the other parts of the soul in the process of becoming good. Indeed, under this view the appetites present distracting and, at times, even dangerous obstacles that we must overcome in our pursuit of justice in the soul.

Alongside the self-mastery model, Socrates also employs images of harmony to describe the nature of justice in the city and the soul. Early in the *Republic*, Socrates refutes Thrasymachus' view that justice is nothing other than the interest of the stronger. He remarks that justice produces "unanimity and friendship" amongst people (351d). In a just city, people live in harmony with each other. One faction of the population does not rule over another faction. Another instance of the harmony model on the level of the city occurs after Socrates presents the image of the sun, the line, and the cave. Socrates explains how they will ensure the establishment of justice in the city by "compelling" those with the best natures to rule (519d). Glaucon objects: "Are we to do them an injustice, and make them live a worse life when a better is possible for them?" (519e). Socrates employs a harmony metaphor to placate Glaucon's concern. They are not concerned with a particular person or class of people doing well, but "the city as a whole, harmoniously uniting citizens by persuasion and necessity, causing them to share with each other the benefit each is capable of providing to the community at large" (520a). A just city functions according to the principles of harmonious engagement with the other, not the principles of mastery of one over another.

The harmony model allows all the parts of the soul to work together to produce justice. Socrates describes justice "with respect to what is within, with respect to what truly concerns him and his own," in precisely these terms (443d). Socrates explains, "he doesn't let each part in him mind other people's business or the three classes in the soul meddle with each other, but really sets his own house in good order and rules himself. He arranges himself, becomes his own friend, and harmonizes the three parts, exactly like three notes in a harmonic scale, lowest, highest and middle" (443d). In contrast to the self-mastery model that prioritizes the rule of the *logistikon* and thereby diminishes the register of the other parts of the soul, the harmony model allows the *epithumetikon* to have a voice in the creation of justices in the soul. It is a necessary note on the harmonic scale of internal justice (443d).

To a certain extent, one can see both these models at work in the positive and negative presentation of the emotions in each of the narrated dialogues. However, I have chosen not to superimpose a conceptual framework found primarily in the *Republic* on the other dialogues. My hope is to follow the narrative commentary of each dialogue and thereby allow each dialogue to sing in its own register. For similar reasons, I refrain from making general statements about the Socratic narrative practice of philosophy until the conclusion, where I draw out the consistent themes that arise in these five narrative portraits of Socrates.

Second, the narrative commentary trains the auditor to become philosophical by drawing attention to important themes in the dialogue. For example, the narrative description of Polemarchus' slave stopping Socrates and Glaucon on their way back to Athens (327c) points to the difference between force and persuasion as modes of human engagement.[18] By underscoring these themes at the beginning of the narrative, Socrates trains the auditor to attend to the ongoing interplay between force and persuasion throughout the dialogue. The auditor learns what to listen and look for as the dialogue progresses by attending to these narrative descriptions along with the other dramatic details of the dialogue.[19]

Third, Socrates' narrative commentary trains the auditor to become philosophical by drawing attention to important dramatic moments in the dialogue. These dramatic moments often coincide with important philosophical arguments and concepts. For example, Socrates describes Thrasymachus' blush to the unnamed auditor of the *Republic*. Socrates' reference to Thrasymachus' blush dramatically symbolizes the fact that Socrates has defeated him in argument (350e). Similarly, Socrates' narrative reference to Polemarchus and Adeimantus' whispered conversation precedes the introduction of the three waves. By calling the auditor's attention to this dramatic moment, Socrates simultaneously focuses the auditor's attention on three important philosophical concepts: the sharing of women and children, the education of women along with men as guardians, and the necessity of the philosopher kings (449a).

Fourth, these narrative markers cause the auditor and, by extension, the reader to enter into a process of ongoing reflection. To explain, Socrates often gives the auditor new information that causes him to reassess what he has just heard. Consider an example from the *Republic*. When Socrates remarks, "even in the middle of our conversation Thrasymachus had repeatedly tried to take control of the discussion, but each time he had been prevented by those sitting around us, who wanted to hear the discussion through to the end" (336b), the auditor must reassess the conversation about justice with the awareness that Thrasymachus had been trying to interrupt throughout the preceding discussion. All of a sudden, he realizes that the discussion might not have proceeded as smoothly as Socrates originally led him to believe. As readers of the dialogue, we must do so as well. When we go back and add new information to the story, we recognize that our previous assumptions about what had transpired are inadequate. We must reassess what we have learned in light of new information. In this way, the narrator's comments train both the auditor and the reader in the process of reflective thinking.

This self-reflective practice prepares the auditor for the highest levels of philosophical thinking. Socrates models this self-reflective practice throughout his narrative remarks. For example, after Socrates recounts the discussion of the desired qualities of the guardian class, that they be both "gentle and full of spirit" (375c), his narrative commentary draws the auditor's attention to this incongruity in the guardian nature. Socrates admits his own dissatisfaction: "I didn't know what to say then. I thought over what we had said, and then tried again" (375d). Socrates' narrative description of his own aporia provides a model of reasoning that the auditor should follow. Like Socrates, the auditor should be willing to reassess the relative value of natural disposition and education in forming the guardian nature. The auditor should recognize that no firm conclusions about the matter can be drawn from the way in which Socrates and his interlocutors have approached the argument.

Finally, the fact that Socrates' narrative commentary typically falls away as each of the narrated dialogues progress offers another invitation for the auditor to become reflective about the narrative he hears from Socrates.[20] As the explicit narrative commentary fades, the auditor has a chance to become more responsible as auditor. What exactly do I mean by this claim? How does this transfer of responsibility work? I suggest that the auditor must take over much of the mediating work that Socrates did as a narrator for him. With this heightened level of interpretive responsibility, the auditor stands positioned to evaluate the information Socrates conveys but also to evaluate Socrates' own role as narrator. In my view, Socrates' narrative commentary has benefits and limitations. It helps the auditor recognize important aspects of the story as it unfolds. However, the rhetorical decisions that Socrates makes about how to tell the story shape the auditor's understanding, much like the shadows on the wall shape the cave dwellers' understanding of reality. However, Socrates is a different sort of image holder. He encourages the auditor to interpret these narrated images. When Socrates stops offering explicit commentary to guide the auditor's understanding, then the auditor must take over this role. With respect to his own role as audience of Socrates' narrative, the auditor must transcend the role of passive listener and start asking questions of the narrative and the narrator. Crito exhibits this capacity to some degree in the *Euthydemus* when he interrupts the narrative (290e–293b) and when he offers his own narrative at the end (304d–305c). In this way, he starts to interpret Socrates' shadows for himself. He starts to loosen his own chains. Like the prisoner in the cave who turns around and sees the light, the auditor begins his own philosophical journey out of the cave. Eventually, the auditor must journey up the philosophical mountain, without the help of Socrates' narrative mediation, which has provided so many footholds to help the auditor along the "rough steep upward way" (515e). As readers of Plato's dialogues, we must do the same.

II. OVERVIEW OF *PLATO'S SOCRATES AS NARRATOR*

In this book, I analyze Socrates' narrative commentary in the *Lysis*, *Charmides*, *Protagoras*, *Euthydemus*, and *Republic*. I describe each dialogue's narrative structure; its narrative setting; Socrates' narrative tone, presence, and persona; and his relationship with his auditor to the extent possible given the details of the text. I then show how Socrates' narrative commentary focuses the auditor's attention on central characters, crucial dramatic moments in the dialogue, and important philosophical themes. New insights about each dialogue emerge when we include these narrative remarks in our overall interpretation of each of these dialogues. More broadly, Socrates' narrative commentary calls us to expand our vision of the practice of philosophy itself. I have chosen to proceed by analyzing each dialogue in its own terms rather than thematically because I believe we will be in a better position to understand the whole of Socrates' narrative practice of philosophy once we understand each of its parts. Socrates interacts with different interlocutors in different ways, tailoring his comments, commentary and speech to their specific needs. We see the specificity of Socrates' narrative approach by examining each dialogue on its own terms. Also, I believe this single dialogue approach will be more helpful to scholars and students who typically focus on one dialogue at a time. Each chapter stands as an independent unit. Taken together, they offer a synoptic view of Socrates' narrative practice of philosophy.

In chapter 2, I show how the narrative aspects of the *Lysis* enhance our philosophical interpretation of the dialogue particularly with respect to our understanding of friendship and the aporetic ending of the dialogue. First, I briefly describe the narrative structure and setting of the *Lysis*. I then show that Socrates' narrative commentary focuses on central characters in the drama. By calling our attention to these characters and their various emotional and intellectual responses to each other, Socrates' narrative commentary underscores the importance of personal autonomy in friendship and in philosophical community. Second, I demonstrate how Socrates' narrative remarks emphasize his mental states, his emotional states, and his responses to his emotions. These self-reflective remarks offer an initial indication of how Socrates' practice of philosophy incorporates the emotional as well as the intellectual dimensions of human experience. Finally, I address how this narrative analysis enhances our ability to see the aporetic nature of the dialogue in positive terms.

In chapter 3, I explore the narrative dimensions of the *Charmides* with an eye toward understanding the complex relationship between philosophy and tyranny. First, I describe the narrative setting and structure of the *Charmides*. Second, I show that Socrates presents the auditor with three models of intemperance: Chaerephon, Charmides, and Critias. Third, I examine how Socrates' *sophrosune* emerges in his narrative remarks that emphasize his emotional states, his response to his emotions, and his awareness of the emotional states of others. This narrative model differs from the dominant account of Socrates that regards him as a thoroughgoing rationalist. Socrates does not simply describe his *sophrosune* as a virtue of reasoned self-control that helps him overcome his desire for Charmides. Rather, Socrates models *sophrosune* as a way of life that involves ongoing self-examination and sustained philosophical inquiry within a communal context. Socrates' relationship with his auditor illustrates this ongoing philosophical community. This narrative analysis promotes an understanding of *sophrosune* that emphasizes social relationships and political obligations, not just the mastery of an individual's desires. Finally, I consider how this narrative portrait of Socrates illustrates the philosopher's capacity to overcome both personal and political tyranny.

In chapter 4, I focus on the narrative structure and setting of the *Protagoras* to show how Socrates' character-driven narrative highlights several fundamental differences between sophistic modes of discourse and Socrates' philosophical practices. I discuss how Socrates' narrative remarks focus on his philosophical practices to a greater degree than in the preceding two dialogues. In these narrative remarks, Socrates draws upon both the emotional and intellectual dimensions of his experience and the experience of his interlocutors and integrates them into his philosophical inquiry. I end this chapter with a reconsideration of Socratic intellectualism in light of the narrative structure of the *Protagoras* and suggest that it depends on a radically impoverished understanding of Socratic philosophical practice.

In chapter 5, I analyze the *Euthydemus* to illustrate the overall effectiveness of Socrates' narrative pedagogical practices. The intricate structure of the *Euthydemus* crystallizes what is apparent in all of the narrated dialogues. Plato presents us with two models of Socrates' pedagogy: the model of Socrates in the temporality of the dramatic events and the model of Socrates as a narrator. On the dramatic level, Socrates often appears combative and adversarial. On the narrative level, he engages in a gentler mode of philosophical provocation, one more suited to his personal relationship with his auditor. I analyze Socrates' dramatic exchanges with Crito to illustrate the personal focus of Socrates' narrative pedagogy. Then, I show how Socrates' narrative commentary underscores the ongoing contrast between eristic and dialectic modes of inquiry. We see the eristic mode when the two foreign sophists (Euthydemus and Dionysodorus) engage two young Athenian boys (Clinias and Ctesippus) in debate. We see the dialectical mode in Socrates' own engagement with the boys. Invariably, Socrates' narrative commentary draws our attention to these different modes of engagement. It highlights the negative effects that the combative mode of sophistic debate has on Clinias and Ctesippus. Socrates' own exchanges with Crito more closely resemble the dialectical mode of engagement he employs with Clinias and Ctesippus.

In the third section, I analyze the final exchange between Socrates and Crito to evaluate the effectiveness of Socrates' narrative pedagogy. In the fourth section, I discuss how Socrates' narrative remarks reveal his inner states of mind. Socrates' self-disclosing remarks, particularly his willingness to present himself as a vanquished victim of the sophists, add additional nuance to the holistic portrait of Socrates that emerges in these narrated dialogues because they show his emotional and philosophical vulnerability. I end this chapter with a brief discussion of the presence of irony in Socrates' narrative descriptions of the brothers. I suggest how Socrates' narrative description of the brothers functions as an additional philosophical provocation for Crito. Generally speaking, Socrates' ironic remarks about the characters in the other narrated dialogues serve this purpose as well.

In chapter 6, I turn to Plato's masterpiece, the *Republic*. I divide my treatment of this dialogue into two chapters. The dialogue is significantly longer than the preceding ones and narrative itself is an important theme in the dramatic action of the dialogue as well as in the narrative frame. I begin by discussing two models of virtue cultivation at work in the dialogue: the self-mastery model and the harmony model. To explain briefly, Socrates regularly offers insights into his own state of mind and provides descriptions of the emotions and motivations of the interlocutors he encounters. Many of these descriptions reinforce the negative view of the emotions often associated with Socratic intellectualism. Socrates' remarks, on the dramatic level, often suggest that he regards self-mastery as the primary means by which humans become virtuous. However, the numerous references to harmony that occur throughout the dialogue and Socrates' narrative self-descriptions point to another way in which we might understand the cultivation of virtue, one that allows for a more nuanced understanding of the role of the emotions in our moral lives. I refer to this alternative mode of virtue cultivation as the harmony model. The harmony model, which Socrates alludes to throughout the *Republic* and that he exemplifies in his narrative commentary, provides a more integrated means of understanding the cultivation of virtue in the soul. The harmony model of justice reinforces the image that I employ in the subtitle of this work, Socrates as philosophical muse.[21]

To elucidate this claim, I describe the self-mastery model in detail and outline some of its practical and conceptual limitations. I then explore the many references that Socrates makes to justice as harmony throughout the *Republic*. In the second section, I analyze Socrates' narrative commentary in Books I, II, and V. Socrates' narrative commentary, along with the dramatic action of the dialogue, draws attention to how Cephalus, Polemarchus, Thrasymachus, Glaucon, and Adeimantus each attempt to achieve self-mastery and how they fail to do so to varying degrees. As a result, each of these characters illustrates at least one practical limitation of the self-mastery model.

In chapter 7, I take up Socrates' critique of Homeric narratives. I consider the criticisms that Socrates offers of the content of Homeric poetry and his critique of its style. Socrates' sustained interactions with Glaucon and Adeimantus throughout this section illustrate the philosophical limitations of these foundational narratives that shaped the warp and woof of Athenian culture. In the second section, I consider Socrates' narrative self-descriptions. Socrates' narrative self-description presents his philosophical practice as more in keeping with the harmony model than the self-mastery model. These narrative comments reveal how Socrates incorporates emotion into his philosophical practice: (1) He discloses his own emotional states to the auditor; (2) He describes his willingness to adapt his philosophic practice to the emotions and desires of his interlocutors; (3) He describes his experience of *aporia* and his willingness to reassess various arguments in emotional terms.

Finally, I consider two central narratives that Socrates tells as a character within his own narrative: the Allegory of the Cave and the Myth of Er. These narratives, along with the self-reflective dimensions of Socrates' narrative commentary, provide another philosophical corrective to Homeric discourse. Socrates improves upon the Homeric narratives that he criticizes. Socrates uses narrative to cultivate critical awareness and self-reflection in his interlocutors. This pedagogical dimension of Socratic narrative helps make sense of Plato's seemingly incongruous rhetorical decision to cast Socrates as a narrator of the *Republic*. He offers us a new philosophical hero, Socrates the narrator, as a corrective to the Homeric heroes and the narratives told about them.[22]

In conclusion, I explore three broader dimensions of this extended narrative analysis. First, I consider the vexing problem of Socratic irony. Irony pervades Socrates' narrative commentary. The presence of irony in these remarks raises questions about his trustworthiness as a reliable narrator about his own experience. Socrates may well be like Hesiod's own muses who "know how to say many false things that seem like true sayings" (27). Here, I analyze the irony in his self-disclosing remarks. Socrates' narrative irony with respect to what he says about other characters, particularly the sophists and their students, seems explicitly adversarial. He uses biting sarcasm and makes numerous hyperbolic remarks about the putative value of sophistic *technai*. I address this aspect of his use of irony in the context of the *Euthydemus* chapter. By contrast, in his self-disclosing remarks, Socrates resembles an Aristotelian *eiron*, someone who presents a façade of excessive modesty. This portrait of Socrates as *eiron* suggests that Plato prefigures Aristotle in recognizing a positive value for the role of the *eiron*. I explore what irony can teach us about the nature of philosophical inquiry itself. I then turn to a consideration of narrative as a productive mode of self-care. Finally, I offer some metaphysical speculations about the narrative relationship between soul and the formal structure of reality that emerge when we take into account the precise ways in which Socrates, Plato's philosophical muse, leads us to the Good.

NOTES

1. On the abandonment of the narrative frame in Plato's "later" works, see Deborah Nails, *Agora, Academy and the Conduct of Philosophy* (Dordrecht: Kluwer, 1995); Harold Tarrant, "Orality and Plato's Narrative Dialogues," in *Voice into Text*, ed. Ian Worthington (Leiden: Brill, 1996), 129–147; Holger Thesleff, "Plato and His Public," in *Noctes Atticae*, eds. B. Amden (Copenhagen: Museum Tusculanum Press, 2002), 289–301; Ruby Blondell, *The Play of Character in Plato's Dialogues* (Cambridge: Cambridge University Press, 2002); and Holger Thesleff, "A Symptomatic Text Corruption: Plato, *Gorgias* 448a5," *Arctos* 38 (2003): 256.

2. Thesleff argues that the *Gorgias* was originally constructed as a dialogue narrated by Socrates and suggests that there may have been an earlier narrated version of the *Theaetetus* and a narrated version of the *Phaedrus*. See "Platonic Chronology," *Phronesis* 34 (1989): 1–26. Socrates also narrated two dialogues of contested authenticity, *The Lovers* and *The Eryxias*.

3. Hesiod attests to nine muses (60–100). Later, each comes to be associated with a particular domain of the creative arts. For an excellent account of the numerous references to the Muses in classical literature, see http://www.theoi.com/Ouranios/Mousai.html (accessed September 23, 2012).

4. Hesiod, *Theogony*, trans. Richmond Lattimore (Ann Arbor: University of Michigan Press, 1988), 50–65.

5. Hesiod, *Theogony*, 34.

6. On dramatic interpretation, see Leo Strauss, *City and Man* (Chicago: Rand McNally, 1964); Jacob Klein, A *Commentary on Plato's* Meno (Chapel Hill: University of North Carolina Press, 1965); Stanley Rosen, *Plato's* Symposium (New Haven: Yale University Press, 1968); Paul Friedländer, *Plato*, trans. Hans Meyerhoff, vol. I–III (Princeton: Princeton University Press, 1964–69); Mitchell Miller, *The Philosopher in Plato's* Statesman (The Hague: Nijhoff, 1980); Charles Griswold, *Self-Knowledge in Plato's* Phaedrus (New Haven: Yale University Press, 1986); James Arieti, *Interpreting the Dialogues: The Dialogues as Drama* (Savage: Rowman and Littlefield, 1991); Gerald Press, ed., *Plato's Dialogues: New Studies and Interpretations* (Lanham: Rowman and Littlefield, 1993); Drew Hyland, *Finitude and Transcendence in the Platonic Dialogues* (Albany: SUNY, 1995); Richard Rutherford, *The Art of Plato: Ten Essays in Platonic Interpretation* (Cambridge: Cambridge University Press, 1995); Kenneth Sayre, *Plato's Literary Garden: How to Read a Platonic Dialogue* (South Bend: Notre Dame Press, 1995); Charles Kahn, *Plato and the Socratic Dialogue: The Philosophical Use of a Literary Form* (Cambridge: Cambridge University Press 1996); Richard Hart and Victorino Tejera, eds., *Plato's Dialogues: The Dialogical Approach* (Lewiston: Mellen Press, 1997); Diskin Clay, *Platonic Questions: Dialogues with the Silent Philosopher* (University Park: Penn State Press, 2000); Christopher Rowe, *Plato and the Art of Philosophical Writing* (Cambridge: Cambridge University Press, 2007); Gerald Press, *Plato: A Guide for the Perplexed* (New York: Continuum, 2007).

7. For a relatively current overview of the state of affairs in Plato scholarship, see Julia Annas and Christopher Rowe, *New Perspectives on Plato, Modern and Ancient* (Washington, D.C.: Center for Hellenic Studies, 2002). For other helpful assessments, see Gerald Press, "The State of the Question in the Study of Plato," *Southern Journal of Philosophy* 34 (1996): 507–32; Francisco Gonzalez, "A Short History of Platonic Interpretation and the 'Third Way,'" in *The Third Way: New Directions in Platonic Studies*, ed. Francisco Gonzalez (Lanham: Rowman and Littlefield, 1995), 1–22; and Ruby Blondell, *The Play of Character in Plato's Dialogues* (Cambridge: Cambridge University Press, 2002), 1–52.

8. See Dorothy Tarrant, "Plato as Dramatist," *The Journal of Hellenic Studies* 75 (1955): 82–89; Harold Tarrant "Chronology and Narrative Apparatus in Plato's Dialogues," *Electronic Antiquity* I, 8 (1994); H. Thayer, "Plato's Style: Temporal, Dramatic and Semantic Levels in the Dialogues," in *Plato's Dialogues — The Dialogical Approach*, ed. Richard Hart and Victo-

rino Tejera (Lewiston: The Edwin Mellen Press, 1997), 85–129; Thomas Szlezák, *Reading Plato* (New York: Routledge, 1999); Leo Strauss, *On Plato's* Symposium, ed. Seth Benardete (Chicago: University of Chicago Press, 2001); Charles Griswold, "Irony in the Platonic Dialogues," *Philosophy and Literature* 26 (2002): 84–106.

9. For an initial formulation of this task, see my essay, "Know Thyself: Socrates as Storyteller," in *Philosophy in Dialogue Form: Plato's Many Devices*, ed. Gary Scott (Evanston: Northwestern University Press, 2007), 82–109. Catherine Zuckert devotes a section of her recent book, *Plato's Philosophers*, to the narrated dialogues. She includes *The Lovers*, often regarded as spurious, along with the five that I consider in this book. Though she offers several insightful observations about the information we glean from Socrates' narrative remarks, they are not the overall focus of her wide-ranging investigation of the portrait of philosophy in the dialogues. Laurence Lampert also devotes a good deal of attention to the narrative frames of the *Protagoras, Charmides*, and *Republic* in his recent book *How Philosophy Became Socratic* (Chicago: University of Chicago Press, 2010). However, the narrative frames themselves are not the main focus of his compelling work.

10. Several scholars have explored the importance of narrative with respect to individual dialogues. See Kenneth Dorter, *Plato's* Phaedo: *An Interpretation* (Toronto: University of Toronto Press, 1982); Patrick Coby, *Socrates and the Sophistic Enlightenment. A Commentary on Plato's* Protagoras (Lewisburg: Bucknell University Press, 1987); Mitchell Miller, *Plato's* Parmenides: *The Conversion of the Soul* (University Park: The Pennsylvania State University Press, 1991). On the *Symposium*, see David Halperin, "Plato and the Erotics of Narrativity," in *Oxford Studies in Ancient Philosophy: Methods of Interpreting Plato and His Dialogues*, ed. Julia Annas, J. C. Klagge, and Nicholas D. Smith (Oxford: Clarendon Press, 1992), 93–129; Alan Bloom, *Love and Friendship* (New York: Simon and Schuster, 1993); Alfred Geier, *Plato's Erotic Thought: The Tree of the Unknown* (Rochester: University of Rochester Press, 2002); and Theodor Ebert, "The Role of the Frame Dialogue in Plato's *Protagoras*," in *Plato's* Protagoras, *Proceedings of the Third Symposium Platonicum Pragense*, eds. Ales Havlicek and Filip Karfik (Prague: OIKOYMENH, 2003), 9–20.

11. Certainly, it is possible to argue for a robust sense of reason that addresses many of the limitations of an intellectualist understanding of virtue. Jill Gordon's *Turning Toward Philosophy* (University Park: Penn State University Press, 1999) is a good example. My work on the narrative contributes to a more comprehensive view of reason.

12. This articulation comes from Alexander Nehamas, who does not share the view he is articulating. See his "What Did Socrates Teach and to Whom Did He Teach It?" *Review of Metaphysics* 46 (1992): 280. For two prominent scholars who hold this view, see Martha Nussbaum, *Fragility of Goodness: Luck and Ethics in Greek Tragedy and Philosophy* (Cambridge: Harvard University Press, 1986); *Cultivating Humanity* (Cambridge: Harvard University Press, 1997); T. Irwin, *Plato's Moral Theory* (Oxford: Oxford University Press, 1977); *Plato's Ethics* (Oxford: Oxford University Press, 1995). For a compelling critique of the basic assumptions that lead to the construction of Socratic intellectualism, see Rosyln Weiss, *The Socratic Paradox and Its Enemies* (Chicago: University of Chicago Press, 2006). This intellectualist reading can be traced back to the influence of Nietzsche's portrait of Socrates on contemporary philosophical discourse and even further back to Aristotle himself.

13. See my essay, "Socratic Reason and Emotion: Revisiting the Intellectualist Socrates in Plato's *Protagoras*," in *Socrates: Reason or Unreason as the Foundation of European Identity*, ed. Ann Ward (Cambridge: Cambridge Scholars Press, 2007): 1–29.

14. I am not developing a typology of emotions with respect to which are harmful and which are helpful to philosophy. Since I am working with the narrative characterization of the emotions in these Platonic five dialogues, I do not wish to superimpose another framework for understanding the emotions. For those seeking a straightforward account of the role of emotions in philosophical experience, and moral psychology in particular, I refer them to Robert Roberts, *Emotions. An Essay in Aid of Moral Psychology* (Cambridge: Cambridge University Press, 2003).

15. "Only then will it become possible for him to give birth not to images of virtue (because he's in touch with no images), but to true virtue (because he is in touch with the true Beauty).

The love of the gods belongs to anyone who has given birth to true virtue and nourished it, and if any human being could become immortal it would be he?" Plato, *Symposium*, 212b.

16. Thesleff notes that the dialogues narrated by Socrates also fall into two types, "Socrates in the house of Kallias and Socrates in Lykeion" (1982, 120). Diogenes Laertius recognized the distinction between dramatic and narrative dialogues, but remarks, "these terms seem better suited to the stage than to philosophy." *Lives of Eminent Philosophers* I–II, trans. R. D. Hicks (Cambridge: Harvard University Press, 1979–80), 321.

17. "Plato's dialogues do contain overt or covert hints, self-focusing devices as U. Eco calls them, about how the reader or interlocutor is to take what will be said. Such hints, if they are to be reliable pointers to the design of the work, must be internal (endogenic) to it." *Rewriting the History of Ancient Greek Philosophy* (Westport: Greenwood Press, 1997), 96. In *Plato's Dialogues One by One,* Tejera remarks, "The self-focusing device is the nearest any dialogue of Plato's comes to giving a stage-direction-or, rather, it is a stage-direction but not extra dialogical, not one that violates the compositional integrity of the dialogue as such." (Lanham: University of America Press, 1999), 111. Charles Segal notes that the prologues of Greek tragedies function in similar ways. "Tragic Beginnings: Narration, Voice, and Authority in the Prologues of Greek Drama," *Yale Classical Studies* 29 (1992): 85–110. See also Harvey Yunis, "Writing for Reading. Thucydides, Plato, and the Emergence of the Critical Reader," in *Written Texts and the Rise of Literate Culture in Ancient Greece*, ed. Harvey Yunis (Cambridge: Cambridge University Press, 2003), 189–212.

18. Lewis Pearson's recent dissertation, *Force and Persuasion in Plato's* Republic (doctoral dissertation, Baylor University, 2009), explores the significance of these numerous references.

19. Gary Scott calls them "narrative precautions." See *Plato's Socrates as Educator* (Albany: SUNY Press, 2000), 193, n6. Another author calls them a "hermeneutic key" that helps unlock the philosophical meaning of the dialogue. Szelzák, *Reading Plato*, 28–29.

20. The *Euthydemus* is the only dialogue narrated by Socrates in which there is an extended return to the temporality of the narrative frame at the end of the dialogue.

21. From the earliest accounts of the Muses, they were strongly associated with music and song. One can see this affinity in the name of the earliest muse worshipped in Greece: Aoide. Aoide's very name means, "to sing." Apollo's ongoing association with the Muses further instantiates these thematic affinities between the Muses and philosophy.

22. On Plato's casting of Socrates as a new Homer, see L. Lampert, *How Philosophy Became Socratic* (Chicago: Chicago University Press, 2010); J. Howland, *The* Republic: *The* Odyssey *of Philosophy* (Philadelphia: Paul Dry Books, 2004); T. Gould, *The Ancient Quarrel between Poetry and Philosophy* (Princeton: Princeton University Press, 1990); R. Klonoski, "The Preservation of Homeric Tradition: Heroic Re-Performance in the *Republic* and the *Odyssey*," *CLIO* 22 (1993): 251–271; R. C. Madhu, "Plato's Homer," *Ancient Philosophy* 19 (1999): 87–95; Bruce Rosenstock, "Rereading the *Republic*," *Arethusa* 16 (1983): 219–46; C. Segal, "The Myth Was Saved," *Hermes* 106 (1978): 315–337; G. R. R. Ferrari, *City and Soul in Plato's* Republic (Chicago: University of Chicago Press, 1999); D. O'Connor, "Rewriting the Poets in Plato's Characters," in *Cambridge Companion to Plato's* Republic, ed. G. R. F. Ferrari (Cambridge: Cambridge University Press, 2007), 55–89; Eva Brann, *The Music of the* Republic (Philadelphia, Paul Dry Books, 2004).

Chapter Two

Listening to Socrates as Narrator of the *Lysis*

Reassessing Friendship, Intellectualism, and Aporetic Endings

In this chapter, I analyze how the narrative aspects of the *Lysis* enhance our philosophical interpretation of the dialogue and point to a reconsideration of the nature of friendship itself.[1] The chapter divides into three parts. First, I briefly describe the narrative structure and setting of the *Lysis*. I then show that Socrates' narrative commentary draws attention to Hippothales, Ctesippus, Lysis, and Menexenus. By describing the emotions, psychological motivations, and behaviors of his main interlocutors, Socrates highlights the differences between their active and passive modes of social engagement. These different modes of social engagement illustrate their capacity for genuine friendship and for philosophical inquiry. Second, I demonstrate how Socrates' narrative remarks highlight his mental states, his emotional states, and his responses to his emotions. These self-reflective remarks offer a preliminary indication of how Socrates' practice of philosophy incorporates the emotional as well as the intellectual dimensions of human experience. This narrative portrait of Socrates presents an initial challenge to the common view of Socrates as an intellectualist. Finally, I address how the narrative relationship between Socrates and his auditor allows us to interpret the aporetic conclusion of the dialogue in positive terms.[2]

I. EXAMINING SOCRATES' NARRATIVE COMMENTARY

A. The Narrative Structure of the *Lysis*

The *Lysis* begins with Socrates speaking at an unknown place and an unknown time. He tells the unnamed auditor,

> I was on my way from the Academy straight to the Lyceum, along the road outside the wall and close under the wall itself. When I got to the little gate by the spring of the Panops, I happened to meet there Hippothales, son of Hieronymus, Ctesippus of Paeania, and with them some other youths, standing together as a group. (203e)[3]

Scholars set the dramatic date of this dialogue at 409 B.C.E.[4] Based on the model of the other narrative dialogues, Socrates probably retells the story soon after the dramatic events took place.[5] However, we do not know with complete certainty where, when, to whom, or under what circumstances Socrates narrates this account. Socrates' auditor listens passively as the narrative unfolds. Socrates narrates the dialogue in a straightforward manner.[6] He does not interrupt the story with any direct questions to his auditor nor does he qualify his ability to remember the events he narrates. His narrative commentary occurs consistently throughout the dialogue.[7] As the *Lysis* ends, it appears that Socrates will conclude his narrative by returning from the timeframe of the dramatic events into the timeframe of the narrative retelling. However, after Socrates explains to the auditor that "in our opinion they had been drinking quite a bit at the Hermaea, so there seemed to be no way to approach them—we were therefore defeated by them, and we broke up our group," he returns to the timeline of the dramatic events (223a). This lack of temporal symmetry draws the auditor into Socrates' aporia about the nature of friendship. To explain, the dialogue ends with Socrates' lament to Lysis and Menexenus; "he who is a friend is we have not yet been able to discover" (223a–b). Because Socrates offers no other concluding remarks to the auditor, the auditor is forced to experience Socrates' aporia about the nature of friendship on the dramatic level more directly. If Socrates had ended his narrative with a description of his aporia that was directed to the auditor himself, the remarks would return the auditor safely back to the temporality of the narrated present. Instead, he remains in the confusion of the aporia that Socrates and the boys are experiencing on the dramatic level. In the last section of this chapter, I explore how the narrative frame allows us to interpret the aporetic ending of the dialogue in philosophically productive terms.

B. Narrating the Social Scene: Hippothales, Ctesippus, Lysis, and Menexenus

Socrates mentions Hippothales and Ctesippus by name early in his narrative (203a). Hippothales and Ctesippus present us with two models of social engagement. Hippothales tends to remain passive in social situations. This aspect of Hippothales' character, along with his extreme emotionality, hinders his ability to achieve the autonomy necessary to function as a genuine friend to his beloved, Lysis. More broadly, it hinders his development as a citizen and as a philosopher. Ctesippus, by contrast, plays an active role in the social dynamics as they unfold. He also recognizes the dangers in Hippothales' excessive emotionality. As a result, he presents a more positive model of the qualities necessary for friendship, citizenship, and philosophy. While Ctesippus does not fully demonstrate these capacities in the course of the dialogue, he represents the sort of student most likely to benefit from Socrates' tutelage.

The dramatic action begins when Hippothales asks Socrates where he is going (203d) and asks Socrates to join them instead: "Come here then. Straight to us. Won't you stop in? It's worth it, you know" (203e). When Socrates hesitates, Hippothales describes their plans in a more enticing light. He mentions the many good-looking youths at this new wrestling school and that "we pass our time with speeches, which we would be pleased to share with you" (204a). Though Hippothales actively encourages Socrates to join them, more careful scrutiny of Hippothales' behavior reveals a passive dimension to his character. He is unwilling to speak for himself. For example, when Socrates asks which of the youths they find most attractive, Hippothales remarks, "each of us has our own opinion" (204b). When Socrates asks Hippothales for his opinion directly, he still does not respond. Hippothales blushes instead (204b). Socrates then tells Hippothales about his ability to discern who people are in love with. Socrates then tells the auditor "On hearing this, he blushed still more" (204c). Socrates uses narrative references such as these to call the auditor's attention to Hippothales' emotional state. It prepares the auditor to make comparisons between Hippothales and the other young boys and ultimately to make comparisons about their aptitudes for philosophy.

For example, after noting that Hippothales blushes for the second time (204c), Socrates shifts his narrative focus to Ctesippus. Ctesippus' entrance into the conversation underscores Hippothales' shyness and passivity. Ctesippus exclaims, "how refined that you blush, Hippothales, and shrink from telling Socrates his name! And yet if he spends even a short time with you, he'll be tormented by hearing you speak it so frequently" (204c).[8] Hippothales will not articulate his erotic feelings in front of Socrates. Indeed, he lets Ctesippus speak for him. We learn about Hippothales' love for Lysis from Ctesippus rather than from Hippothales himself. For example, when Socrates presses Hippothales for details about his behavior (205b), Hippothales refuses to speak for himself. Instead, he challenges Ctesippus to reveal everything: "Surely this fellow will tell you. For he understands it and remembers precisely as if, as he says, he's been talked deaf from always hearing me" (205b).

Ctesippus happily complies. He remarks, "In fact, it's ridiculous, Socrates. For how can it not be ridiculous that he—who's a lover and who has his mind on the boy more than the others do—has nothing private to say which even a boy couldn't tell" (205b).[9] Hippothales forces his feelings on his friends. He "compels us to listen to him speaking and singing these things" (205b). Ctesippus' remarks paint Hippothales' shyness in a negative light. For example, when Hippothales admits that he loves Lysis, but denies that he composes love songs and prose pieces (205a), Ctesippus breaks in and calls him "not well, foolish, and raving" (205b). Socrates then tells the auditor, "When I heard this I said, 'Ridiculous Hippothales, are you composing and singing a song of praise about yourself before you've won the victory?'" (205d). By repeating the same word, *ridiculous*, that Ctesippus uses to describe Hippothales, Socrates suggests that the auditor should view Hippothales' overly emotional behavior as Ctesippus does. Then, Socrates warns Hippothales that he will receive "ridicule" if Lysis gets away (206a).[10]

To his credit, Hippothales explicitly asks Socrates for help: "it's because of these things, Socrates that I'm consulting with you. And if you have anything else, give your advice as to what to say in conversation or what to do so that someone might become endeared to his favorite" (206c). However, after this straightforward expression of his need for help, Hippothales reverts to his passive stance. Hippothales wants to watch Socrates demonstrate "what you need to say to him in conversation" (206c). Indeed, Hippothales develops an elaborate plan to facilitate this process:

> For if you enter with Ctesippus here and then sit down and converse, I suppose that he will come to you himself—for he is exceedingly fond of listening, Socrates. Moreover, since they're observing the Hermaea, the youths and the boys are mingled in the same place; so he'll come to you. And if not, he's well-acquainted with Ctesippus because of the latter's cousin, Menexenus. He happens to be a closer companion to Menexenus than to anyone else. Let Ctesippus here call him, then, if it turns out that he doesn't come himself. (206d)[11]

Hippothales' comments reveal how much he is attuned to the social dynamics of his peers. He knows of Lysis' fondness for listening, the status of his relationship with Ctesippus and Menexenus respectively, and the likelihood that he will approach Socrates and Ctesippus. Hippothales uses this knowledge of his peers to manipulate the situation to his advantage. Hippothales entices Socrates into an elaborate plan aimed at satisfying his erotic desire for Lysis. Socrates seems quite willing to engage in this social subterfuge. He responds favorably to Hippothales' plan; "That's what needs to be done" (206e).

At this juncture Socrates' narrative voice intervenes at length. Socrates describes the physical setting and social setting inside the wrestling school.

> And at the same time I took Ctesippus and went into the palaestra. The others went after us. When we entered, we found that the boys had offered a sacrifice there and that what they had to do with the victims was already nearly done. The boys were playing with knucklebones, and all of them were dressed up. Now the majority was playing outside in the courtyard, but some were in the corner of the dressing room, playing at odd-and-even, with a great many knucklebones which they selected from some little baskets. There were others standing around them and looking on. Among the latter was Lysis. He was standing among the boys and youths, crowned with a wreath, and he stood out by his appearance as someone worth being spoken of not only for being beautiful, but because he was beautiful and good. We went over to the opposite side of the room and sat down—for it was quiet there—and we began some conversation with each other. Then Lysis started to turn around frequently to look at us. Evidently, he desired to come over and he shrank from coming over to us alone. But Menexenus, in the middle of his playing entered from the courtyard, and when he saw Ctesippus and me, he came to sit down beside us. On seeing him, Lysis then followed and he sat down beside us along with Menexenus. Then all the others also came toward us. And in particular Hippothales, when he saw rather many of them standing nearby, screened himself behind them and approached to where he supposed Lysis wouldn't see him, for he feared to incur his hatred. And in this way he stood near and listened. (206e–207b)

This extended narrative passage reinforces the ongoing comparison between Ctesippus and Hippothales in three ways. First, Socrates indicates his preference for Ctesippus over Hippothales by taking Ctesippus along with him. While Ctesippus goes with Socrates, Hippothales becomes one of the nameless others who follow them. Second, Socrates uses the plural verbs and pronouns throughout this passage to indicate his association with Ctesippus and to reinforce his separation from Hippothales. Third, Ctesippus dominates the social scene. He draws a crowd around him. Menexenus comes over when he sees Ctesippus and Socrates then Lysis follows. Hippothales, in contrast, hides in the crowd because, according to Socrates, "he might incur the hatred of Lysis" (207b). Ctesippus' social prominence indicates the active role that he takes in his interactions with others. This active aspect of Ctesippus' character makes him a more suitable dialogical partner for Lysis than Hippothales. Hippothales wants to manipulate the situation so that Lysis will find him attractive. He exhibits no desire to converse with Lysis about substantive philosophical matters himself. Far from wanting to engage Lysis in conversation, Hippothales avoids even being seen by Lysis.

Socrates' extended narrative commentary also shifts the auditor's focus to Lysis and Menexenus. Lysis and Menexenus both exhibit qualities of the active and passive models of social behavior. In many ways, Lysis shares Hippothales' social passivity. Menexenus, like Ctesippus, is socially dominant. In addition to describing Lysis' physical appearance, Socrates provides insight into Lysis' character. Lysis wants to participate, he even strongly desires it, but hesitates because of his shyness. Socrates' narrative commentary draws out this comparison by mentioning that Hippothales was hiding right after he tells the auditor about Lysis following Menexenus over to them. Despite his social hesitancy, the effect that Lysis' beauty has on other people aligns him more closely with Ctesippus. His beauty commands attention from the social group. The group follows Lysis over to Ctesippus and Socrates (207b) just as the other boys followed Ctesippus and Socrates into the wrestling school (206e).

Socrates starts his inquiry by focusing on Menexenus rather than Lysis, perhaps suggesting that Menexenus is a more engaging conversational partner. Menexenus has a more socially dominant personality than Lysis. Menexenus immediately comes over to join Socrates and Ctesippus, whereas Lysis holds back. At first, Menexenus takes an active role by answering Socrates' first two queries (207c). Lysis says nothing. Socrates does not describe Lysis' participation in the conversation until Socrates asks which of them is older and which is nobler. Then, he asks if they argue about which of them is better looking. Here, Socrates tells the auditor, "they both laughed" (207c).[12] This dual reference indicates that Lysis has entered as a conversational partner along with Menexenus. They answer his next two queries together (207c and 207d).

Socrates now tells his auditor,

> "After that I was attempting to question them as to which one was juster and wiser. But in the middle of this, someone came up to fetch Menexenus, saying that the gymnastic master was calling. It was my opinion that this was because he happened to be supervising the sacred rites. So then Menexenus had departed, and I began to question Lysis." (207d)

Socrates' description of Menexenus reveals that Menexenus maintains a social dominance over Lysis.[13] Lysis enters the conversation only after Menexenus leaves. Socrates' narrative comments also suggest that Menexenus' interest in the conversation with Socrates is not his first priority. His social obligations take precedence over philosophical conversation.

Socrates and Lysis engage in a prolonged discussion of love and friendship. They focus on familial love and obligation and how these personal commitments enable self-improvement (207c–210a). Other than telling the auditor that Lysis "laughs" (208d), Socrates' narrative remarks offer no additional information beyond reporting the conversation until he reduces Lysis to aporia (210e). Socrates' narrative voice intervenes here to underscore the significance of Lysis' admission of aporia and Socrates' philosophical assessment of him. He is "not yet thoughtful" and "still thoughtless" (210d). He also turns the auditor's attention back to Hippothales:

> And when I heard him I looked over toward Hippothales and almost committed a blunder. For it came over me to say, "This, Hippothales is how one needs to converse with his favorite, by humbling him and drawing in his sails instead of puffing him up and spoiling him, as you do." But then I caught sight of him in agony and disturbed by what had been said, and I recalled that though he was standing near Lysis, he wished to escape his notice. And thus I recovered myself and held back from speech. (210e–211a)

Once again, Socrates' narrative remarks focus on Hippothales' passivity and his emotionality. Although Socrates consistently portrays Hippothales in a negative light, we should be careful about drawing conclusions concerning Socrates' view of the emotions based on his characterization of Hippothales. Socrates does not condemn Hippothales' emotions as such but rather how he allows his shyness to dictate his behavior in ways that are potentially harmful to himself and to others. To explain further, Socrates mentions that the manner in which Hippothales expresses his love for Lysis is harmful to Lysis' character. Because Hippothales is "in agony and disturbed by what had been said" (210e), he cannot learn from watching the conversation between Socrates and Lysis. He exhibits no desire to change his behavior and he never becomes an active participant in the conversation. Hippothales' unwillingness to change his situation points to a limitation in his character that tells us something important about the nature of both friendship and philosophy. Both are practices that necessitate active engagement with others and a willingness to be affected by that engagement. In this way, Socrates seems to suggest that there is a place for emotionality in the philosophical life. The problem is not Hippothales' emotional experience as such, but that he cannot use his emotions in a way that furthers his moral development or Lysis' for that matter.

As a means of underscoring this limitation in Hippothales, Socrates shifts his narrative focus to Menexenus and Lysis: "Menexenus, meanwhile, came back and sat down beside Lysis, which is where he had risen from. Then Lysis whispered to me very boyishly and in a friendly way—unobserved by Menexenus—and he said, 'Socrates, tell Menexenus too what you've been saying to me'" (211a). In addition to describing Lysis' motivation, Socrates reports that Lysis' remark is unnoticed by Menexenus. This brief remark should cause the auditor to observe a similarity in the behavior of Lysis and

Hippothales. Each wants Socrates to engage someone else on his behalf rather than to approach the person directly.

As their private conversation unfolds, Socrates encourages Lysis to converse with Menexenus. Lysis agrees that he will do so in the future, but he wants Socrates to "speak to him about something else, so I too may listen, until it's time to go home" (211b). Lysis explains his unwillingness to engage Menexenus directly; Menexenus is exceedingly contentious (211c). Lysis thinks that Menexenus needs to be chastened by Socrates (211c). Lysis' true motive is unclear. On the one hand, he realizes Menexenus will benefit from the encounter with Socrates, but on the other hand, the use of the word κολάζω suggests that Lysis wants to punish Menexenus in some public way.[14] David Bolotin reads Lysis' motivation in rather dark terms, "Lysis' action, while playful and harmless enough, contains the seeds of betrayal."[15]

Socrates, perhaps sensing some ulterior motivation on Lysis' part, lists several reasons why he is hesitant to engage Menexenus in debate: because of his reputation, because he is Ctesippus' student, and because Ctesippus himself is present. Lysis implores him, "Don't be concerned about anyone, Socrates. But come on, converse with him." Socrates agrees (211c). Socrates allows Lysis to observe him in conversation just as he let Hippothales do earlier. In some ways, it seems odd that Socrates would encourage their passive behavior given that he places such a primacy on being an active participant in philosophical conversation. His willingness to accede to these plans illustrates his philosophical adaptability. Socrates' adaptability should not be seen as an "anything goes" mentality. Rather, it is a fitting response to the situation in which he finds himself. He adapts his philosophical plans to accommodate the emotional needs of the young boys. In all likelihood, Socrates hopes they will learn from watching the exchange and become more active social participants like Ctesippus and Menexenus. Socrates underscores this contrasting behavior when he mentions that Ctesippus confronts their secrecy and demands that the rest of them be "given a share of the speeches" (211d). Socrates hopes the more reticent boys will gain confidence and imitate Ctesippus' eagerness to engage in conversation.

Socrates and Menexenus discuss the reciprocal nature of love and whether it is possible to love someone who does not love in return (211d–213e). Throughout this exchange, Socrates' narrative remarks do not offer any additional insight beyond recording the dynamics of the conversation. Then Menexenus' admits aporia: "By Zeus, Socrates, for my part I can't find my way at all" (213c). Socrates asks him to consider the matter in a different light: "Can it be, Menexenus, that we were seeking in an altogether incorrect fashion?" (213d). Lysis, silent up until now, remarks, "Yes—at least in my opinion, Socrates" (213d). At this point, Socrates' narrative voice intervenes:

> And at the same time as he said this, he blushed. I had the opinion that what had been spoken escaped him involuntarily, because of his applying his mind intensely to what was being said—an attitude which was evident also while he was listening. And so, since I wished to give Menexenus a rest and was also pleased by that one's love of wisdom, I turned to Lysis and began to make my arguments to him. (213e)

Socrates links Lysis' blushing with Hippothales' blushing. However, the two events stand in stark contrast to one another. Hippothales blushes because his erotic interest in Lysis was revealed. Lysis blushes because of the intensity of his philosophical engagement with Menexenus' aporia and his understanding of the reasons behind it. Whereas Hippothales' blushing does nothing to stimulate a change of behavior in him, Lysis' blush signifies that the philosophical exchange has engaged him to such an extent that he cannot remain passive.[16] It compels him to become an active participant in the conversation. Hippothales never emerges from his state as a passive observer. Socrates also mentions Lysis' innate love of philosophy. In doing so, he highlights the fact that he and Hippothales are unlikely to become genuine friends who pursue philosophical inquiry together. Even though Hippothales loves Lysis, he does not share Lysis' love of philosophy.

Socrates appears pleased by Lysis' entry into the conversation. Socrates affirms Lysis' philosophical insight (213e). He then suggests they take a different conversational path: "But let's not go in that direction any longer, for indeed that examination appears to me like a quite difficult path. Instead, we need to go on, in my opinion, from where we turned aside—by examining the things according to the poets" (213e–214a). Socrates seems to recognize that the return to the poets will appeal to Lysis and help him understand the inquiry into friendship. Socrates reports their final conversation about the poets and their views on friendship without significant narrative commentary (214a–218c).[17] After Socrates provisionally concludes "that whatever is neither bad nor good is itself, because of the presence of an evil, a friend of the good," he addresses the auditor directly:

> They [both] entirely assented and granted that this was so. And what is more, I rejoiced greatly myself, as if I were a hunter and had, to my satisfaction, what I had been hunting [for myself]. But then some most strange suspicion came over me—from where I don't know—that the things we had agreed to were not true, and at once I said in vexation, "Woe is me, Lysis and Menexenus! I'm afraid it was a dream that we've been wealthy." (218c)

In his final narrative remarks, Socrates offers the auditor one additional clue about the nature of genuine friendship. Socrates presents Menexenus and Lysis as a pair (218b–c) after he has gone to some lengths to separate them in his previous narrative remarks (213d–e). By joining Menexenus and Lysis back together in his remarks, Socrates prepares them and the auditor to understand the last discussion of friendship (218d–222a). Friendship requires ongoing dedicated association with each other even in the face of repeated obstacles, such as those presented by the argument itself. Socrates creates a semblance of this ongoing association by joining them together in his speech. Even though Menexenus takes over as the primary conversational partner, Socrates still refers to the boys together at 219b and again four times in rapid succession as the exchange with Menexenus draws to a close at 221e.

Then, Socrates explains that genuine friendship requires more than ongoing association. They must also have a kinship of soul (222a). At this crucial juncture, Socrates reports that Menexenus says "Certainly." Then Socrates notes that "Lysis was silent" (222a). Here Socrates' narrative remark, though brief, is telling because it separates the two boys from each other again. Lysis' silence suggests that he sees the conclusion they have reached in different terms than Menexenus does. Lysis is silent. Menexenus is not. Lysis' silence seems to indicate that he finds the conclusion more difficult to accept than Menexenus does.

At this point, Socrates mentions Hippothales for the first time since observing how "distressed and disturbed" Hippothales was at seeing Lysis being reduced to aporia (211a). He tells the auditor "Hippothales radiated all sorts of colors as a result of his pleasure" (222b). Hippothales blushes because he wants Lysis to see him as a genuine friend. Francisco Gonzalez perceptively remarks, "What the deluded Hippothales fails to hear is Socrates' distinction between the genuine lover and the feigning lover. Given all that we have learned about love and friendship in this dialogue, it is not hard to see that Hippothales is not a genuine lover."[18] After watching this extended conversation, Hippothales remains unchanged. He does not recognize their unsuitability as genuine friends. As if to underscore Hippothales' unsuitability, Socrates says nothing about Hippothales as his narrative ends. Though Hippothales instigates the conversation, he plays no part in its conclusion. Instead, Socrates includes Lysis and Menexenus in his aporia about the nature of friendship: "Now, Lysis and Menexenus, we have become ridiculous—I, an old man, and you. For these fellows will say, as they go away, that we suppose we're one another's friends—for I also put myself among you—but to what he who is a friend is we have not yet been able to discover" (223).

II. A SOCRATIC SELF-PORTRAIT

In this section, I explore how Socrates' narrative commentary gives the auditor insight into Socrates' internal state of mind.[19] When Socrates discloses his mental and emotional states to the auditor, he paints a detailed portrait of the philosopher in action. I consider three elements of this narrative portrait. First, it illustrates Socrates' intellectual adaptability. Second, it reveals Socrates' interrogative stance and his sustained commitment to philosophical inquiry in the face of ambiguity and uncertainty. Third, it shows how Socrates' interest in eros particularly and the emotions more generally are woven into the very fabric of his philosophical inquiry. These aspects of Socrates' philosophical practice are important to observe because they provide the auditor with a model of the qualities that are required for genuine friendship. Furthermore, they teach the auditor, at least indirectly, how to philosophize.

Socrates illustrates his adaptability from the very beginning of his narrative. Socrates presents himself to the auditor as someone on a journey to a specific destination: "I was on my way from the Academy straight to the Lyceum, along the road outside the wall and close under the wall itself. When I got to the little gate by Panops spring, I happened to meet there Hippothales . . ." (203a). While this opening scene may seem mundane, Socrates conveys that he has a particular plan in mind and that he remains open to what this chance encounter with Hippothales may offer him.[20] Hippothales and his group diverted Socrates from his going on to the Lyceum to a recently built and unnamed wrestling school. Socrates shows this same adaptability at other places in the dialogue as well. For example, when Menexenus has to return to his obligations with the sacred rites, Socrates immediately begins to question Lysis instead (207d). Another example of his adaptability occurs when Socrates goes along with Lysis' spontaneous plan to refute Menexenus upon his return to the conversation (211a).[21]

From the beginning of his narrative, Socrates presents himself as an inquisitive person.[22] He asks several questions of the boys: who they are, what their pastimes are, who teaches at the Lyceum (204a). Socrates finds his interrogative behavior important enough to include in the opening of his narrative. In doing so, he models curiosity about human affairs and a willingness to engage in social encounters. Both of these qualities illustrate the socially embedded nature of Socrates' philosophic practice. He maintains this interrogative stance throughout the dialogue. He questions Menexenus and Lysis together (207c–d), Lysis alone (207d–210e), Menexenus alone (211d–213d), Lysis again (214a–218b), and Menexenus and Lysis together (218c–222e). Throughout his recounting of these events, Socrates presents himself as someone thoroughly committed to the interrogative activity that philosophical dialogue demands.

Socrates continues his philosophical questioning even when his interlocutors are ready to give up. For example, when his review of the argument ends, Socrates remarks to Menexenus and Lysis, "What, then, might we still make of the argument? Or is there clearly nothing . . . if nothing among these is a friend, I no longer know what to say" (222e). Socrates implies that he has given up on the possibility of further conversation with the boys. However,

Socrates' narrative remarks intervene just after this admission of aporia. They focus the auditor's attention on Socrates' willingness to start another conversation with different interlocutors: "But as I said these things, I already had in mind to set in motion something else among the older fellows" (222e). Socrates could have ended his narrative on this final note "we were therefore defeated." However Socrates' narrative commentary expresses his philosophical optimism. He will continue his search for the meaning of friendship despite the obstacles he encounters.

In addition to underscoring Socrates' willingness to continue his philosophical inquiry, his narrative commentary also underscores his interest in the emotions. Scholars often regard Plato and Socrates as philosophers who are deeply suspicious of emotional experience and the role the presence of it and even the expression of it plays in philosophy. Socrates is frequently associated with an intellectualist viewpoint which "seems to identify virtue with knowledge and therefore appears to consider the affective side of our nature irrelevant to our virtue, to what counts as a good life."[23] Martha Nussbaum goes so far as to claim that Plato attempts to create "a pure crystalline theater of the intellect" in his dialogues.[24] To be sure, there are many aspects of the Platonic dialogues that support a strong distinction between emotion and reason as well as a prioritization of reason over emotion and a corresponding denigration of emotional experience.[25] However, Socrates' narrative commentary provides a different picture of the relationship between reason and emotion in the philosophical life. Socrates' narrative comments in the *Lysis*, and even more so in the other narrated dialogues, demonstrate an understanding of reason and emotion more in keeping with the one found in other aspects of Greek culture like poetry and theater. Ismene Lada explains, "In Greek theatrical experience emotion is a privileged way of getting access to the truth, of reaching both understanding of others and, most importantly, self-realisation."[26] Socrates' narrative commentary provides a model of a philosopher in action. Socrates does not offer a model of philosophy as an abstract practice of reason, but a model of philosophy as a balanced practice that responds to and incorporates the emotional richness of everyday life.

Socrates' interest in eros is one indication of the emotional dimensions of his philosophical inquiry. His interest in eros first manifests when the erotic turn of the conversation overcomes any initial hesitancy he may have had about joining the boys. Indeed, Socrates seems particularly interested in meeting Lysis, the object of Hippothales' intense erotic fascination (206d). The fact that Socrates presents himself as interested in matters of love is important because it reveals willingness to engage in the emotional dimensions of human experience. Indeed, his interest in the erotic matters between these young boys occasions the entire philosophical inquiry into the nature of friendship. Consider the moment when Hippothales' emotional response to

Lysis motivates Socrates' philosophical involvement in the dialogue (206e). This empathy for Hippothales' emotional suffering leads Socrates into this extended encounter at the wrestling school. Socrates uses his emotional awareness of Hippothales to teach him something about the proper way to love. Even if one wanted to argue that Socrates' interest in the emotional states of the young boys is something of a rhetorical pretext, a sort of enacted role that he uses to lure the boys into the practice of philosophy, it is nonetheless striking that he is willing to engage in philosophy on the emotional level. He does not demand that the boys give up their emotional entanglements to practice philosophy. Rather, he presents philosophy in the emotionally saturated social context in which they interact with each other.

As this narrative unfolds, Socrates paints a vivid picture of the scene inside the wrestling school (206e–207c). Not only does he present himself as someone with a highly honed ability to sense the psychological motivations and emotional needs of others, he also describes his own actions, thoughts, and feelings directly to the auditor. Some of the thoughts and actions Socrates includes are fairly mundane. For example, he tells the auditor: "I took Ctesippus with me and went into the palaestra" (206e). Other times, Socrates' narrative comments can be quite revealing. Sometimes Socrates shows himself in a potentially unfavorable light. For example, after refuting Lysis (207e–210e), Socrates tells the auditor: "And when I heard him I looked over toward Hippothales and almost committed a blunder. For it came over me to say, 'This, Hippothales, is how one needs to converse with his favorite, by humbling him and drawing in his sails instead of puffing him up and spoiling him as you do!'" (210e). Lysis' admission of aporia and what Hippothales should learn from it so excites Socrates that he momentarily forgets that Hippothales wishes to keep his interest in Lysis a secret. Socrates certainly did not have to include this detail about his emotional enthusiasm in the narrative. That Socrates does so suggests that he wants the auditor to see him as someone who experiences intense emotional responses to his circumstances. Socrates describes his inner state, "But then I caught sight of him in agony and disturbed by what had been said, I recalled that though he was standing near Lysis, he wished to escape his notice. And thus I recovered myself and held back from speech" (210e–211a). Though Socrates depicts himself as very excited, he maintains control of himself and refrains from speaking. One might interpret this passage as an indication of Socrates' self-mastery over his emotion. It is true that Socrates does control himself in a way that Hippothales does not. However, it is important to see that Socrates does not simply ignore or repress his emotions as a means of garnering control. Rather, he feels them quite profoundly and deeply. His emotions help him understand Hippothales' current state. In fact, he uses his emotional awareness of Hippothales' state and his own to stimulate further inquiry on his part. In this way, Socrates channels his emotions back into his philosophical questioning and thereby allies his emotions with his intellect. By including his emotional responses in his narrative, Socrates gives the emotions an ongoing place in his philosophical discourse. Nor does he characterize his emotions in negative terms. He does regain control of himself but he does not characterize the loss of control that his intense emotional response creates as a negative state of affairs. Indeed, he finds it important enough to include in his account of the conversation to the auditor. Both the emotional response and the response to his emotions are important for the auditor to hear.

To explain further, just as Socrates presents his philosophical conversation with Lysis as a corrective model for Hippothales, Socrates presents his ability to moderate his emotions in a difficult social situation as a model for the auditor. One could argue that Socrates' ability to control his emotions is also a corrective model for Hippothales, but Hippothales is, in fact, unaware of Socrates' near blunder and subsequent recovery. By providing the auditor with this information, Socrates moves the pedagogical work of the dialogue to the narrative level. To explain, the narrative commentary implicitly asks for a response from the auditor just as Socrates' *elenchus* asks for a response from the boys within the dramatic level of the dialogue. The auditor should recognize that Socrates' balanced response to his emotions is more desirable than Hippothales' lack of ability to deal with his strong attractions. Hippothales simply retreats into shyness. He has no way to act upon his emotions in positive terms. Socrates, in contrast, models a more positive response. The fact that Socrates includes these emotional moments in the narrative when he retells it to the auditor shows that he has not overcome his emotions by banishing them from his experience but that he manages his emotions by incorporating them into the narrative dimensions of his philosophic practice.

Socrates frequently links these observations about his inner mental states with crucial dramatic moments in the dialogue. One example occurs when Lysis admits aporia (213d). Socrates reports that "at the same time as he said this, he blushed. I had the opinion that what had been spoken escaped him involuntarily, because of his applying his mind intensely to what was being said—an attitude which was evident also while he was listening" (213d). The fact that Socrates notices Lysis' embarrassment illustrates his ongoing interest in the emotions of others. When Socrates attributes a particular motivation for this blush, he demonstrates an empathetic understanding of Lysis' existential state. Even more importantly, Socrates' narrative commentary links his philosophical assessment of both Lysis and Menexenus with his observation of Lysis' emotional state. Socrates' ability to observe their emotional state also dictates his next course of action. Immediately after describing Lysis' blush, Socrates tells the auditor: "And so, since I wished to give Menexenus a rest and was also pleased by that one's love of wisdom, I turned to Lysis and began to make my arguments to him" (213d–e). These comments suggest that Socrates uses the information that he gains from his emotional sensitivity of others to shape his philosophical assessment of them.

Throughout his narrative commentary, Socrates describes his response to the argument in emotional terms. For example, Lysis' philosophical aptitude pleases him (213e). Socrates also uses emotional language to describe his response to philosophical argument at his next significant narrative intervention (218c). He "rejoiced greatly" at their apparently successful conclusion. Socrates vividly describes his emotional state; he compares himself to a cheerfully contented hunter basking in the delight of a kill.[27] Then he is vexed and annoyed when he fears the wealth of the argument was but a dream (218c). Though Socrates' emotional displeasure may well arise because he wants to adopt a view supported by reason, his recurrent use of emotionally charged language to explain his response to rational argument suggests that his understanding of reason is closely aligned with his emotional states. Though we often think of the Socratic *elenchus* as a movement away from emotions and toward reason, Thomas Schmid notes that the *elenchus* itself, the hallmark of the Socratic Method, depends upon a strong engagement with the emotions. He writes, "It is the self-expressive, self-revealing, and potentially self-reformative nature of the *elenchus*, the fact that it involves the interlocutor's desires and emotions as well as his belief in the dialectical situation, which makes it such a powerful tool for moral inquiry."[28]

Furthermore, aspects of Socrates' narrative commentary imply he does not depend on reason alone to reach his philosophical conclusions. One example occurs when Socrates tells his auditor that "a very strange suspicion comes over him" (218c6). Though Socrates does not refer to his daimon here, his description of the event accords with other instances of the appearance of the daimon.[29] The daimon typically intervenes to keep Socrates from proceeding along an incorrect course of action.[30] Here, Socrates presents himself to the auditor as being swayed by something beyond the argument itself to change his mind about the conclusion of the argument. While it is possible that Socrates senses the logical implications of their argument and changes his mind according to the dictates of reason, he does not describe the experience in rational terms. Though Socrates chooses to tell the auditor about this strange suspicion, he does not tell Lysis and Menexenus about it. To them, Socrates uses emotional language to describe his hesitancy about their conclusions: "I'm afraid it was a dream that we've been wealthy" (218c). Even when Menexenus directly asks him, "Why do you say that?" Socrates does not tell him about the strange suspicion. He reiterates his fear that the arguments are false. In this response, Socrates links his fear with the argument explicitly: "I'm afraid that we have come across some false arguments about the friend" (218d). Menexenus still does not understand Socrates. He asks Socrates again, "What do you mean?" Still, Socrates says nothing about the strange suspicion (218d) but attempts to explain the limitations of the argument (218d–222a). If we paid attention to the dramatic level of the dialogue alone, Socrates' philosophic practice does seem to focus primarily on argument. However, when we take into account the narrative level of Socrates' philosophic practice, then our understanding of Socratic argumentation and the different rhetorical strategies he deploys needs to expand to include his emotional sensitivity and how he incorporates that into his philosophic practice.

A little later, Socrates' narrative focuses on another interplay of emotion and reason: "Now [both] Lysis and Menexenus, with difficulty, somehow nodded yes, but Hippothales radiated all sorts of colors as a result of his pleasure" (222a–b). Here, Socrates juxtaposes Hippothales' pleasure with his own philosophical process. Socrates "wishes to examine the argument" (222b). At this juncture, Socrates presents his own reasoning process as superior to a solely emotional response. It might be tempting to conclude that Socrates' juxtaposition of his reasoning process with Hippothales' emotional response suggests that Socrates always prioritizes reason over emotion. However, the fact that Socrates includes his own emotional responses in the narrative along with his rational thought process demonstrates that he sees both reason and emotion as important components of the story he tells the auditor.

Admittedly, the narrative descriptions of Socrates' emotional states are not as robust as one might hope. The other narrated dialogues I will examine through the course of this book offer additional, and more detailed, examples of how Socrates interweaves emotion and reason into the narrative dimensions of his philosophic practice. At this point, we can provisionally claim that Socrates' narrative remarks reveal an interested awareness of the emotional states of the young boys. Indeed, he tethers his philosophical encounters with them to their various emotional responses to him and to each other. His philosophical inquiry with them is partially shaped by his ability to relate to them on an emotional level. Furthermore, Socrates depicts himself as having emotional responses to the argument as it unfolds. Unlike Hippothales, Socrates moderates his response to his emotional states in such a way that he can continue to engage in philosophical conversation.[31] In doing so, Socrates allows a space for his emotional responses to people, events, and arguments to shape the direction of his philosophical engagement with others. The evidence of Socrates' narrative commentary does not suggest that the emotions play a cognitive role that trumps his dependence on reason, but his comments do clearly illustrate that Socrates allows the arguments about friendship to unfold based on his awareness of his emotions and the emotions of his interlocutors.

III. NARRATIVE, APORIA, AND FRIENDSHIP

Scholars are generally divided with respect to how we should interpret the lack of positive philosophical conclusions about friendship in the *Lysis*.[32] Some simply regard this dialogue as a prelude to the more fully developed expositions of love and friendship found in the *Phaedrus* and *Symposium*.[33] Vlastos sees it as indicating the lack of a place for genuine love of the individual in Plato's philosophy.[34] Some read dark overtones in the aporetic ending.[35] Others find the aporetic conclusion less troubling. For example, Gadamer thinks the young age of his interlocutors demands it.[36] Some scholars even see positive value in the aporetic conclusion. Gonzalez, for example, sees Socrates as enacting philosophical friendship: "by leading others into that kinship or belonging that is a realization of their greatest potential as 'intermediate' beings, Socrates' philosophizing is itself the highest act of friendship."[37] The narrative dimensions of the *Lysis* reinforce these more positive interpretations because they portray Socrates' attempt to lead the auditor into philosophical kinship with the good. Because of the presence of the auditor, Socrates is not a solitary figure, alone with his thoughts, as the dialogue begins.

Despite the fact that we do not witness any social interaction between Socrates and the auditor, three aspects of the dialogue suggest Socrates may be on intimate terms with the auditor. First, Socrates tells him this lengthy narrative. He assumes the auditor would find the narrative interesting. Second, Socrates relates how he almost revealed Hippothales' infatuation with Lysis to Lysis himself (210e). When Socrates tells his auditor about this social blunder, Socrates displays a level of trust between himself and his auditor that is not present between himself and the characters in the dramatic events. Third, Socrates tells the auditor about a "strange suspicion" that overcomes him (218c). Though he has ample opportunity to do so in his conversation with Menexenus, Socrates keeps the focus on the limitations of the argument. This personal disclosure about his trust in his strange suspicion suggests a greater level of intimacy between Socrates and the auditor than is present between Socrates and the young boys. Because of the narrative relationship between Socrates and the auditor, the conditions for the possibility of friendship are present from the beginning of the dialogue. In fact, the narrative level of the dialogue provides us with a concrete example of Socrates extending love to an individual person. What precisely does this Socratic love involve? Socrates' narrative is an act of love because it offers an ongoing invitation to the philosophical life. By recounting this narrative, Socrates imitates his own actions for the auditor. The auditor then has the opportunity to enter into the same discussion. Through the act of narrating, Socrates offers the auditor the opportunity to become better through the practice of philosophy. In the preceding sections, we have explored how the narrative commentary draws the auditor's attention to philosophically important aspects of Socrates' account. Ultimately, the auditor should move beyond a dependence on Socrates' narrative commentary and begin to take a more active role in the joint, dialogic character of philosophical inquiry that Socrates exhibits himself and tries to instill in his interlocutors on the dramatic level.

Several instances of this invitation occur as the dialogue progresses. First, the narrative dimensions of the text should cause the auditor to recognize his own status as passive observer of the narrative. Just as Socrates allows Hippothales and Lysis to remain passive observers with the hope that they will learn to become more active participants in the social and philosophical domain, Socrates has the same hope for the auditor. Socrates narrates to provoke the auditor into the active practice of philosophy just as Lysis himself is provoked.

Second, as a character in his own narrative, Socrates reveals more about his thoughts and emotions to the boys themselves (211e, 214b–d, 214e). Socrates has made similar self-disclosing remarks to the auditor from the beginning of the narrative. Here, Socrates makes them within the temporal context of the drama. By this point in the narrative, the auditor should be sufficiently trained to notice these comments about Socrates' inner states even though Socrates does not make these observations to the auditor directly. In this way, the auditor can move beyond his dependence on Socrates' narrative commentary.

The turn to the discussion of poetry offers another chance for the auditor to extend the inquiry beyond the confines of the dialogue. Socrates tells Lysis: "Instead, we need to go on, in my opinion, from where we turned aside—by examining the things according to the poets. For the poets are, as it were, our fathers in wisdom and our guides" (213e). This consideration of poetry comes immediately after Socrates explicitly tells the auditor that Lysis' aptitude for philosophy pleases him. If Lysis is so good at philosophy, why does Socrates now turn to a consideration of poetry? This turn toward poetry perhaps indicates that the auditor should read a level of ironic hesitancy into the remark he just heard about Lysis' philosophical ability.

Finally, Socrates does not report how the young boys respond to his final admission of aporia (222e). Instead, he addresses his auditor directly:

> But as I said these things, I already had in mind to set in motion something else among the older fellows. But then, like some daemons, the attendants—the one of Menexenus and the one of Lysis—came forward, bringing their brothers. And they called to them, and bade them to leave for home. For it was already late. Now at first, we and those standing around tried to drive them away. Yet since they paid no heed to us, but showed irritation and kept calling out none the less with a somewhat foreign accent—and in our opinion they had been drinking quite a bit at the Hermaea, so there seemed to be no way to

approach them—we were therefore defeated by them and we broke up our group. (223a)

Socrates' last remarks to the auditor underscore the failure of the inquiry. Socrates has reached an impasse with the young boys and hopes to find new conversational partners. The auditor may well become such a conversational partner. Pangle remarks, "The *Lysis* provides no model of a '"friendship based on kinship between those who have become both wise and substantially self-sufficient."'[38] However, she overlooks the possibility of the narrator/ auditor relationship. If the auditor achieved some level of philosophical autonomy by listening to the narrative and taking up the invitations to philosophy contained within it, he would become precisely what Socrates most ardently seeks: a genuine friend. Together, they would have a reciprocal friendship of equals who could participate in the philosophical life together.

Unfortunately, we cannot be certain of this reciprocity because we do not see how the auditor responds to Socrates' invitation. Nonetheless, Socrates' narrative commentary is an ongoing exhortation to philosophy. Through it, Plato extends philosophical friendship to the audience of the dialogue.[39] By paying attention to the narrative dimensions of this text, we see another level of what Gadamer calls "the Doric harmony of logos and ergon which Plato's philosophical utopia will subsequently construct—although again only in words."[40] The narrative retelling harmoniously records Socrates' deeds in Socrates' own words. The saying, the retelling of the logos of the *Lysis*, is the work of friendship.

NOTES

1. On Plato's *Lysis*, see Laszlo Versenyi, "Plato's *Lysis*," *Phronesis* 20 (1975): 185–198; David Bolotin, *Plato's Dialogue on Friendship* (Ithaca: Cornell University Press, 1979); Hans-Georg Gadamer, "Logos and Ergon in Plato's *Lysis*," in *Dialogue and Dialectic: Eight Hermeneutical Studies on Plato*, trans. P. Christopher Smith (New Haven: Yale University Press, 1980), 1–20; James Haden, "Friendship in Plato's *Lysis*," *Review of Metaphysics* 37 (1983): 327–356; Aristide Tessitore, "Plato's *Lysis*: An Introduction to Philosophic Friendship," *Southern Journal of Philosophy* 28 (1990): 115–132; Brian Mooney, "Plato's Theory of Love in the *Lysis*," *Irish Journal of Philosophy* 7 (1990): 131–159; Francisco Gonzalez, "Plato's *Lysis*: An Enactment of Philosophical Kinship," *Ancient Philosophy* 15 (1995): 69–90; Gary Scott, *Plato's Socrates as Educator* (Albany: SUNY Press, 2000); Lorraine Pangle, "Friendship and Human Neediness in Plato's *Lysis*," *Ancient Philosophy* 21 (2001): 305–323; Alfred Geier, *Plato's Erotic Thought* (Rochester: University of Rochester Press, 2002); Francisco Gonzalez, "How to Read a Platonic Prologue: *Lysis* 203a–207d," in *Plato as Author: The Rhetoric of Philosophy*, ed. Ann Michelini (Leiden: Brill, 2003), 15–44; and T. Penner and C. Rowe, *Plato's* Lysis (Cambridge: Cambridge University Press, 2005).

2. My thanks to Mary Nichols for reading a penultimate draft of this chapter. I have also benefited greatly from her recent book, *Socrates on Friendship and Community: Reflections on Plato's* Symposium, Phaedrus, *and* Lysis (Cambridge: Cambridge University Press, 2009).

3. I use Bolotin's translation throughout. I have also consulted Stanley Lombardo's translation in *Plato Complete Works*, ed. John Cooper (Indianapolis: Hackett, 1997), 687–707. Where

I have cited Plato's Greek, I follow Johannes Burnet, *Platonis Opera* (Oxford: Oxford University Press, 1903).

4. Deborah Nails, *The People of Plato* (Indianapolis: Hackett, 2002), 316–317.

5. See *Republic*, 327a; *Protagoras*, 309b; *Euthydemus*, 271a; and *Charmides* 153a.

6. Planeaux points out a number of incongruities in the story that Socrates tells the auditor. For example, his opening description of the way to Lyceum is not accurate (60) and that Socrates was unaware of the presence of the wrestling school (62). See "Socrates, an Unreliable Narrator? The Dramatic Setting of the *Lysis*," *Classical Philology* 96 (2001): 60–68. Given that Planeaux acknowledges Socrates' "half truths" (67) are meant to be seen through by the auditor, they do not detract from Socrates' general reliability.

7. 218e–222a is the longest passage without narrative commentary.

8. Like Socrates, Ctesippus himself mentions Hippothales' blushing twice (204c and 204e). On the blushing, see Geier, *Erotic Thought*, 75.

9. In this passage, Ctesippus twice refers to Hippothales as "ridiculous." On this point, see Tessitore, "Plato's *Lysis*," 129n6.

10. Socrates also accuses Hippothales of making Lysis "savage through speeches and songs" (206b).

11. On the Hermaea festival, see H. D. Parke, *Festivals of Athens* (Ithaca: Cornell University Press, 1977), 107–120.

12. Bolotin insightfully points out, "Yet concealed within their common laughter there may also be difference between the boys. For we assume in part from everyone's silence about Menexenus' appearance, that Lysis is manifestly the better looking of the two." *Plato's Dialogue*, 81.

13. On this point, see Geier, *Erotic Thought*, 87.

14. H. G. Liddell and Scott list "to curtail, dock, prune and punish along with to chastise as meanings of the verb." *An Intermediate Greek-English Lexicon* (Oxford: Clarendon Press, 1986), 441.

15. Bolotin, *Plato's Dialogue*, 106.

16. Scott notes that Lysis himself becomes an auditor of Socrates. See *Socrates as Educator*, 72.

17. He tells the auditor that Lysis nods (214d) and notes the change in speaker at 216a and 218b.

18. See Gonzalez, "Philosophical Kinship," 85.

19. See Drew Hyland, "Eros, Epithumia, and Philia in Plato," *Phronesis* 13 (1968): 32–46, for a helpful treatment of Plato's use of these terms.

20. Geier provides an excellent account of Socrates' initial state of mind and his hesitancy to join in the conversation with the young boys, *Erotic Thought*, 68–77.

21. See also 206e, 223a.

22. Cohen sees Oedipus' questioning as the model Plato has in mind for Socrates' questioning, "The Aporias in Plato's Early Dialogues," *Journal of the History of Ideas* 62 (1962): 164–165.

23. Alexander Nehamas, "What Did Socrates Teach and to Whom Did He Teach It?" *Review of Metaphysics* 46 (1992): 280.

24. Martha Nussbaum, *Fragility of Goodness: Luck and Ethics in Greek Tragedy and Philosophy* (Cambridge: Harvard University Press, 1986), 133.

25. See, for example, *Republic*, 491d–507c, and *Phaedo*, 64c–67c.

26. Lada, "'Empathic Understanding': Emotion and Cognition in Classical Dramatic Audience-Response," *Proceedings of the Cambridge Philological Society* 39 (1993): 94–140.

27. This hunting imagery appears throughout Socrates' narrative remarks in the *Euthydemus* as well.

28. Schmid, *Plato's* Charmides *and the Socratic Ideal of Rationality* (Albany: State University of New York Press 1998), 65.

29. For several good essays on the daimon, see *Reason and Religion in Socratic Philosophy*, eds. Nicholas D. Smith and Paul B. Woodruff (Oxford: Oxford University Press, 2000).

30. See *Apology*, 31d.

31. Socrates' emotional responses are even more extreme in the other narrated dialogues. See *Charmides*, 155c–3; *Republic*, 336d; *Protagoras*, 328d, 339e; and *Euthydemus*, 303b–c.

32. On the range of scholarly opinion, see Versenyi, "Plato's *Lysis*," and Gonzalez "Philosophical Kinship." Most famously W. K. C. Guthrie remarks, "Even Plato can nod." *A History of Greek Philosophy* (Cambridge: Cambridge University Press, 1975), 143. See also Julia Annas, "Plato and Aristotle on Friendship and Altruism," *Mind* 86 (1997): 32–554.

33. Oscar González-Castán, "The Erotic Soul and its Movement towards the Beautiful and the Good." *Revista de Filosofia* 21 (2000): 75–86; and C. Rowe, "The *Lysis* and the *Symposium*: Aporia and Euporia?" in Robinson and Brisson (2000), 205–215.

34. Vlastos, "The Individual as the Object of Love in Plato," in *Platonic Studies* (Princeton: Princeton University Press, 1973), 3–11.

35. Tindale notes that the final image of the dialogue is one of Socrates standing alone. "Plato's *Lysis*," 107.

36. Gadamer, "Logos and Ergon," 6. Scott agrees with Gadamer. See his *Socrates as Educator*, 52.

37. Gonzalez, "Philosophical Kinship," 86. On more positive readings of the ending, see Vernesyi "Plato's *Lysis*"; Scott, *Socrates as Educator*; and Geier, *Erotic Thought*.

38. Pangle, "Human Neediness," 322.

39. On this point, see Bolotin, *Friendship*; Tindale, "Plato's *Lysis*"; and Pangle, "Human Neediness."

40. Gadamer, "Logos and Ergon," 20.

Chapter Three

Chastening Charmides

In this chapter, I explore the narrative dimensions of the *Charmides*.[1] I argue that Socrates' narrative descriptions of his interlocutors and his narrative self-presentation offer an opportunity to reconsider the nature of *sophrosune* itself and the complex relationship between philosophy and politics.[2] *Sophrosune* is usually translated as temperance. It also means sound-mindedness, moderation, self-restraint, or self-control. These standard translations present *sophrosune* as virtue that largely concerns individual self-comportment. Unfortunately, they obscure the social and political meanings of *sophrosune* that were central to its usage throughout the fourth and fifth centuries B.C.E.[3] Because Socrates' interlocutors lack this deeply political virtue, they attempt to control the social situations in which they find themselves by exerting mastery over others rather than cooperating with others to achieve their goals. Genuine philosophical conversation and sustained inquiry into the nature of the good depend upon cooperative harmonious engagement with others. I show how Socrates' *sophrosune* emphasizes his emotional states and his responses to his emotions. Socrates does not exhibit *sophrosune* simply as a virtue of reasoned self-control that helps him strengthen his intellectual pursuit of the good and overcome his erotic desire for Charmides.[4] Through his narrative commentary, Socrates models *sophrosune* as a way of life that involves ongoing self-examination, emotional awareness, and sustained philosophical inquiry within a communal context.[5] Finally, I consider how this narrative portrait of Socrates illustrates the philosopher's capacity to resist the temptation of both personal and political tyranny.[6]

I. SETTING THE STAGE

A. The Narrative Setting of the *Charmides*

The *Charmides* begins with Socrates reporting that "We got back the preceding evening from the camp at Potidaea, and since I was arriving after such a long absence I sought out my accustomed haunts with special pleasure" (153a).[7] As in the *Lysis*, we do not know where, why, or to whom Socrates tells this story. Scholars typically assume that the narrative retelling takes place the day following his return from battle in 429 B.C.E.[8] However, Socrates could be retelling this story at some unspecified later time.[9] If so, Socrates, as narrator, dates the narrated events for the auditor by telling him that these events occurred the day after he returned from the famous battle of Potidaea. Why should we consider this later dating of the narrative setting? Almost every commentator on the *Charmides* notes that understanding the dramatic irony of the dialogue involves knowing what fate befalls Critias and Charmides. Critias leads the Thirty Tyrants. Charmides was also one of the Thirty and was involved with several sacrilegious crimes. Neither survives the aftermath.[10]

If the narrative retelling occurs the day after the conversation with Charmides and Critias, then Socrates could not be exploiting this tragic irony on the narrative level because the fates that befall Charmides and Critias have yet to occur. Furthermore, another dimension of this tragic irony, at least on the level of the reader of the dialogue, involves knowing of Socrates' historical fate as well. Perhaps the auditor knows of Socrates' pending trial and has sought him out for that reason. If so, the date of the narrative telling would be almost thirty years after the events Socrates narrates. Given these possibilities, the temporal setting of the narrative retelling remains uncertain.

This uncertainty has two main functions. First, as was the case in the *Lysis*, it forces the reader to confront a certain level of aporia, a certain level of not knowing, at the very outset of the dialogue. On this minimal level, we become like Socrates, whose self-knowledge depends upon a profound awareness of knowing what he does not know. Second, it illustrates the way in which narrative connects the present moment with the events of the past. The self-knowledge that Socrates exhibits on the narrative level connects past events with the present moment in which he finds himself. That we do not know when the narrative is retold suggests that it could be at anytime, that the story and the necessity of self-inquiry are relevant regardless of the context in which we, as readers, find ourselves.[11]

Though the exact identity of Socrates' auditor is unknown, Christopher Bruell suggests that the auditor "is perhaps a foreigner led to Athens by his interest in the way of philosophizing practiced by Socrates. Socrates repays his interest by narrating to him his encounter with Charmides and Critias."[12]

The fact that Socrates explains to his auditor why the people in Athens had not heard the news of the battle supports Bruell's observations (153b). A native Athenian would be familiar with these circumstances particularly if the narrative retelling occurs the day following Socrates' return from battle. Benardete agrees that the auditor is a foreigner and suggests that he may be Theodorus.[13] Brann muses that "Perhaps we are supposed to think it's Plato."[14] Laurence Lampert agrees with her suggestion. He provocatively maintains, "Let the auditor of the *Charmides* be the author of the *Charmides*. Let an author who never speaks in his writing show himself listening. The problem of transmitting Socrates' philosophy would thus be transmitted to the one who transmitted it successfully."[15]

Regardless of the auditor's identity, three aspects of Socrates' narrative suggest that he and Socrates have a friendly, perhaps even intimate, relationship. First, Socrates directly addresses him as a "friend."[16] Martin McAvoy notes that each of the direct addresses occur when Socrates describes the erotic effect that Charmides has on him. He suggests that these references "establish an intimate understanding between Socrates and his hearer."[17] Benardete sees these references as evidence that the auditor exhibits "a certain priggishness in sexual matters, so Socrates addresses him twice in a row when he speaks of the erection he suffered when he saw the things within Charmides' cloak."[18] While I agree that these direct addresses to the auditor occur at highly charged erotic moments, the text does not indicate that the auditor is embarrassed. Second, Socrates reports his willingness to mislead Charmides about having a cure for his headache (155b).[19] As was the case in the *Lysis*, Socrates' willingness to reveal his subterfuge demonstrates a degree of trust and honesty between himself and his auditor that was not present in his encounter with Charmides and Critias. Within the confines of the narrative relationship, Socrates can speak and act in a way that he could not during the events that he now narrates. Third, Socrates' ongoing revelation of his emotions suggests a level of intimacy between himself and his auditor. In the *Lysis*, Socrates' narrative remarks focus primarily on the emotional states that he observed in others.[20] In this dialogue, Socrates includes his own emotional responses in the narrative along with his ongoing observations about the emotions of his interlocutors.[21] For instance, Socrates mentions his pleasure at going to the Palaestra (153c), his amazement at Charmides' stature and appearance (154c), his overwhelming response to the glimpse inside Charmides' cloak (155d), and the subsequent return of his self-confidence (156d). This self-disclosure suggests that he knows the auditor well enough to reveal personal details about his inner life, details the auditor would find of interest.

B. The Opening Scene (153a–154b)

Socrates describes the scene inside the Palaestra:

> I found a number of persons, most of whom were familiar though; there were some, too, whom I didn't know. When they saw me coming in unexpectedly, I was immediately hailed at a distance by people coming up from all directions and Chaerephon, like the wild man he is, sprang up from the midst of a group of people and ran towards me and seizing me by the hand, exclaimed, "Socrates, how did you come off in the battle?" (153b)

Chaerephon immediately mentions another report about the battle. He heard that the fighting was heavy. Socrates confirms the accuracy of the account (153c).[22] Chaerephon asks if Socrates was present at the battle. Socrates confirms that he was. Chaerephon then tells Socrates, "Sit down and give us a complete account, because we've had very few details so far" (153c). Socrates reinforces Chaerephon's references to other narratives as he tells the auditor:

> While he was still talking he brought me over to Critias, the son of Callaeschrus, and sat me down there. When I took my seat, I greeted Critias and the rest and proceeded to relate the news from the camp in answer to whatever questions anyone asked, and they asked plenty of different ones. (153d)

These references to various narrative exchanges underscore the social aspects of the encounter. For example, as Socrates reports the narrative, he draws out the social nuances of his situation. Socrates remarks that he knows most people, but not everyone. The fact that Socrates does not recognize everyone reinforces his initial narrative observation that he had been away for some time (153a). Furthermore, the inclusion of this detail shows Socrates' willingness to narrate the account of the battle to this group even though he does not know everyone well. Third, a friend approaches him and asks to hear the account of the battle. In fact, Chaerephon more or less forces Socrates to relate the events of the battle. Chaerephon runs to Socrates, seizes his hand and asks five direct questions of him. Finally, Chaerephon commands Socrates to narrate and physically sits him down next to Critias (153b). The inclusion of this detail may suggest that Socrates does not initially want to give an account of the battle, but that he acquiesces to the demands of the social situation. The auditor may have asked about this battle or Socrates' conversation with Charmides and Critias in a similarly insistent manner.

Nonetheless, the fact that Plato writes this dialogue as a narrative reinforces the social context because the entire dialogue unfolds within the relationship between Socrates, qua narrator, and his auditor. Indeed, this social context between the auditor and Socrates itself seems more important than the particular details Socrates narrates to the auditor. For example, Socrates does not report the events of the battle to the auditor. Schmid and Hyland both correctly observe that this omission illustrates Socrates' *sophrosune* because he does not wish to dwell on the atrocities of war.[23] Furthermore, Socrates' omission of these details from his narrative retelling suggests that he sees the social context of the narrative retelling of the battle events as more important to convey to the auditor than the particular details about the battle.[24]

Why might Socrates choose to prioritize these details about the social context of his narrative over the details of the battle itself? By focusing his narrative on the activity of narrating, Socrates implicitly asks the auditor to reflect on his narrative relationship with Socrates. For example, the auditor should recognize the similarity between the situation he finds himself in as audience of Socrates' narrative and the narrative situation that Socrates reports to him. The auditor should ask himself what responsibility he has as the audience to Socrates' narrative performance. What does this role require of him? Is he only called upon to listen attentively or should he offer a response to the narrative?

Socrates reinforces his emphasis on the narrative relationality by mentioning how those present at the Palaestra respond to his narrative. After Socrates tells the narrative of the battle, the audience questions him. Socrates emphasizes that they ask many questions (153d). The inclusion of this detail illustrates Socrates' focus on the social context of narrative over the content of what is narrated. Simply put, Socrates starts his narrative by giving his auditor a model of how to respond to a narrative. If the auditor follows Socrates' narrative cue, then he should recognize that he should engage Socrates the narrator by asking him questions about the narrative he tells just as those present in the Palaestra questioned Socrates after his report of the battle. He should engage in this social practice actively and enthusiastically. Socrates emphasizes the importance of this reciprocity between himself and his narrative audience in the Palaestra by mentioning that their questions of him generate further questioning. Their queries give Socrates the opportunity to question them and turn the conversation toward philosophical matters. This social reciprocity continues as Socrates moves the conversation explicitly toward philosophy.

He reports, "When they had had enough of these things, I in my turn began to question them with respect to affairs at home, about the present state of philosophy and about the young men, whether there were any who had become distinguished for wisdom or beauty or both" (153d).[25] If the relationship between Socrates and the auditor is to become a philosophical one, then the auditor must do more than passively listen as the narrative unfolds. He must become an active conversational partner. Unfortunately, the auditor seems unwilling or unable to take up this challenge. As in the *Lysis*, the auditor simply listens as Socrates tells his story. He does not interrupt Socrates' narrative to ask any questions. Because the dialogue ends in the temporality of the narrated events, we do not see how the auditor responds to Socrates' narrative, or if he does so at all. As in the *Lysis*, we are left to take up the philosophical provocation of Socrates' narrative. We must ask the philosophical questions that the auditor fails to ask.[26] This ambiguous ending provokes a continuation of the dialogue outside the text. Surely, Plato's motivation for crafting the dialogue in this intricate manner is to instantiate the sort of inquiry in us, the readers of the dialogue.

For example, as readers of the dialogue, we must confront the limits of our minimal knowledge about the narrative setting and the identity of the auditor. Careful attention to the narrative structure of this dialogue places us in a mild state of aporia. This initial aporia foreshadows the ongoing association between Socrates' narrative commentary and the aporetic moments that occur in the dramatic action of the dialogue.[27] It prepares us for the moments of philosophical perplexity that will occur as the dialogue unfolds. If we are honest about our epistemological stance toward the narrative setting, we must realize that we do not have anything like complete knowledge about the events themselves. Likewise, we must acknowledge the limitations of the various definitions of *sophrosune* that we will encounter as the dialogue unfolds.

II. THREE MODELS OF INTEMPERANCE

A. Chaerephon

Socrates' inclusion of the Chaerephon interlude suggests that he knows the auditor well enough to know that he will find this extended discussion of Chaerephon of interest and that the auditor will benefit from hearing about it.[28] Socrates describes Chaerephon in these terms: "Chaerephon, like the wild man he is, sprang up from the midst of a group of people and ran towards me and seizing me by the hand, exclaimed, 'Socrates! How did you come off in the battle?'" (153b). While Chaerephon's outburst is understandable, given that he is a close friend of Socrates' since childhood and has no doubt been quite worried about him, Socrates presents Chaerephon as excessively emotional.[29] Socrates calls him a "wild man." He details his frenzied and frantic actions. Chaerephon "sprang up out of the crowd" (153b). He runs toward Socrates; he seizes Socrates by the hand (153b).

Socrates presents himself as the passive object of Chaerephon's enthusiastic eagerness.[30] Not only does Chaerephon seize Socrates' hand, he also demands that Socrates give them an account of the battle (153c).[31] Chaerephon brings him over to Critias (153c). Similarly, after Socrates describes how Charmides affects everyone in the Palaestra (154c–d), he tells the auditor that "Chaerephon called to me and said, 'Well, Socrates, what do you think of the young man? Hasn't he a splendid face?'" (154d). Socrates answers favorably. He agrees that Charmides' face is "extraordinary" (154d). After securing Socrates' agreement, Chaerephon makes an even more immoderate comment: "If he were willing to strip, you would hardly notice his face, his body is so perfect" (154d). Socrates then notes: "Everyone else said the same things as Chaerephon" (154d). By emphasizing Chaerephon's behavior, Socrates presents the auditor with an image of the negative social consequences of an individual's immoderate behavior. Initially, Chaerephon's emotional greeting of Socrates merely distinguished him from the group. Now, Chaerephon influences the group to follow his immoderate desires.

Ironically, Socrates opens this exploration of *sophrosune* with a detailed portrait of someone who lacks this virtue.[32] By starting the narrative with this extended example, Socrates' pedagogical motivation becomes apparent.[33] By providing the auditor with a concrete example of immoderation, Socrates helps the auditor identify immoderation in others and offers a way to best respond to it. Socrates offers a model of cooperative engagement that his auditor might emulate in his interactions with others. Furthermore, by giving the auditor the opportunity to observe the limitations of Chaerephon's character, Socrates also provides the auditor with the opportunity to recognize those same limitations within himself. If those limitations are present, he can work to overcome them by emulating the model of *sophrosune* that Socrates will exemplify as the narrative unfolds. The dialogue as a whole provides its contemporary readers with the same opportunity to overcome the tendency toward tyranny in themselves and in their interactions with others.

Socrates illustrates the necessity of taking this turn by deliberately moving the conversation away from the immoderate direction toward which Chaerephon leads the crowd. Socrates shifts the conversation from Charmides' body toward Charmides' soul. In doing so, he suggests that philosophy requires an appreciation of the beauty of soul.[34] He tells Chaerephon, "By Heracles, you are describing a man without an equal—if he should happen to have one small thing in addition . . . a well-formed soul?" (154d). One would expect Chaerephon to continue with his enthusiastic praise of Charmides' many attributes, but curiously, Critias, not Chaerephon, first responds to Socrates' inquiry about Charmides' soul (154d). On one level, the fact that Critias answers rather than Chaerephon illustrates Critias' impatient desire to enter the conversation, but it also suggests that Chaerephon has little interest in Charmides' soul. Though Chaerephon is an enthusiastic and vocal admirer of Charmides' body, he has nothing to say about Charmides' soul. From his silence about Charmides' soul, we can assume that Chaerephon's eros is directed toward Charmides' body, not his soul. Given Chaerephon's interest in Charmides' body, it is not surprising that after this conversational shift to Charmides' soul, Socrates does not mention Chaerephon again. Socrates leaves Chaerephon behind as his narrative moves forward toward more philosophical considerations of Charmides' attributes. Just as Socrates shifted the initial conversation away from Chaerephon's immoderate interest in the details of the battle, now he moves beyond Chaerephon's immoderate interest in Charmides' body. In doing so, Socrates implicitly asks the auditor to leave Chaerephon and his immoderate desires behind and turn toward the philosophical considerations of *sophrosune* itself.

B. Charmides

As Socrates reports Charmides' entrance into the Palaestra, he addresses the auditor directly, calling him "*etaire*," a friend or comrade (154b). Socrates tells the auditor:

> You mustn't judge by me, my friend. I'm a broken yardstick as far as handsome people are concerned, because practically every one of that age strikes me as beautiful. But even so, at the moment Charmides came in he seemed to me to be amazing in stature and appearance, and everyone there looked to me to be in love with him, they were so astonished and confused by his entrance, and many other lovers followed in his train. That men of my age should have been affected this way was natural enough, but I noticed that even the small boys fixed their eyes upon him and no one of them, not even the littlest, looked at anyone else, but all gazed at him as if he were a statue. (154b–d)

Socrates emphasizes Charmides' importance by describing him in extraordinary terms. He underscores Charmides' extraordinary presence in the next set of narrative remarks as well. After Critias predicts that Charmides will soon join them, Socrates describes the situation in detail:

> [This] is just what happened. He did come, and his coming caused a lot of laughter, because every one of us who was already seated began pushing hard at his neighbor so as to make a place for him to sit down. The upshot of it was that we made the man sitting at one end get up, and the man at the other end was toppled off sideways. (155c)

Charmides' unusual beauty disrupts normal social decorum. Socrates' narrative remarks focus on how Charmides affects those around him. Young boys are attracted to him, not just older men. In their frenzy to be close to him, people lose their seats and topple sideways. They swarm around Charmides in a circle. Socrates casts the scene in a comedic light by referring to their laughter (155c).[35] Nonetheless, dark undertones lurk beneath Socrates' humorous description. For example, Socrates compares Charmides to a lion that will devour the fawn (155d). Socrates' use of Cydias' verse should strike the auditor as odd. Charmides does not seem like a dangerous predator. Indeed, Charmides appears somewhat meek and shy. He has yet to speak a word at this point in Socrates' account. Nonetheless, Socrates describes Charmides in this strange manner. In doing so, Socrates alerts the auditor to some hidden aspect of Charmides' character that has not yet become apparent. That Charmides' beauty disrupts the social decorum is not intrinsically problematic. Indeed, Socrates' philosophical inquiries often result in similar disruptions of the social situation. Perhaps Socrates' initial description of Charmides being like a statue, an object without a soul, is suggestive of what is hidden from view. Charmides' soul is hidden from himself.

On one level, Charmides seems eager to find out about these unknown aspects of himself. He appears eager to improve himself. He asks Socrates if he has a cure for headaches. After Socrates admits that he does, Charmides immediately wants to know what the cure is (155d). Socrates reports that he tells Charmides about the headache cure, which includes a leaf and a charm to sing along with it. In response, Charmides tells Socrates that he "will write it down immediately at your dictation" (156a). Charmides' eagerness is perhaps a bit too eager. His response reveals his willingness to take something that has not yet been offered to him. Indeed, he implicitly commands Socrates to dictate the charm to him. Socrates recognizes Charmides' attempt to control him and asks Charmides if he will do so "With my permission or without it?" (156a). Socrates notes that Charmides laughs in response. His laughter suggests that he recognizes that he has exceeded the social boundaries of Socrates' offer. He takes from others rather than search within himself to fill his own needs.

Charmides also illustrates his eagerness to learn by admitting he knows Socrates by his reputation amongst the youth and because he remembers Socrates from his previous visits with Critias (156a). This remark illustrates his eagerness to meet Socrates and to improve himself through association with Socrates. Socrates responds favorably to Charmides' admission that he remembers Socrates: "I shall speak more freely about the nature of the charm" (156b). However, on another level, Charmides' admission may indicate that he is a willing participant in Critias' plan to engage Socrates in conversation with him.[36] Charmides' desire to meet Socrates may have led Critias to orchestrate this encounter between them. At the very end of the dialogue, Charmides tells Socrates "our plotting is all done" (176c). In doing so, he alludes to his own involvement in this plan.

Though Charmides appears eager to learn from Socrates, other aspects of his behavior suggest that he is content to remain in the background, to remain hidden from view and from the obligations of direct engagement with Socrates. To explain, Socrates tells Charmides a brief narrative about how he acquired this cure from "one of the Thracian doctors of Zalmoxis" (156d–157c). As he concludes the story, Socrates tells Charmides, "If you are willing, in accordance with the stranger's instructions, to submit your soul to be charmed with the Thracian's charms, first, then I shall apply the remedy to your head. But if not, there is nothing we can do for you, my dear Charmides" (157c).[37] One would expect to hear how Charmides responds to Socrates' offer, but Socrates reports that Critias answers for him (157d). Critias' rapid response reveals Critias' desire for social control and Charmides' willingness to let Critias speak for him.

Socrates forces Charmides to distinguish himself from Critias. He must step out of the passive role that he has grown accustomed to in his relationship with Critias if he is going to engage in philosophical conversation with Socrates. Socrates addresses Charmides immediately after Critias has spoken for him and describes the superior lineage of Critias and Charmides (157e–158b).[38] Socrates tells Charmides to answer for himself (158c). Socrates emphasizes the importance of Charmides' first response by telling the auditor, "At first, Charmides blushed and looked more beautiful than ever, and his bashfulness was becoming at his age. Then he answered in a way that was quite dignified, he said that it was not easy for him, in the present circumstances, either to agree or to disagree with what had been asked." (158c)

Charmides' blush could indicate that he is shy and bashful. However, it may also reveal Charmides' discomfort at the prospect of overcoming his passivity and assuming an active role in the conversation, particularly given the social complexity of the situation. Charmides shows some insightfulness as he explains the difficulty he faces:

> If I should deny that I am temperate, it would not only seem an odd thing to say about oneself, but I would at the same time make Critias here a liar, and so with the many others to whom, by his account, I appear to be temperate. But if, on the other hand, I should agree and should praise myself, perhaps that would appear distasteful. So I do not know what I am to answer. (158d)

Charmides' first response is more an articulation of an unwillingness to answer more than it is an answer. It nonetheless conveys a rudimentary sense of what *sophrosune* entails. Nonetheless, Socrates affirms Charmides' sense of the situation (158e). Socrates then gets Charmides to agree to answer the questions about this aspect of his nature (158e–159b). Socrates asks Charmides "to help us decide whether it resides in you or not" and asks him to say, "What, in your opinion, temperance is" (159b). Socrates' narrative commentary emphasizes Charmides' unwillingness to speak for himself: "At first he shied away and was rather unwilling to answer. Finally, however, he said that in his opinion temperance was doing everything in an orderly and quiet way, things like walking in the streets, and talking and doing everything else in a similar fashion" (159b). Charmides finally gives Socrates a definition, "what you ask about is a sort of quietness" (159b).

Socrates and Charmides discuss this tentative definition (159c–160e). After Charmides admits to the inadequacy of his first answer, Socrates exhorts him to start again (160e). Socrates describes Charmides' response at this crucial dramatic juncture: "He paused, and looking into himself very manfully said, 'Well, temperance seems to me to make people ashamed and bashful, and so I think modesty must be what temperance really is'" (160e). Socrates does not simply report what Charmides said, but describes the manner in which Charmides speaks. This additional information gives the auditor the opportunity to assess Charmides' character. For example, when Charmides pauses, the auditor might think that Charmides exhibits the same shyness Socrates mentioned earlier. Here, however, Socrates' description of Charmides' "entirely manful" demeanor suggests that Charmides possesses courage to overcome his shyness. Socrates also notes that Charmides looks inward. Like Lysis, Charmides evinces some aptitude for philosophy. Socrates uses his narrative commentary to alert the auditor to Charmides' philosophical potential by mentioning his courage in offering a second definition of *sophrosune* and his willingness to examine himself.

Unfortunately, Charmides does not seem committed to this second definition. After Socrates quickly refutes the definition, Charmides tells Socrates, "What you say has quite convinced me" (161b). Then Charmides challenges Socrates, "Give me your opinion of the following definition of temperance. I have just remembered having heard someone say that temperance is minding one's own business. Tell me if you think the person who said this was right" (161b). Charmides' forceful action differs quite starkly from the hesitancy he has exhibited in the two previous definitions. Just as Charmides wanted to write down the instructions for the headache cure without Socrates' permission and implicitly commanded Socrates to dictate them, here he commands Socrates to answer him. Charmides' sudden change in comportment shows that his shyness is a façade. It masks Charmides' own desire to control the social situation, a desire that matches Critias' own.

Socrates, for his part, recognizes this affinity between them because he answers Charmides' challenge with a pointed accusation: "You wretch, you've picked this up from Critias or from some other sophist" (161b). Critias denies Socrates' suggestion (161c) and Charmides seems to support Critias' denial. He asks Socrates, "What difference does it make, from whom I heard it?" Socrates responds, "None at all, since the question at issue is not who said it, but whether what he said is true or not" (161c). Socrates then refutes this definition and challenges Charmides to answer again, "Then what in the world, is 'minding your own business'? Are you able to say?" (161c–162b). Charmides then admits aporia and shifts Socrates' attention away from his inability to answer by suggesting, "Perhaps the one who said it didn't know what he meant either" (162b).

At this crucial dramatic moment, Socrates tells the auditor, "When he said this he smiled and looked at Critias" (162c). Socrates' narrative emphasis on Charmides' smile gives the auditor insight into Charmides' psychological motivation. Charmides' smile could indicate that he is sympathetic with Critias' social discomfort. If Charmides had smiled after Socrates revealed the subterfuge, the smile might be best taken as a smile of social sympathy. That Charmides smiles at his own revelation of Critias' involvement suggests that he takes pleasure in this action, which leads to Critias' discomfort. Indeed, the narrative description of Charmides' smile should cause the auditor and the reader to recall Socrates' earlier narrative characterization of him as a lion rather than a fawn. The quiet modesty that Charmides exhibited earlier, his fawnlike appearance, now seems to be a social façade. Charmides' desire for control, exhibited in his willingness to command Socrates and in his unmasking of Critias as the author of the definition, reveals his true nature. Charmides escapes the snares of Socrates' argument by turning Critias into its prey. In this case, his ability to exert social control exceeds Critias' ability to do so. Charmides is a lion after all.

Socrates reinforces this assessment of Charmides:

> In my opinion, what I suspected earlier was certainly true, that Charmides had picked up this saying about temperance from Critias. And then Charmides, who wanted the author of the definition to take over the argument rather than himself, tried to provoke him to it by going on to point out that the cause was lost. (162d)

Though Socrates does not report exactly what Charmides says, his remarks reveal that Charmides forces Critias to take over his own argument. Charmides' direct challenge to Critias' authority illustrates that there is more to Charmides' character than his quiet modesty would suggest. Just as Charmides' arrival in the Palaestra caused disorder in the seating arrangement, he disrupts the social order in his relationship with Critias. He is unwilling to remain under Critias' control.

Just as Socrates pushes Lysis toward personal autonomy, Socrates supports Charmides' attempt to overcome Critias' social control of him. For example, after Critias takes up Charmides' challenge, "Do you suppose, Charmides, that just because you don't understand what in the world the man meant who said that temperance was 'minding your own business,' the man himself doesn't understand either?" (162c–e), Socrates answers for Charmides (162e). Socrates intervenes on Charmides' behalf to force Critias into upholding his own definition. While Socrates may be interested in arguing with Critias because Critias is a more worthy intellectual adversary, Socrates' decision to engage Critias in debate also gives Charmides time to separate himself from Critias.

Though Charmides exhibits some of the self-control and self-reflection that philosophy requires, his willingness to allow Socrates to engage Critias for him suggests that he lacks the inner resources to become a philosopher who can engage on an equal footing with other philosophers. Ironically, Charmides may well have achieved his desired end by having Socrates argue with Critias. He has manipulated Socrates into challenging Critias' authority for him. Having accomplished this goal, Charmides recedes into the background of the drama. Indeed, Socrates does not mention him again until the close of the dialogue (175d–176d). There, Charmides reveals his complicity in plotting with Critias to engage Socrates in conversation. We see Charmides' willingness to use force against those who oppose him. The dialogue ends with Charmides illustrating his tyrannical tendencies even as he admits he needs to submit himself to Socrates' charms every day.[39]

C. Critias

When Socrates finishes narrating the events of the battle, a narrative he alludes to but does not share with the auditor, he asks "about the present state of philosophy and about the young men, whether there were any who had become distinguished for wisdom or beauty or both" (154d). Socrates then tells the auditor that Critias "glancing towards the door and seeing several young men coming in and laughing with each other, with a crowd of others following behind," answers him (153d–154a).[40] Critias presents Charmides' attributes so that they will entice Socrates into conversation: "As far as beauty goes, Socrates, I think you will be able to make up your mind straight away, because those coming in are the advance party and the admirers of the one who is thought to be the handsomest young man of the day, and I think that he himself cannot be far off" (154a). Critias' description intrigues Socrates. Socrates then asks Critias several questions about Charmides (154b). Critias appears confident that Socrates will find Charmides "not only a philosopher but also, both in his own opinion and that of others, quite a poet" (155a).[41]

As Charmides' guardian, Critias is quite understandably concerned for Charmides' reputation. However, Socrates' descriptions of Critias show him to be excessively concerned with social standing and reputation. Throughout the dialogue, Critias attempts to control whatever social situation arises. For example, in his opening exchange with Socrates (153c–155d), Socrates suggests that they call Charmides over to them. Initially, Critias seems willing to let Socrates dictate how the conversation will unfold. However, Critias soon takes control of the situation. Socrates tells the auditor: "He immediately spoke to his servant and said, 'Boy, call Charmides and tell him I want him to meet a doctor for the weakness he told me he was suffering from yesterday'" (155b). The fact that Critias exerts his authority over his servant illustrates his desire for social control, as does the fact that he commands Charmides through the servant. Furthermore, Critias tells the servant that it is his own desire that Charmides join them. He hides the fact that it was Socrates' idea initially.[42] By commanding his servant in this way, Critias presents himself as the one who is in control of the social situation. Critias also engages in another, more explicit, deception to entice Socrates into conversation with Charmides. Critias enlists Socrates in his plan: "You see, just lately he's complained of a headache when he gets up in the morning. Why not pretend to him that you know a remedy for it?" (155b). Though Socrates plays along with this social deception, just as he did in the *Lysis*, the deception here is Critias' idea.

Socrates also places Critias in a negative light by associating him with Charmides' headaches, a symbol of the lack of *sophrosune*. Hyland suggests that these headaches result from Charmides' intemperate behavior the evening before.[43] Each time Socrates mentions Charmides' headache, he mentions Critias as well (155b, 155d, 156b, and 157d). Similarly, each time Socrates refers to his own loss of self-control, he refers to Critias as well (155c and 155d). Socrates' inclusion of Critias' name at these moments where *sophrosune* eludes him cannot be accidental. By linking Critias with these moments, Socrates associates Critias with a lack of *sophrosune*.[44] Another example of this linking occurs when Socrates asks Charmides if he will submit his soul to the Thracian's charm (157c). At that point, Critias interrupts their conversation and answers for Charmides. Critias wants Socrates to view Charmides favorably. He informs Socrates: "Charmides not only outstrips his contemporaries in beauty of form, but also in this very thing for which you say you have the charm" (157d). Critias then asks Socrates: "It was *sophrosune* wasn't it?" (157d). The fact that Critias appears to forget that they are talking about *sophrosune* suggests that Critias has little interest in the virtue. Generally speaking, Critias is regarded in quite negative terms in the secondary literature. Schmid characterizes Critias as "a man concerned with his own advantage and honor, not with justice or truth."[45] Brann goes so far as to call Critias an "inchoate evil."[46]

Socrates' narrative descriptions of Critias provide ample evidence for these negative assessments.[47] For example, when Charmides offers his definition of *sophrosune* as minding one's own business, Socrates describes the very moment that Critias loses self-control. He reports, "It was clear that Critias had been agitated for some time and also that he was eager to impress Charmides and the rest who were there. He had held himself in with difficulty earlier, but now he could do so no longer" (162c). Socrates describes the scene for the auditor:

> Critias seemed to me to be angry with Charmides just the way a poet is when his verse is mangled by the actors. So he gave him a look and said, "Do you

suppose, Charmides, that just because you don't understand what in the world the man meant who said that temperance was 'minding your own business,' the man himself doesn't understand either?" (162e)

Just as Critias engages Socrates in a duplicitous plan to get Charmides to speak with him, here Socrates' narrative commentary suggests Critias' involvement in another similar plan: he may have coached Charmides about what to say in conversation with Socrates. In this way, Critias exerts his control over the social situation by attempting to control the content and direction of the conversation itself. He uses the mechanism of logos, of speech, to exert his social tyranny. Unfortunately, Charmides' enactment of the argument does not hold up against Socrates' refutation of it. Critias' impatience now turns into agitation and misdirected anger. Beversluis aptly notes that Critias gets mad at Charmides while he should be mad at Socrates.[48] In all likelihood, he is mad at himself since his planning failed to bring about his desired aim.

Socrates' narrative commentary does more than describe these dramatic interactions. It also leads the auditor into autonomous philosophical reflection about the nature of this virtue that both Critias and Charmides lack. For example, when Socrates mentions that prior to this point Critias has restrained himself, but with difficulty (162d), the auditor must reflect back on what Socrates told him and add this new information about Critias into the picture.[49] The auditor should recognize that Socrates is not narrating events exactly as they happened. This recognition should cause the auditor to move beyond his dependence on Socrates' narrative commentary and assess for himself Critias' character and the limitations of his arguments. Socrates' narrative commentary trains the auditor to overcome his dependence on its authority. When the auditor recognizes the limits of Socrates' narrative authority, he begins to think for himself.

This narrative provocation to philosophical autonomy intellectually prepares the auditor to hear the rest of the discussion with Critias. Once Critias takes over as primary interlocutor (162d), Socrates offers no additional narrative commentary on their discussion of *sophrosune* as minding one's business (163a), as the doing of good things (163e), as self-knowledge (164e), as a science (165c), as a science of itself and of other sciences and the absence of science (166e). Socrates does not interrupt his report of their conversation with any narrative remarks, beyond those necessitated by the "I said" and "he said" constructions of reported discourse until 169c. In this philosophically complex part of the dialogue, Socrates does not give the auditor any additional commentary to help him reason through the philosophical perplexities of each definition. In the absence of this commentary, the auditor must grapple with these philosophical complexities for himself.

So, what should the auditor observe concerning Critias' arguments about *sophrosune*? First, the auditor should see that the definitions that Critias provides focus on external actions which are associated with an aristocratic value system, i.e., doing one's own things and doing good things (161b–163e),[50] or on an intellectual understanding of *sophrosune* as the science of science (164d–167a). Critias does not define *sophrosune* in terms of self-control or the regulation of desire. Notomi puts the point this way: "Critias' definitions are obviously one-sided in that they entirely ignore the common meaning of 'self-control' (i.e. control of appetites and pleasures)." He emphasizes further that "all the definitions presented by Critias show his aristocratic (or oligarchic) and intellectualist bias."[51]

Second, the auditor should recognize that Socrates wishes to separate himself from the understanding of *sophrosune* as the science of science. The auditor should notice the moment when Socrates admits his inability "to accept *sophrosune* as such a science" (169b). Socrates challenges Critias, "To first clear up this point, that what I just mentioned is possible and then, after having shown its possibility, go on to show that it is useful. And so, perhaps, you will satisfy me that you are right about what temperance is" (169c). Socrates' narrative voice intervenes here for the last time. Perhaps Socrates chooses this moment to insert more directive comments because he fears that the auditor may be overwhelmed with the complexities of the argument.[52] Perhaps Socrates worries that Critias' intellectualist definition of *sophrosune* will sway the auditor away from an understanding of *sophrosune* that requires emotional awareness along with the regulation of desire. This simultaneous integration and regulation of emotions is particularly important with regards to the social context of the virtue. Social situations are always complicated, complicated partly by the competing interests of those involved and the varying degrees of emotional involvement. If one disregards the emotional dimensions of social exchange, one becomes, quite simply, a tyrant to reason.

To help the auditor recognize the risk of overly intellectualizing a situation, Socrates' narrative voice underscores the fact that Critias cannot face Socrates' challenge to his definition about s*ophrosune* as the science of science. Critias cannot explain either how such a science of science is possible or that it is useful (169c). In fact, Critias experiences Socrates' aporia about the usefulness of *sophrosune* when viewed in these intellectualist terms. Socrates focuses the auditor's attention on this point:

> When Critias heard this and saw that I was in difficulties, then, just as in the case of people who start yawning when they see other people doing it, he seemed to be affected by my troubles and to be seized by difficulties himself. But since his consistently high reputation made him feel ashamed in the eyes of the company and he did not wish to admit to me that he was incapable of

dealing with the question I had asked him, he said nothing clear but concealed his predicament. (169d)

Socrates' final narrative remarks reinforce how Critias' oligarchic worldview requires the acclaim of others. As a result, he engages in subterfuge to preserve his social reputation rather than admit the inadequacy of his definition. Critias cannot follow Socrates on the inward path of philosophical inquiry because he cannot overcome his need for public acclaim. His sense of worthiness demands that he put his own concerns before the concerns of others. Because Critias overlooks an understanding of *sophrosune* that involves an inward turn, Critias has no other resources to appeal to when his social reputation fails him. As a result, Critias chooses a path of deception over the path of truth that philosophy requires. Christopher Bruell notes that Socrates does not tell the auditor exactly how Critias answers at this point.[53] Just as Socrates omits the details of the battle, in the narrative retelling, he also omits the details of Critias' attempted response. The auditor only knows that Critias conceals his true predicament, not how he did so. In fact, the contrast between Critias and Socrates is heightened by the fact that Socrates performed well in the battle of Potidaea and still chooses not to seek out the public acclaim that Critias so clearly seeks in attempts to control his conversation with Socrates. Socrates wins this battle with Critias and chooses not to dwell on the details of the victory. When Socrates focuses on this moment of deception, he presents the auditor with a choice. The auditor can choose Critias' path of immoderate deception in the social sphere or he can choose the path of Socratic *sophrosune*.

D: Critias and Charmides Together Against Socrates (169e–176d)

Socrates' narrative voice does not intervene again. However, the preceding narrative commentary has provided the auditor and the reader with enough interpretive clues to assess Socrates', Critias', and Charmides' behavior in the final moments of the dialogue. First, Socrates makes the argument go forward (169d). That he does so, suggests that Critias cannot handle the intellectual demands of the conversation. Socrates explores two complex issues: (1) the practical limitations of seeing *sophrosune* as the science of science and (2) if knowing what one knows and does not know is the same thing as knowledge of self (169d–172c). Critias, by contrast, says very little here. His responses are curt. Critias agrees with Socrates' argument without challenge until he accuses Socrates of "speaking strangely" (172e). Critias then asks Socrates to explain so that "we may understand" (173a). Despite this apparent willingness to look at *sophrosune* differently, Critias will not give up his view of *sophrosune* as a science. Even when Socrates forces Critias to acknowledge that *sophrosune* hinges on knowledge of good and evil (173c), Critias does not relinquish his position. Socrates calls him a "wretch *miare*" and accuses Critias of concealing his knowledge (174b) just as he previously covered up his inability to answer Socrates' query (169d).[54] In the earlier passage, Socrates' narrative commentary emphasized Critias' willingness to conceal his true situation. The auditor must recognize this important point without the help of Socrates' narrative commentary.

Throughout this exchange, Charmides plays no obvious role. While Charmides may be listening intently, he does not participate until Socrates finally brings him back into the conversation (175d–e). Socrates expresses his frustration that the argument has been inconclusive. He also worries for the sake of Charmides. Socrates laments to Charmides about the possibility that "with such a body and, in addition, a most temperate soul, you should derive no benefit from this temperance nor should it be of any use to you in this present life" (175e). As the dialogue draws to a close, Socrates tells Charmides that "*sophrosune* is a great good, and if you truly have it, you are blessed. So see whether you do have it and are in no need of the charm—because if you do have it, my advice to you would rather be to regard me as a babbler, incapable of finding out anything whatsoever by means of argument, and yourself as being exactly as happy as you are temperate" (176a).

Even though Socrates' narrative commentary does not intervene beyond reporting that Charmides spoke, the auditor should sense the importance of this dramatic moment. Will Charmides recognize that he lacks genuine *sophrosune* and join Socrates in further discussion or will he find his current mode of existence acceptable? Charmides, for his part, expresses aporia about whether or not he does have *sophrosune* at all (176b). In this way, Charmides aligns himself with Socrates' willingness to admit aporia and with his search for the answer that eludes them (176c). Given Charmides' eagerness to be charmed by Socrates, the dialogue appears to end more positively than the *Lysis*. There, Socrates reaches an impasse with the young boys and hopes to continue his conversation with the others present. But they are called away. As a result, Socrates stands alone in his search to understand the nature of friendship (223a). Here, Charmides appears to align himself with Socrates' search for *sophrosune*.

However, even though Charmides tells Socrates that he wants to "be charmed by you every day until you say I have had enough" (176b), the auditor should realize that this ongoing association will never occur. The fact that Charmides sees the charming as something Socrates will do to him rather than something that he will do for himself or, together with Socrates, illustrates Charmides' desire to remain in his passive social role. He is unwilling to assume responsibility for cultivating his own *sophrosune*. That Charmides does not want to repeat the charm himself suggests that he does not possess the resources within himself to cultivate *sophrosune* and turn away from the social acclaim of the crowds who surround him. Furthermore, when Charmides expresses his willingness to submit to Critias' command, he maintains his passive stance in his relationship with Critias as well (176c). This comment suggests that both Critias and Charmides are more attached to their particular social roles than to learning the truth about how best to pursue the cultivation of *sophrosune*.

The ending exchange between Socrates, Charmides, and Critias makes their choice even more apparent (176b–176d). As many scholars note, the conclusion of the dialogue foreshadows the tyrannical end of Critias and Charmides in several ways.[55] First, Critias orders Charmides to be charmed. In doing so, Critias yields to the temptation of overt social control through the command of others. Critias' desire to exert overt social control culminates in his involvement with the Thirty Tyrants. As leader of this regime, he rules over all other Athenian citizens. Second, Charmides willingly obeys Critias just as he will later do as one of the Ten chosen by the Thirty to govern Piraeus. Third, Socrates asks what they are plotting (176c). Charmides emphatically says, "Nothing." Then, he immediately admits that they have been plotting all along by saying, "Our plotting is all done" (176c). This admission reinforces Socrates' previous allusion to their rehearsing of the arguments (162d). The repeated use of *bouleo* also reinforces these political overtones.[56]

Fourth, Socrates continues to use language with political overtones, asking: "Are you going to use force and not give me a preliminary hearing?" (176c).[57] It is telling that Charmides himself responds rather than Critias. Charmides' final words express his allegiance to Critias over Socrates, "We shall have to use force . . . seeing that this one here has ordered it" (176c). With these words Charmides expresses his willingness to do as Critias commands, but with his next words, he exhibits his own desire to exert control. He warns Socrates: "Take counsel as to what you will do" (176c). Charmides' direct warning to Socrates illustrates Charmides' tendency to exert tyrannical control over others. He does not simply want to follow Critias' dictates but to control people himself. Socrates warns him about the implications of his choice to use force: "What use is counsel? Because when you undertake to do anything by force, no man living can oppose you" (176d). Historically, of course, Socrates does oppose them. He refuses to participate in the unlawful arrest of Leon (*Apology*, 32c).[58] Krentz rightly notes that "Socrates did not try to prevent others from arresting Leon, nor did he endeavor to warn Leon himself. He went home." Nonetheless, Krentz concludes: "Socrates must have been unusual in opposing the government even this much."[59]

Charmides' last words leave no room for dissension or debate. He orders Socrates not to oppose him (176d4). By choosing overt control over cooperative philosophical council, Charmides reveals his tyrannical aims. Charmides chooses the path of tyranny over the path of temperance. Socrates' narrative both begins and ends with examples of intemperance. Socrates alone emerges as the model of *sophrosune*.

III. SOCRATIC *SOPHROSUNE*

Socrates' narrative commentary presents a model of *sophrosune* that contravenes the various manifestations of immoderation exhibited by Chaerephon, Charmides, and Critias. Socrates' narrative remarks focus on his emotional states and how he responds to his emotions throughout the course of his philosophical inquiry.[60] This aspect of Socrates' self-presentation counteracts the pervasive view in the secondary literature that Socratic *sophrosune* involves the ability to overcome the conflict between emotions and reason with a higher appeal to reason.[61] Because these narrative comments include the emotional dimensions of Socrates' own experience, they suggest that Socrates exhibits *sophrosune* not merely by overcoming his emotions in the way that he illustrates within the dramatic events, but also by incorporating the insights gained from his emotional responses to Charmides into his philosophical practice, which he recreates on the communal level of the narrative retelling.

In the *Lysis*, Socrates does not directly say anything about his emotional state until well into the dialogue (210e). In the *Charmides*, by contrast, Socrates mentions his emotional state in the opening line of his narrative. After returning from Potidaea, Socrates "gladly returns to his accustomed pastimes" (153a).[62] Socrates does not merely report what he did, but how he feels about it. Socrates then notes that he saw people he knew as well as people he did not (153a). In all likelihood, Socrates is happy to see those he recognized and eager to meet new people. The detail of Socrates' narrative commentary, both with respect to his physical surroundings and his emotional state, contrasts with the laconic brevity of the answers he gives to Chaerephon. Even though Chaerephon specifically asks, "How did you come off in the battle?" Socrates does not respond in any detail. Rather he says, "Exactly as you see me" (153b). Socrates does not reveal that he examines his emotional state on the dramatic level. He does not want to bring that dimension of self-disclosure into his conversation with Chaerephon.

On the narrative level, on the other hand, Socrates shares his emotional awareness with the auditor. For example, after Charmides' entrance into the Palaestra, Socrates describes Charmides' effect on him: "At the moment Charmides came in he seemed to me to be amazing in stature and appearance" (154c–d). Socrates reports how the closeness of Charmides' presence overwhelms him; he is "in difficulty" (155c). His former bold courage disappears completely (155c). Socrates describes the full force of Charmides' gaze as "inconceivable" (155d). Once he sees inside Charmides' cloak, Socrates is "inflamed and no longer in himself" (155d). Socrates then employs a vivid poetic metaphor to describe Charmides' effect on him: "It occurred to me that Cydias was the wisest love-poet when he gave someone advice on the subject of beautiful boys and said that 'the fawn should beware lest, while taking a look at the lion, he should provide part of the lion's dinner,' because I felt as if I had been snapped up by such a creature" (155d). After Socrates persuades Charmides that he must cure the whole body along with his headache, Socrates again describes his emotional state to the auditor: "When I heard his approval, I took heart, and little by little, my former confidence revived and I began to wake up" (156d). Socrates seems to be suggesting that his emotional state was not itself problematic but the manner in which he initially responded to his emotions needed to change. Given the traditional focus on the Socratic Method as something primarily concerned with the *elenchus*, the philosophical importance of these sorts of narrative remarks is often disregarded. However, remarks such as these suggest that Socrates' method of self-care extends to every level of human experience.

Socrates' narrative commentary also shows how he responds to the strong pull of his emotions. For example, when Socrates expresses his overwhelming awe at the beauty and stature of Charmides (154c–d), he also tells the auditor "You must not judge by me, my friend. I'm a broken yardstick as far as handsome people are concerned, because practically everyone of that age strikes me as beautiful" (154c). Similarly, despite being overcome by his glimpse inside Charmides' cloak, Socrates recalls the wise advice of Cydias the love poet (155d). The appeal to Cydias calms Socrates. This therapeutic use of poetry runs counter to the largely negative treatment of poetry in the *Republic* and Socrates' negative remarks about poetic wisdom in the *Apology* and the *Ion*. Here, Socrates portrays poetry as an important mechanism by which he gains his bearings in this unusual situation. Indeed, Socrates presents himself as taking refuge in the teachings of Cydias. His knowledge of poetry helps him continue his philosophical quest. Far from undermining his philosophical ability to reason, poetry upholds his philosophic practice.[63] With this poetic observation firmly in mind, Socrates tells Charmides about the leaf, the charm, and the method of treatment for his headache. Rutherford describes Socrates' ability to compose himself: "It was through the power of reason that Socrates had dominated his passionate satyr-like nature. Part of the purpose of the *Charmides* is to demonstrate this aspect of Socrates' character, for throughout the rest of the dialogue he speaks freely and without reserve, showing no sign of desiring him [Charmides] or wanting to seduce him."[64] As I mentioned in the introduction, scholars often regard Plato and Socrates as philosophers who are suspicious of emotional experience, particularly with respect to the positive value it might have for philosophical inquiry.[65] Under this view, one might reasonably conclude that Socratic *sophrosune* involves the strong redirection of, if not outright suppression of, his bodily desires and appetites. For example, Rutherford acknowledges that "Plato's Socrates is not simply an embodiment of reason. His philosophic religion has its irrational side also (his inexplicable 'divine voice'), and here we see that for all his self-discipline he is a man of strong passion." Nonetheless, he maintains, "It is clear from the *Charmides* and from the later, fuller account of his behavior by Alcibiades in the *Symposium*, that his passion was contained and controlled."[66] Though Rutherford allows some room for a more emotional Socrates, the emotions are still clearly subservient to Socrates' rational side throughout his fine book, *The Art of Plato*.

However, the narrative commentary in the *Charmides* supports a more nuanced understanding of the interplay between the appetites, emotions and reason.[67] Socrates does not compose himself by characterizing his response to Charmides as unwarranted. Nor does he compose himself by appealing to a rational argument about why his response to Charmides is harmful to the philosophic task at hand. Socrates seems to compose himself through his heightened emotional awareness of the very moments when reasoned self-control fails him. Landy notes, "In giving an account of these things to his nameless listener, Socrates shows what could be considered an essential ingredient of temperance; knowledge of himself, his appetites and weaknesses, and he eventually recovers his composure."[68] This view seems paradoxical, but the paradox is partially resolved because the failure is not complete or permanent. The narrative level of the dialogue shows us a Socrates recomposed. As I mentioned previously, Socrates recalls Cydias' poetic verse immediately after feeling outside himself and shortly after that engages Charmides in philosophical conversation (155d). Nonetheless, on a deeper level, this paradoxical sense of self-control remains. As McAvoy aptly observes, "He is acknowledging his susceptibility to Charmides as real, and not simply pretense, and also demonstrating his way of overcoming it by first recognizing its power over him."[69] The self-control that Socrates exhibits by engaging Charmides in conversation does not involve denying his intense desire for him. Indeed, he fully acknowledges the power of his erotic desire and emphasizes how deeply he is in the grasp of it by comparing Charmides to a lion that has snatched him up.

Simply put, Socrates' narrative activity is a part of his ongoing quest for self-knowledge. Socrates describes his desire to know what sort of creature he is in the *Phaedrus*: "Am I a beast more complicated and savage than Typhon, or am I a tamer, simpler animal with a share in a divine and gentle nature?" (230a). Socrates engages in this ongoing query by telling narratives about himself. By telling these narratives, Socrates models a mode of being that diminishes the strong conflict between reason and emotion because it includes both his emotional experiences and intellectual experiences in the narratives he tells. Socratic self-examination becomes a therapeutic model of self-care. This narrative model of self-examination as self-care offers guidance to the auditor as he seeks to integrate the emotional and intellectual dimensions of his own life. These narratives are acts of self-representation by which he comes to a deeper level of self-understanding. Once we regard Socrates' narrative commentary as an integral part of his search for self-knowledge and as an integral part of the path that he models for others to follow, maintaining a strict priority of reason over emotion in Plato's presentation of Socratic self-knowledge and philosophic practice becomes more difficult.[70] Socrates does not seek to control the narrative with his reason alone. His narrative allows space for his emotions to exist in the story, just as they should have a place in our lives. By denying them a place, we make reason a tyrant in our lives. This Socratic narrative model of self-examination provides a concrete model for us to follow as we seek to bring both reason and emotion into our own philosophical lives.

One could still argue that Socrates' references to his overwhelming emotional responses are simply meant to show precisely how dangerous the emotions are to reasoned philosophical discourse. Socrates could be telling this narrative to show why the philosopher must turn away from the emotions and embrace the path of reasoned discourse. However, there are two problems with upholding this interpretation. First, it simply reasserts the intellectualist reading which the evidence of the narrative frame calls into question. Second, Socrates includes these emotional moments in the narrative he tells. Without the narrative frame, we would have no way of knowing that Socrates was attracted to Charmides at all. The narrative commentary allows us to see the emotional dimensions of Socrates the character. Indeed, Socrates seems quite willing to disclose these aspects of himself to the auditor. He does not present himself as a philosopher unaffected by emotions and desires, but as a philosopher who practices philosophy in the midst of experiencing a full range of emotions and desires as a means of acquiring self-knowledge.

So precisely what kind of knowledge does Socrates display on the narrative level? I suggest that it is a sense of knowledge based in an ongoing discursive praxis, rather than a content or propositionally based knowledge. Narrative self-knowledge is best understood as a type of self-care. We care for ourselves, we continue to grow into ourselves, to "become who we are" at least in part by constructing and listening to the narratives we tell about ourselves through the course of our engagement with others. Marina McCoy's analysis of Sophocles' rather bleak play, *Philoctetes*, is an excellent example that illustrates the importance of not "getting trapped" in our narratives. For Philoctetes to know himself more fully, to know himself as other than he is, he needs a new narrative to tell about himself.[71] Plato portrays Socrates as doing precisely this work. He is not content to explore "what kind of creature he is" merely through his interactions with others. He reconsiders what he gains from those explorations by telling narratives about his experience, at least as Plato tells the story. In doing so, Socrates illustrates how self-knowledge is an ongoing practice aimed at overcoming our own limitations.

IV. NARRATIVE SELF-KNOWLEDGE: AUTONOMY, COMMUNITY, AND OVERCOMING TYRANNY

Most of the scholarly discussion about *sophrosune* as self-knowledge centers on the various definitions of knowledge presented in Socrates' exchanges with Critias (165c–175d).[72] Some scholars do notice that the narrative frame of the dialogue points to an additional way of understanding Socratic self-knowledge because of the self-reflective portrait Socrates creates in his narrative. This fruitful line of interpretation moves the discussion beyond the theoretical dimensions of self-knowledge that emerge when we focus primarily on the argument between Socrates and Critias and toward a richer understanding of how Plato portrays Socrates' practice of self-knowledge in the dialogues. For example, Richard McKim notes that "Although his *characters* may be confused about what sort of self-knowledge 'knowledge of knowledge' can be, Plato provides his *readers* with an unmistakable clue as to what sort we are to take it to be—namely, Socratic self-knowledge."[73] Francisco Gonzalez explains the differences between Socrates' understanding of knowledge and Critias' in this way: "We see no good in Critias' contentious employment of definitions, but the good is revealed in the way in which Socrates examines and refutes definition."[74] I suggest that awareness of Socrates' narrative activity contributes to an even richer portrait of Socrates in action. Though neither Gonzales nor McKim discusses the narrative representation of Socrates' activity, it is on this narrative level that Socrates most adequately "*shows us what it means to be good.*"[75] It does so in two primary ways. First, Socrates' reported narrative about his search for *sophrosune* illustrates the ongoing nature of his philosophical inquiry. It also illustrates the deeply communal nature of Socratic philosophical inquiry. By retelling this conversation, Socrates opens the whole discussion of *sophrosune* for reconsideration by himself and the auditor. He continues his philosophical quest for self-knowledge and for knowledge of the good by telling a narrative about himself engaged in that very quest. Second, as I suggested in the previous section, Socrates' narrative commentary suggests that self-care is an integral part of self-knowledge. Part of how Socrates cares for himself is to constantly ask questions about himself and others. Drew Hyland calls this preserving of the questioning stance "responsive openness."[76] Indeed, Socrates' narrative retelling of this conversation embodies his responsive openness to the possibility of new philosophical insight about the matters at hand by engaging with the auditor. Socrates' receptive philosophical openness models a form of respectful engagement with the auditor that contrasts with the tyrannical methods of social engagement that Critias and Charmides employ. While Critias and Charmides seek to control their interactions with Socrates and with each other, Socrates' narrative invites the auditor into a philosophical engagement with the narrative. The Socratic invitation does not dictate how the auditor will respond. Socrates' narrative invites him to respond and take up the task of philosophical inquiry for himself.

However, some scholars regard Socrates' narrative commentary as an attempt to control the auditor's response to these events. Benardete notes:

> The auditor learns that Socrates at this moment was no longer in himself (*en emautou*); he learns this when Socrates is fully in control: as narrator he can say and not say what he wants about himself and everyone else. Self-control in the strict sense seems to be possible only if there is complete control of everyone else. Narration is the retrospective equivalent of what in the present would be universal tyranny.[77]

Under this view, the control that Socrates maintains over the retelling of the events can become the philosophical equivalent of tyranny. While some would argue that this tyranny exists in any narrative situation, Plato portrays Socrates as resisting this temptation. Socrates resists this temptation toward narrative tyranny by allowing his narrative commentary to diminish over the course of this dialogue. Socrates' commentary disappears from 162e–169c and does not occur at all after 169c. Once Critias takes over as the primary interlocutor, the auditor must follow the argument and make assessments about his character largely without the benefit of Socrates' guidance. Furthermore, the fact that Socrates' narrative voice does not return at the end of the dialogue also diminishes the totalizing effect of Socratic narrative perspective. In relinquishing this control, Socrates illustrates that he does not have the final view or supreme perspective on the events that transpired, the definitions and arguments, or even his self-understanding. This diminishing of narrative control gives the auditor the space to interpret the narrative for himself.[78] The auditor must look inward to find answers to the questions that remain unanswered by Socrates' narrative depiction of his philosophical questioning. Hopefully, the auditor will seek out and help to bring about a community of others to continue this self-inquiry just as Socrates has done by telling this narrative to him.

Why might Plato dramatize this provocation to philosophical reflection on the narrative level? One answer involves the strong political undertones of the dialogue. To explain, on the dramatic level, Charmides and Critias succumb to the temptation of social tyranny over Socrates and over each other. This social tyranny illustrated in the drama of the dialogue foreshadows the political temptation of tyranny that both succumb to during the tumultuous events following the Peloponnesian War. On the historical level, Socrates does oppose Critias and the Thirty Tyrants. Plato may want to remind the audience of Socrates' ethical resistance to political tyranny.

On a deeper level, the *Charmides* raises the issue of the role of philosophy in the polis and philosophy's own temptations with various forms of tyranny. Though Socrates the individual philosopher resists the Thirty Tyrants, the temptation to use philosophy for tyrannical ends remains present for anyone who takes up the philosophical life. The temptation toward tyranny remains because the philosopher recognizes the lure of political power like any person, but also because philosophy requires a level of autonomous insight into the nature of reality that may lead one to take less seriously the demands that society places upon the individual. Another aspect of the temptation of tyranny lies with the intellectual arrogance that often comes along with philosophical insight. That arrogance can lead one to believe that the philosopher, because the philosopher has a heightened understanding of truth, should rule the polis.

Within the dramatic confines of the story, Socrates fulfills his political obligations by participating in the war and fulfills his social obligations by reporting the facts about the battle to those at the Palaestra. After reporting the events of the battle, Socrates immediately asks about the city more broadly, about the youth, and particularly, if any of them has an aptitude for philosophy (153d). With these queries, Socrates shows that his interest in the social sphere extends beyond the obligations of war.[79] By turning the conversation away from politics toward philosophy, Socrates reveals that his fundamental interest lies in philosophical inquiry rather than political affairs, at least when narrowly understood. Unlike the other Athenians who surround him, Socrates' passion is for philosophy, not for "war fever."[80] Socrates illustrates this same preference on the narrative level. He does not recount the details of the battle to his auditor but instead relates the details of his philosophical encounter with Critias and Charmides.

For a politically oriented society such as Athens, this preference becomes problematic. "Philosophers are a political problem" because they are willing to question received communal wisdom, institutional power structures, and the role of the individual in society.[81] Philosophy promotes a level of autonomy and freedom of thought that moves the individual beyond the socially constructed confines of the polis.[82] Philosophy, however, is not a wholly private matter. Philosophers seek to bring others into the philosophical life. Indeed, as Tucker Landy puts it, "Socrates is naturally interested in educating the young, especially the most talented and ambitious, toward a life of philosophy."[83] Unfortunately, educating the youth highlights these competing interests between philosophy and the polis. The polis seeks to create citizens who will uphold the values of the polis. The philosopher motivates others to become philosophers who will seek truth beyond the confines of the polis. Landy puts it this way, "philosophy is distinguished, not by any set of doctrine or rigor of method, but above all by its tendency to view wisdom as having value independently of whatever public reputation or political power it may bring."[84] Socrates' turn from discussions of war to philosophic conversation, on both the dramatic and narrative level, exemplifies what Drew Hyland refers to as "the apolitical nature of philosophy."[85] This claim does presuppose a certain view of politics, as commonly practiced, as intractably non-philosophical. Philosophy, in turn, becomes the domain of true politics. Differently put, philosophy might better be regarded as prepolitical politics. Within the political sphere where power dictates the decision-making process, philosophy must, by necessity, become apolitical if it is to maintain a space for its own existence.

This apolitical aim of philosophy does not mean that philosophy is noncommunal. The philosopher seeks to create a community in which philosophy can occur. This desire for community is best seen on the narrative level. Socrates, qua narrator, instantiates a community for philosophical inquiry to continue. Socrates invites the auditor to experience philosophy along with him. In doing so, Socrates brings philosophy into the public sphere rather than allow it to remain his own private task for self-understanding. His continued search for self-knowledge may involve sustained silent individual reflection, as exhibited in the *Symposium* trance (175a), but it also involves sharing his ongoing self-reflection with others via philosophical discussion and via the narratives he tells. Socratic *sophrosune* involves both an inward and outward orientation. Socrates exemplifies the inner orientation of *sophrosune* by telling a story about himself. Ultimately, however, the presentation of his self-reflection is outwardly directed toward the auditor. As Socrates brings the auditor into philosophical community, he exhibits the outward orientation of *sophrosune*. As a result, the narrative dimensions of the dialogue portray Socrates' own "form of self-knowledge, a volitional habit of rationality that both sustains and helps create moral autonomy and community."[86] By telling this narrative about himself, Socrates instantiates a community between himself and the auditor that requires philosophical autonomy from both members. Socratic *sophrosune* illustrates how the inner and outer levels of the virtue are mutually reinforcing. True political community demands both individual and communal space. On this point, Paul Stern argues that Socrates' *sophrosune* stands in defense of politics by showing that one thing true politics shares with the philosophic quest is awareness of the enduring questionableness of human wholeness.[87]

This different model of community enacted on the narrative level prioritizes a model of social inclusivity rather than a model of political exclusivity. According to Peter Krentz, the tendency to exclude people from political power was a central feature of Ancient Greek tyranny. The Thirty, for example, disenfranchised increasing numbers of the Athenian populace.[88] Socrates' narrative philosophy, in contrast, is inclusive. He draws the auditor into the philosophical experience by telling this narrative about his philosophical experience. The inclusive openness that Socrates exhibits in telling the narrative illustrates the very opposite of the tyrannical tendency to exclude.[89] Socrates' narrative presentation of *sophrosune* presents a model of individual autonomy that overcomes the temptations of tyranny because it includes receptive openness to ongoing inquiry and an inclusive willingness to engage others.[90] Viewed in this way, Socrates redefines the political associations of *sophrosune* itself. As mentioned previously, *sophrosune* was generally regarded as an oligarchic virtue. Socrates' exemplification of *sophrosune* on the narrative level democratizes the virtue because it invites others into association with him.

Socrates' narrative retelling of this encounter between a philosopher and two tyrants illustrates one of the ways that Socrates chooses temperance over tyranny. On the narrative level, Plato portrays Socrates as overcoming the philosophical temptation of tyranny by relinquishing his narrative control as the dialogue progresses. Socrates' forgoing of narrative control exemplifies a model of the philosopher doing politics fruitfully. To be sure, he engages in the communal sphere by telling a narrative to the auditor but Socrates qua narrator does not explicitly dictate how the auditor should respond to the story based on his own understanding of truth or on the powerful advantages that accrue from his heightened intellectual or moral development. Socrates gives the auditor the intellectual space to think for himself. As Socrates' narrative commentary diminishes, the auditor has the opportunity to interpret the events for himself, to come to his own moral assessments about the characters in the story, his own intellectual assessments of the philosophical arguments, and his own decision about how to apply the lessons of the narrative to his own life.

Socrates' narrative gives the auditor the opportunity to cultivate the resources he needs to overcome his internal struggles with intemperance and to oppose the external forces of tyranny. Whether the auditor will apply this narrative charm more successfully than Charmides does on the dramatic level remains an open question. The openness of this question, in turn, invites the reader into the community instantiated by the narrative and asks the reader to cultivate the inner resources necessary to choose a philosophical life over a tyrannical one. In sum, I will briefly note that Laurence Lampert believes that Plato himself is the auditor of the *Charmides* and that Plato's presence as auditor of the text signifies that he has learned the lessons that Charmides and Critias have not. Under this view, Plato's presence as auditor ensures that philosophy will not succumb to these temptations.[91] The auditor achieves what the interlocutors cannot. In this way, Plato places himself in the text as a model for us all.

NOTES

1. My thanks to Jill Gordon for reading an early draft of this chapter.
2. The following studies are particularly insightful on the narrative dimensions of the dialogue: Christopher Bruell, "Socratic Politics and Self-Knowledge: An Interpretation of Plato's *Charmides*," *Interpretation* 6 (1977): 141–203; Seth Benardete, "On Interpreting Plato's *Charmides*," *Graduate Faculty Philosophy Journal* 11 (1986): 9–36; Thomas Schmid, *Plato's Charmides and the Socratic Ideal of Rationality* (Albany: State University of New York Press, 1998); and Andrew Reece, "Drama, Narrative, and Socratic *Erōs* in Plato's *Charmides*," *Interpretation* 26 (1998): 65–76.
3. See Helen North, *Sophrosyne: Self-Knowledge and Self-Restraint in Greek Literature* (Ithaca: Cornell University Press, 1966). Thomas Tuozzo also offers a detailed exploration of the social context of this virtue in his *Plato's Charmides* (Cambridge: Cambridge University Press, 2011).
4. See Nussbaum, *Fragility*; Nussbaum, *Cultivating Humanity*; Irwin, *Moral Theory*; and Irwin, *Plato's Ethics*.
5. On the political overtones of the dialogue, see Drew Hyland, *The Virtue of Philosophy: An Interpretation of Plato's Charmides* (Athens: Ohio University Press, 1981); Thomas Tuozzo, "What's Wrong with These Cities? The Social Dimension of *Sophrosune* in Plato's *Charmides*," *Journal of the History of Philosophy* 39 (2001): 321–350; Eva Brann, "The Tyrant's Temperance," in *Music of the Republic* (New York: Paul Dry Books, 2004), 66–87; and Paul Stern, "Tyranny and Self-Knowledge: Critias and Socrates in Plato's *Charmides*," *The American Political Science Review* 93 (1999): 399–412.
6. See Francis Coolidge, "On the Grounds for Aristocracy and the Rejection of Philosophy: A Reflection on Plato's *Charmides*," *Journal of Speculative Philosophy* 9 (1995): 208–228, and Tucker Landy, "Limitations of Political Philosophy: An Interpretation of Plato's *Charmides*," *Interpretation* 26 (1998): 183–199.
7. I use Sprague's translation in *Plato Complete Works*, ed. John Cooper (Indianapolis: Hackett 1997), 640–663. I have also consulted *Plato's Charmides*, trans. Thomas West and Grace Starry West (Indianapolis: Hackett, 1986). Where I refer to Plato's Greek, I follow Johannes Burnet, *Platonis Opera* (Oxford: Oxford University Press, 1903).
8. See Martin McAvoy, "Carnal Knowledge in the *Charmides*," in *Dialogues with Plato*, ed. Eugenio Benitez (Edmonton: Academic Printing and Publishing, 1996), 62–102, and Christopher Planeaux, "Socrates, Alcibiades, and Plato's *Ta Poteideia*: Does the *Charmides* Have an Historical Setting?" *Mnemosyne* 52 (1998): 72–77.
9. For a later date of the narrative retelling, see N. Van Der Ben, *The Charmides of Plato: Problems and Interpretations* (Amsterdam: B. R. Grüner, 1985), 4.
10. On the rule of the Thirty, see Nails, *People of Plato*, 111–114; Peter Krentz, *The Thirty at Athens* (Ithaca: Cornell University Press, 1982); and G. Tuckey, *Plato's Charmides* (Cambridge: Cambridge University Press, 1951), 14–17. On Charmides, see Nails, *People of Plato*, 17–20. On Critias, see Tuozzo, "Plato's *Charmides*."
11. I discuss both these aspects of narrative uncertainty in the concluding chapter.
12. Bruell, "Socratic Politics," 142.
13. Benardete, "Plato's *Charmides*," 9. Benardete's assumption would support a much later dating for the narrative retelling.
14. Brann, "Tyrant's Temperance," 72.
15. Lampert, *Philosophy Became Socratic*, 236.
16. Socrates uses three different forms of address: *etaire* (154c), *phile* (155c), and *gennāda* (155d). For a thorough exploration of Socrates' use of friendship terms, see E. Dickey, *Greek Forms of Address from Herodotus to Lucian* (Oxford: Clarendon, 1996).
17. Benardete, "Plato's *Charmides*," 78n28. Tuozzo also agrees that these references are meant to heighten the auditor's interest in Charmides' beauty. He notes further, "we may suppose that Plato, too, plans to bring his intended readers into a similar frame of mind and then to carry them along in the move toward beauty of the soul." "Plato's *Charmides*," 105.
18. Benardete, "Plato's *Charmides*," 9.
19. Cf. *Lysis* 206b and 210e.

68   Chapter 3

20. Socrates refers to his emotional state twice in the *Lysis* (211a and 218c).
21. Socrates mentions the emotions of Chaerephon, Critias, and Charmides at 153b, 158c, 159b, 160e, 162c, 169d.
22. All the dialogues with non-Socratic narrators refer to other narrative situations in their opening scenes. See *Phaedo*, 58a; *Symposium*, 172b; *Theaetetus*, 142d; and *Parmenides*, 126c–127a.
23. Schmid, *Socratic Ideal*, 4, and Hyland, *Virtue of Philosophy*, 29.
24. See Stephen Halliwell, "Between Public and Private: Tragedy and Athenian Experience of Rhetoric," in *Greek Tragedy and the Historian*, ed. Christopher Pelling (Oxford: Clarendon, 1997), 121–141.
25. Tucker Landy draws attention to an important distinction between Socrates' interests and the interests of his audience. See "Political Philosophy," 187.
26. Andrew Reece explains, "Plato gives his readers to opportunity to assume the role of the 'friend' and to evaluate Socrates' own commentary on the previous day's events." Reece, "Drama, Narrative," 65.
27. 155c, 162c, 169c.
28. Bruell suggests that the auditor knows Chaerephon and that his relationship with Chaerephon has led him to Socrates. "Socratic Politics," 142.
29. This highly emotional portrait of Chaerephon corresponds to the observations Socrates makes about him at *Apology*, 21a and also with the presentation of him in comedy. See Nails, *People of Plato*, 86–87.
30. Lampert interprets the relationship between Socrates and Chaerephon somewhat differently. Lampert observes that the laconic exchanges between Chaerephon and Socrates should refer us to the *Odyssey* and specifically when Odysseus reveals himself to Telemachus after a long time away and then references to Penelope waiting for his return. Under this reading, Chaerephon and Socrates are symbolically linked to Penelope and Odysseus. His reading makes for a more moderate Chaerephon but it certainly enhances the emotional association between the two. See Lampert, *Philosophy Became Socratic*, 149–153.
31. Chaerephon's excessive interest in the details of the battle also illustrates his immoderate character.
32. See Schmid, *Socratic Ideal*; Hyland, *Virtue of Philosophy*; Benardete, "Plato's *Charmides*"; Bruell, "Socratic Politics"; and T. F. Morris, "Knowledge of Knowledge and of Lack of Knowledge in the *Charmides*," *International Studies in Philosophy* 21 (1989): 49–61.
33. The pedagogical motivation for Socrates' narratives will become increasingly apparent in the more detailed presentations of the relationship between Socrates and his auditor in the *Protagoras* and in the *Euthydemus*.
34. This shift from body to soul is similar to the opening steps of the philosophical journey that Diotima describes to Socrates in the *Symposium* (210b).
35. Benardete observes, "The laughter belongs to the narrative level: the auditor should find it funny." See "Plato's *Charmides*," 15.
36. For other examples in the dialogues where this sort of social collusion becomes apparent, see *Symposium*, 177a and *Republic*, 327c–328a.
37. Socrates' use of these friendship terms references, "dear son of Glaucon and my dear Charmides" (158b) illustrates Dickey's view that they are a means by which Socrates conveys superiority not intimacy with his interlocutor.
38. Plato shares this lineage. See Nails, *People of Plato*, 243–252.
39. Tuozzo reads Charmides' response in a more charitable light. He argues that Charmides realizes he "really has nothing comparable to offer Socrates in return. The playful threat to use violence, much as it is at the beginning of the *Republic*, a way of acknowledging the fact that in the view of those that threaten the violence, in their conversation with Socrates it will always be they who receive the greater benefit." See "Plato's *Charmides*," 300.
40. On the historical Critias, see Nails, *People of Plato*, 108–111; Notomi, "Origins of Political Philosophy"; and Krentz, *The Thirty*.
41. On this point, see Coolidge, "Rejection of Philosophy," 25.

42. This action foreshadows Critias' willingness to pass off Socrates' definitions of *sophrosune* as his own. On Critias' use of Socratic philosophy, see Lampert, *Philosophy Became Socratic*.

43. (41). Coolidge argues that "Charmides is, at some level, oppressed or weighed down by the mindless adulation that is being given him." See "Rejection of Philosophy," 32. McAvoy mentions, "If the dramatic date is 429, [then]a pain in the head (followed by the eyes) was also the first symptom of the plague." See "Carnal Knowledge," 95n 69.

44. Notomi traces the historical development of this negative image of Critias in "Critias and The Origins of Political Philosophy," in *Plato: Euthydemus, Charmides. Proceedings of the V Symposium Platonicum. Selected Papers*, vol.13, eds. Tom Robinson and Luc Brisson (2000): 237–249. For more favorable assessments of Critias, see Voula Tsouna, "Socrates' Attack on Intellectualism in the *Charmides*," *Apeiron* 30 (1997): 63–78; Tuozzo, "Plato's *Charmides*"; Arthur Madigan, "*Laches* and *Charmides* v. the Craft Analogy," *New Scholasticism* 59 (1985): 377–87.

45. Schmid, *Socratic Ideal*, 131.

46. Brann, "Tyrant's Temperance," 81.

47. Tuozzo offers a compelling vindication of Critias. See particularly his analysis of the historical references to Critias and Critias' own writing in Part One, sections 2–4. See "Plato's *Charmides*."

48. J. Beversluis, *Cross-Examining Socrates* (Cambridge: Cambridge University Press, 2000), 142.

49. Socrates' description of Thrasymachus' behavior at *Republic*, 336b, and Phaedo's description of Apollodorus at *Phaedo*, 117d, function in similar ways.

50. On this point see North, *Sophrosune*; and Tuozzo, "Plato's *Charmides*."

51. Notomi, "Origins of Political Philosophy," 248, and Coolidge, "Rejection of Philosophy."

52. Diotima's asides to the young Socrates serve a similar dramatic function. See *Symposium* 210a, 210e, and 211d.

53. Bruell, "Socratic Politics," 184.

54. Scholars differ about Socrates' attitude toward Critias at this juncture. Schmid reads it as hostile. *Socratic Ideal*, 138. Tuozzo reads *miare* in a more friendly fashion. "Plato's *Charmides*," 330.

55. Tuozzo offers a much more nuanced assessment of Plato's allusion to these events through "Plato's *Charmides*." He suggests that "there was much in Critias' own political thought that Plato thought valuable, and that he subsumed into his own, much more sophisticated philosophical theory. "Plato's *Charmides*," 302. Tuozzo sees this reference merely as an attempt to "call into question the worth of their dialectical contributions to the dialogues." See "Plato's *Charmides*," 302. I do not find Tuozzo's view completely compelling based only on the evidence of the dialogue, his extensive research into the historical documents about Critias is more convincing (see Part One, Section two of "Plato's *Charmides*"). Nonetheless, his reading is a welcome call to rethink facile assumptions about Plato's political views and motivations.

56. See Brann, "Tyrant's Temperance," 86.

57. Tuozzo regards this reference to receiving a hearing as a Platonic allusion to the fact that the Thirty, following a Spartan model, wanted to limit the number of citizens to three thousand. He writes, "All those who were not among that number were denied access to normal judicial procedure; they could be put to death without trial by the Thirty." See "Plato's *Charmides*," 301.

58. Mary Renault offers an intriguing reading of this moment in her historical novel, *The Last of the Wine* (New York: Vintage, 1984). As she tells the story, all of Socrates' followers were certain that this refusal would lead to his death. She suggests that Plato himself intervened on Socrates' behalf and kept Critias from retaliating against Socrates. *Wine*, 384.

59. Krentz, *The Thirty*, 83.

60. Rutherford argues that Socrates' commitment to reason overcomes his emotional orientation. See *Art of Plato*, 87. See also McAvoy, "Carnal Knowledge."

61. Reece, "Drama, Narrative," 70, and Rutherford, *Art of Plato*, 89.

62. The word, *diatribe*, conveys some emotional affect. It can mean amusement as well as serious employment study or a way of life.

63. I will return to this point at greater length in my discussion of the *Republic*. But let me say that I am personally quite sympathetic to a largely ironic understanding of Plato's negative assessment of poetry. Given that the dialogues themselves are works of art, filled with poetry, drama, and appeals to the emotions, their very existence seems to undermine any attempt to take the negative assessment of the arts in a straightforward manner. However, in that many people do interpret the critique of poetry quite prosaically, particularly those who hold an intellectualist view of Socrates and Plato, it seemed prudent to me to recognize that it is a viable interpretive option for many whom I wish to reach with my own argument. Miriam Byrd has a helpful way of navigating the ground between various dramatic, ironic, esoteric readings of Plato and more doctrinal ones. She argues that passages such as this one in the *Charmides* function as intentional contradictions in the text that alert the reader to Plato's intention. She sees them as functioning as a "summoner" does in the context of the *Republic* (522e-525a), a contradiction that leads the mind to higher and higher stages of cognition, understanding, and ultimately truth. See M. Byrd, "Summoner Approach," *Journal of the History of Philosophy* 47 (2007): 365-381. I am thankful to an anonymous reviewer for calling my attention to this important article.

64. Rutherford, *Art of Plato*, 89. See also Reece, "Drama, Narrative," 70.

65. See R. F. Stalley, "*Sophrosune* in the Charmides," in *Plato:* Euthydemus, Charmides. *Proceedings of the V Symposium Platonicum. Selected Papers vol.13*, eds. Tom Robinson and Luc Brisson (2000): 265–277.

66. Rutherford, *Art of Plato*, 89.

67. Patrick Yong, "Intellectualism and Moral Habituation in Plato's Earlier Dialogues," *Aperion* 29 (1996): 49–61.

68. Landy, "Political Philosophy," 189. See also McAvoy, "Carnal Knowledge," 88, n57.

69. McAvoy, "Carnal Knowledge," 89.

70. See Kahn, *Philosophical Use*, 188 and 188fn8.

71. M. McCoy, *Sophocles* (Oxford: Oxford University Press, 2012).

72. See Tuozzo, "What's Wrong," 324.

73. McKim, "Socratic Self-Knowledge," 62.

74. Gonzalez, *Dialectic and Dialogue*, 58.

75. Ibid. See also Benardete, "Plato's *Charmides*," 9.

76. Hyland, *Virtue of Philosophy,* 53–54.

77. Benardete, "Plato's *Charmides*,"15. See also Brann, "Tyrant's Temperance," 74.

78. C. Dewald explores the relinquishing of first-person narrative control in Herodotus. See "Narrative Surface and Authorial Voice in Herodotus' *Histories*," *Arethusa* 20 (1987): 147–150.

79. See Benardete, "Plato's *Charmides*"; Hyland, *Virtue of Philosophy*; Brann, "Tyrant's Temperance"; and Schmid, *Socratic Ideal*.

80. Schmid, *Socratic Ideal*, 4.

81. Hyland, *Virtue of Philosophy,* 75.

82. T. Landy, "Philosophy, Statesmanship, and Pragmatism in Plato's *Euthydemus*," *Interpretation* 25 (1998): 184–200.

83. Landy, "Philosophy, Statesmanship," 187. See also Landy, "Political Philosophy," and D. O'Connor, "Socrates and Political Ambition: The Dangerous Game," *Proceedings of the Boston Area Colloquium in Ancient Philosophy* 15 (1999): 31–51. See P. Stern, "Tyranny and Self-Knowledge: Critias and Charmides in Plato's *Charmides*," *American Political Science Review* (1999): 399–412.

84. Landy, "Political Philosophy," 183.

85. Hyland, *Virtue of Philosophy*, 75. See also L. Strauss, "Plato," in *History of Political Philosophy*, 3rd ed., eds. Leo Strauss and J. Cropsey (Chicago: University of Chicago Press, 1987), 33–89.

86. Schmid, *Socratic Ideal*, 85.

87. Stern, "Tyranny and Self-Knowledge," 211.

88. See chap. three of Krentz, *The Thirty*.

89. Notomi, "Origins of Political Philosophy," 250. See also Coolidge, "Rejection of Philosophy."
90. On receptive openness, see Hyland, *Finitude*, 15–17.
91. Lampert, *Philosophy Became Socratic*, 236.

Chapter Four

Performing Philosophy in the *Protagoras*

In fields ranging from neuroscience to economics and from biology to psychology, the concept of rationality has undergone a radical reassessment. Even within philosophical circles, the primacy of reason is deeply scrutinized.[1] However, despite this ongoing reassessment of the nature of reason and rationality, the view of Socrates and Plato as strong advocates of the primacy of reason and as vigorous opponents of the role that the emotions play in the intellectual life remains firmly entrenched in academic circles. Martha Nussbaum's portrait of Socrates in both the *Fragility of Goodness* and in *Cultivating Humanity* typifies this view.[2] In *Cultivating Humanity*, she regards Socrates as a beneficial pedagogical model precisely because he exemplifies a rigorous commitment to rational self-examination. For example, she characterizes the Socratic rationalist ideal as

> A life that accepts no belief as authoritative simply because it has been handed down by tradition or become familiar through habit, a life that questions all beliefs and accepts only those that survive reason's demand for consistency and for justification. Training this capacity requires developing the capacity to reason logically, to test what one reads or says for consistency of reasoning, correctness of fact, and accuracy of judgment.[3]

Throughout the previous two chapters, I have argued that Socrates' role as narrator of the *Lysis*, and the *Charmides*, illustrates that the standard view of Socrates as a thoroughgoing rationalist is based on an incomplete assessment of Plato's portrait of Socrates. In this chapter, I focus on Plato's *Protagoras*. The *Protagoras* is central to my argument for two reasons. First, rationalist accounts of Socratic philosophy often draw upon Socrates' argument with

Protagoras, particularly 358b–d, to bolster the intellectualist position.[4] Irwin defines Socratic intellectualism as the view that "knowledge is sufficient to virtue and that therefore all the virtues can be identified with knowledge of the good."[5] Alexander Nehamas notes further that Socratic intellectualism "appears to consider the affective side of our nature irrelevant to our virtue, to what counts as a good life."[6] This intellectualist reading is widely held and forcibly articulated by a number of prominent scholars.[7] Given the weight of tradition, it is not surprising that we typically regard Socrates' philosophical practice as an exhortation to the life of reason.

Second, the finely drawn narrative dimensions of this dialogue, i.e., the enacted prologue with the auditor, the Hippocrates/Socrates encounter, and Socrates' narrative descriptions of the sophists and his encounters with them, all demonstrate how Socrates engages in a variety of pedagogical practices that draw upon a heightened sensitivity to a broad range of human experience. This holistic portrait emerges both in how Socrates tethers his narrative to the emotional and psychological needs of the auditor and Hippocrates and in how he discloses his own inner states of mind in his narrative commentary. Ultimately, I argue that the view of Socrates as a rational intellectualist emerges when we prioritize the importance of his *elenchic* activity without seeing the broader pedagogical context in which these practices occur. This view hinders our capacity to see philosophy as a practice that includes a positive regard for the role of the emotions. Socrates' narrative practice illustrates how he presents philosophy to his auditors in ways that make the practice relevant to their everyday lives and concerns because he integrates emotionality into this practice.[8]

With these larger aims in mind, I divide this chapter into four parts. First, I discuss the outer framing conversation between Socrates and the auditor. Second, I show how Socrates' narrative commentary highlights the pedagogical relationship between the sophists and their students. Third, I discuss how Socrates' narrative remarks reveal his inner experiences and his emotional responses to the various sophistic speeches. These emotional remarks underscore the difference between Socrates' philosophical practices and sophistic speeches by focusing on the dynamics of oral performance. Finally, I show how the narrative dimensions of Socrates' philosophical practice call for a reconsideration of Socratic intellectualism and the unity of the virtues.[9]

I. THE OUTER FRAME

The *Protagoras* starts with an exchange between Socrates and an unnamed auditor (309a–310a).[10] The auditor asks Socrates: "Where have you just come from?" (309a).[11] Though the beginning of the *Protagoras* is enacted rather than reported, it exhibits many structural parallels with the openings of the *Lysis* and *Charmides*. For example, the setting is indeterminate. Though the conversation between Socrates and the auditor takes place almost immediately following the events that Socrates will soon narrate, we do not know exactly where or when this conversation occurs.[12] Second, we do not know the auditor's identity. Though we learn more about the auditor's character than we do in the *Lysis* or the *Charmides*, we still do not know exactly who the auditor is, nor do we know anything about the other members of the narrative audience (310a). Third, like the auditors of the *Lysis* and the *Charmides*, the auditor and the others who are present remain passive recipients of Socrates' account.[13]

Despite these thematic similarities, the beginning of the *Protagoras* differs from the *Lysis* and the *Charmides* in an important way. The opening dramatic exchange between Socrates and the auditor allows us to observe the social context in which Socrates tells a narrative. The enacted opening scene provides information about the character of Socrates' auditor and Socrates' relationship with him. As a result, we can observe how Socrates tailors his account directly to the auditor to a greater degree than was possible with the limited textual evidence in the preceding dialogues. Because we learn more about the auditor, we can more carefully consider Socrates' pedagogical motivations for telling narratives and gauge the possible pedagogical effects.

Though Robert Bartlett correctly observes that the auditor is referred to as a *hetairos* (a companion), rather than the more intimate *philos* (friend), he and Socrates seem to know each other fairly well.[14] For example, he observes some aspect of Socrates' demeanor that enables him to answer his own opening query about Socrates' activity. He remarks: "Or is it indeed clear that you have been hunting Alcibiades who is in his prime?" (309a). Socrates acknowledges that his assumption is correct (309b). The joking manner in which they converse about the appropriate age for a beloved and about Socrates' interest in Alcibiades also suggests at least a passing familiarity between them, if not a more intimate relationship. Additionally, Socrates wants to tell the auditor about "something strange" that happened to him (309b). Just as the auditor knows Socrates well enough to surmise that he had been with Alcibiades, Socrates knows the auditor well enough to recognize that a story about Protagoras will eclipse his interest in Alcibiades. Indeed, after Socrates mentions Protagoras, the auditor does not refer to Alcibiades again. Chris Long suggests that Socrates had been planning to meet the auditor all along and indeed it is the meeting with the auditor that motivates Socrates' desire to leave the gathering at Callias' house (336b). He has simply been waylaid by Hippocrates and then further delayed by his extended conversation with Protagoras at Callias' house. If Long is correct in this assumption, their prearranged meeting supports the fact that Socrates and the auditor know each other well.[15] The fact that the auditor ascertains that Socrates has the leisure to narrate the account (310a) also suggests that they are on familiar terms. The auditor knows Socrates well enough to recognize that he does not always want to report on his evidence. The auditor's polite inquiry contrasts with Chaerephon's commanding insistence that Socrates narrate the account of Potidaea (*Charmides*, 153b). Socrates seems more willing to narrate this account than he was in the opening of the *Charmides*. In fact, Socrates confirms his enthusiasm for the task, saying "I'd count it a favor [*charin*] if you'd listen" (310a). The auditor affirms that the feeling is reciprocal. Socrates then repeats that he would consider it a favor, this time calling it a double favor (310a). The fact that Socrates repeats the word, *charin*, emphasizes gratitude on both sides of the relationship. This opening scene presents a model of reciprocity between speaker and listener that has not been explicitly present in the preceding dialogues. Unfortunately, this model of reciprocity remains only a possibility that we can consider, at least within the textual confines of the dialogue, because we do not see how the auditor responds to Socrates' narration at any point during the narration or at the end of the narration. Nonetheless, that this reciprocity is present at the beginning of the dialogue is significant. It places the importance of reciprocity in philosophical conversation at the forefront of the reader's mind. Marina McCoy sees this emphasis on reciprocity as a key distinction between philosophic and sophistic modes of discourse. She writes, "While Protagoras makes a clear separation between the speaker, who is active, and the audience, who is passive, Socrates treats both the questioner and answerer as active participants in the conversation."[16] Of course, she is describing the exchange between Socrates and Protagoras in the dramatic action of the dialogue, but it is interesting to note that this theme emerges in the opening exchange between Socrates and the auditor as well.

What does the opening scene tell us about the auditor himself? First, the auditor is fascinated with the relationship between Socrates and Alcibiades. The auditor remains focused on Alcibiades even when Socrates confesses that he forgot all about him (309b–c). The auditor's fascination with Alcibiades is, in many ways, not surprising. Deborah Nails notes that Alcibiades "was descended on both sides from families that were among Athens' first and most powerful, deploying both wealth and influence."[17] At the dramatic date of the dialogue, Alcibiades was about twenty years old and an extremely popular figure. He was strong, handsome, intelligent, showing great aptitude for political success. Nails puts it well when she remarks "Athens was alternately besotted and infuriated with him [Alcibiades]."[18] As Socrates relates the story to the auditor and his companions, the average Athenians would have been besotted with Alcibiades and his potential for leadership. Infuriation, after his numerous betrayals, would follow years later.

From the auditor's intense curiosity about this relationship, which he assumes to be erotic, we can extrapolate that the auditor is motivated by eros in a more general sense.[19] The fact that Socrates brings up other examples of lover-beloved relationships in his narrative commentary bears out this assumption. Socrates mentions Eryximachus and his beloved Phaedrus (315c) and Pausanias and the young and lovely Agathon (315d). Just after these two erotic pairs, Socrates refers to Alcibiades again (316a). This reference to Alcibiades would reinforce the auditor's assumption about the erotic nature of the relationship between Socrates and Alcibiades. That Socrates does not chastise him for this assumption suggests that Socrates does not find his interest in eros intrinsically problematic.

Second, Socrates refers to the auditor as an "admirer of Homer" (309b). Socrates makes this descriptive comment in response to the auditor's query about his relationship with Alcibiades. In this way, Socrates links the auditor's questions about Alcibiades with his enthusiasm for Homer. In doing so, Socrates equates the specificity of the auditor's erotic interests with an orientation toward emotionality more generally. Socrates' exploration of Homeric poetry in the *Republic* makes clear that Homer appeals to the emotional dimensions of human experience. It is not surprising, then, that the auditor, given his interest in erotic matters, would admire Homer. References to Homer occur throughout Socrates' narrative. Lombardo and Bell note that Homer is mentioned five times in this dialogue.[20] Socrates also paints the scene at Callias' house as a Homeric vision (315c, 315d). He quotes Homer in his appeal to Prodicus for help (340a) and in his attempt to keep Protagoras engaged in the conversation (348c).

Third, the auditor does not inhabit the same intellectual circles as Socrates. He does not know about Protagoras' arrival in Athens.[21] However, once the auditor learns of Protagoras' presence, his focus shifts from Alcibiades to Protagoras. This quick shift in focus suggests that his emotionality also colors his enthusiasm for the sophist. Many aspects of the auditor's behavior indicate his lack of enthusiasm for intellectual matters in and of themselves. For example, in addition to being unaware of Protagoras' presence in Athens, he seems not to sense any irony in Socrates' remarks regarding Protagoras' wisdom (309c). Also, the auditor does not interrupt Socrates at any point to ask questions and we do not see how the auditor responds to Socrates' narrative at the end of the dialogue.

Interpretations of the auditor's silence vary in the secondary literature. Patrick Coby takes the auditor's silence to indicate his lack of intellectual aptitude. He wants to be entertained by Socrates' account of Protagoras, much like one would be entertained by listening to a muse recounting a Homeric tale. Coby remarks, "the companion, therefore, is one of those vulgar human beings who are entertained by the speech of others" (347c–e); he is not a *kalos kagathos*, a true gentleman, who participates in a conversation and submits himself to its testing.[22] However, Robert Bentley sees the auditor's enthusiasm for Protagoras as a reflection of deeper intellectual interests. Some aspects of the text support Bentley's interpretation. For example, though the auditor seems eager to know "what is up" with Alcibiades and Socrates (309b), after he hears about Protagoras, the auditor becomes even more insistent about hearing Socrates' account: "Well sit right down, if you're free now, and tell us all about it" (310a).[23] I suggest that the auditor has the intellectual aptitude that Bentley attributes to him, but has little interest in developing the aptitude he has for philosophical dialogue. Chris Long's suggestion that Socrates planned to meet the auditor prior to his encounter with Hippocrates also reinforces a more positive regard for the auditor's philosophical aptitude.[24] He is someone Socrates plans to meet and converse with.

In the following section, I analyze how Socrates starts his narrative by telling the auditor about Hippocrates, another highly emotional character. I argue that Socrates includes the details of this meeting to help the auditor recognize the potential harm of an overly emotional orientation toward life, but at the same time, the Hippocrates encounter upholds the absolute necessity of the emotions in our philosophical lives. If the auditor attends to the details of Socrates' conversation with Hippocrates, he will encounter a model of philosophical exchange that creates a space where he can fuse his emotional interests with his intellectual ones. If the auditor allows himself to listen, Socrates will become his philosophical muse.

II. SOCRATES' NARRATIVE DESCRIPTIONS

A. Hippocrates

Even though Socrates professes to be eager to report his "quite long conversation with Protagoras" and the auditor is eager to hear it (310a), Socrates starts his account by describing his early-morning encounter with Hippocrates (310b–314c).[25] Whereas we could only speculate about the similarities between Chaerephon and the auditor in the *Charmides*, due to the lack of character development of the auditor, in the *Protagoras* the similarities between the auditor and Hippocrates should be apparent to the careful reader. The fact that Socrates refers to Hippocrates' relationship with his slave, Satyrus, provides an explicit parallel with the auditor who just told his own slave to make room for Socrates. Coby notes that Socrates has just taken the place of the auditor's slave to tell this narrative. As he takes the slave's place, Socrates symbolically enslaves himself to the auditor. From this "enslaved" position, he tells the auditor a story about a person who cannot control his slave even though he approaches him as "a tool for his use."[26] Socrates, for his part, uses this opportunity to teach the auditor about the "enslaved" status of the auditor's own soul, by telling the auditor this narrative about Hippocrates.[27]

Though the auditor has more control over his slave than Hippocrates does over Satyrus, Hippocrates shares the auditor's emotional enthusiasm, his erotic nature, and his enthusiasm for Protagoras. We see all these traits in Hippocrates' extended exchange with Socrates. Hippocrates appears at the beginning of Socrates' narration: "just before daybreak, while it was still dark, Hippocrates, son of Apollodorus and Phason's brother, banged on my door with his stick, and when it was opened for him he barged right in and yelled in that voice of his, 'Socrates, are you awake or asleep?'" (310b). Socrates presents Hippocrates as an aggressive, loud, excitable person. The Aristophanic character of this passage also reinforces the erotic dimensions of Hippocrates' character; Socrates paints Hippocrates in an Aristophanic light to underscore both his emotionality and eroticism for the auditor.[28] As Socrates' narrative progresses, Hippocrates' behavior becomes increasingly erotic. He enters Socrates' bedroom, locates the bed and sits at his feet (310c). Hippocrates' entrance into the bedroom casts the entire scene in an erotic light. The name of Hippocrates' slave, Satyrus, adds to the erotic overtones of this episode. To explain briefly, satyrs had strong sexual appetites and erotic drives. Alcibiades famously compares Socrates to a satyr because of his ability to attract people to him (*Symposium* 215b).[29]

The details that Socrates includes in his narrative enable us to see how Hippocrates' emotional exuberance creates instability in his daily life. For example, his slave has run away (310c). Hippocrates intends to tell Socrates about this event, but he forgets (310c). Because of his inability to control his slave, Hippocrates does not learn of Protagoras' arrival until later. Symbolically, Hippocrates' inability to control Satyrus suggests his inability to control the direction of his life. After his brother tells him about Protagoras, Hippocrates wants to see Socrates immediately (310d). Realizing it is too late to visit Socrates, Hippocrates eats and sleeps.[30] However, Hippocrates' excitement about Protagoras' arrival is so great that he disregards social convention and arrives early at Socrates' house.[31]

Even after he arrives at Socrates' house, Hippocrates' exuberance for seeing Protagoras remains unchecked. He wants to go to Callias' house immediately (311a). Socrates cautions him about the early hour. Instead, Socrates leads Hippocrates from his own bedroom into the outer courtyard. The change in physical location symbolizes Socrates' desire to move Hippocrates (and the auditor) away from their emotionally driven enthusiasm for Protagoras and toward a more cautious stance with respect to what they can learn from the sophist. Just as Socrates physically moves him from the erotically charged setting of the bedroom into a more neutral one, Socrates engages him in philosophical discussion to move him away from his unreflective enthusiasm for Protagoras' teaching toward a more thoughtful consideration of what he will learn from Protagoras (311c–314c). As Hippocrates and Socrates move from the darkness of the bedroom into the light of the courtyard, they symbolically leave Hippocrates' unreflective enthusiasm for Protagoras behind. The fact that Protagoras is usually found indoors and that Socrates conducts his various activities outdoors in the agora reinforces this symbolic movement (311a). By moving Hippocrates outdoors and by having him walk around in the light, Socrates channels Hippocrates' exuberance into a more discerning stance that will serve him well as he goes on to meet the sophist himself.

The narrative dimensions of the dialogue allow us to see Socrates' pedagogy on two levels. First, within the temporality of the dramatic events, Socrates provides an external restraint for Hippocrates' emotional exuberance. Second, on the narrative level, by starting with this episode about Hippocrates, Socrates restrains the auditor's enthusiasm to hear about Protagoras. Just as Socrates makes Hippocrates wait for daylight and engage in conversation with him before they head to Callias' house, Socrates makes the auditor wait to hear about his encounter with Protagoras. Just as Socrates provokes Hippocrates into considering what he hopes to gain from study with Protagoras, Socrates uses narrative to provoke the auditor into reflection about his enthusiasm for Protagoras. Throughout this passage, Socrates intersperses various narrative comments that illustrate these pedagogical parallels on the dramatic and narrative level.

Some examples follow. When Socrates engages Hippocrates in *elenchus*, his narrative remarks convey his pedagogical purpose: "I wanted to see what Hippocrates was made of, so I started to examine him with a few questions" (311b). Socrates interrogates Hippocrates about Protagoras; "What is he, and what do you expect to become?" (311c). As Socrates' *elenchus* continues, he emphasizes, on the one hand, the technical nature of what the sophists offer by drawing a comparison between doctors and sculptors and, on the other hand, the fact that Protagoras charges a great deal of money for his teachings.[32] Socrates asks him what he would learn from a physician and from a sculptor and Hippocrates answers easily (311c–312e). After Socrates asks Hippocrates what he wants to learn from Protagoras, Hippocrates admits that he wants to become a sophist (312a).[33] On the narrative level, Socrates calls attention to this moment by telling the auditor "he blushed as he said this" (312a). Socrates also tells the auditor that the daylight allows him to see the blush (312a). Socrates does not say precisely how he interprets the blush. Hippocrates could be embarrassed or excited, ashamed or even angry. Nonetheless, he calls attention to it twice. Regardless of what specific emotional state the blush signifies, Socrates' double reference to the blush signals the importance of Hippocrates' emotional state to the auditor. This narrative comment again shows how Socrates' pedagogy works on two levels. Just as Socrates leads Hippocrates to blush when he admits his desire to become a sophist, Socrates underscores this moment in his narrative to evoke a similar reversal and recognition in his auditor. The auditor should feel the force of Hippocrates' blush within himself.

After Hippocrates admits aporia: "By God, I really don't know what to say" (312e), Socrates explicitly tells the auditor: "I went on to my next point" (312a). As in the preceding dialogues, Socrates' narrative remarks highlight the aporetic moments that he and his interlocutors experience. Here, this brief comment suggests that Socrates does not see aporia as the end of his inquiry, but rather as a new starting point. By calling attention to these aporetic moments, Socrates' narrative commentary trains the auditor to move beyond this aporetic stance toward a consideration of what wisdom is best for the soul to pursue. In other words, he enacts the very same pedagogical strategy that he employs on the dramatic level. On the dramatic level, Socrates cautions Hippocrates about the potential harm to his soul (313b–314c). Hippocrates agrees to choose carefully the nourishment he gives his soul. Socrates emphasizes the shared agreement by telling the auditor: "Having agreed on this, we set out" (314c). As his narrative unfolds, Socrates describes the effect that his conversation has on Hippocrates: "When we got to the doorway we stood there discussing some point which had come up along the road and which we didn't want to leave unsettled before we went in. So we were standing there in the doorway discussing it until we reached an agreement" (314d).[34] Though Hippocrates' initial excitement led to his impatient banging at Socrates' door, now Hippocrates waits at Callias' door until he and Socrates settle their discussion. Hippocrates can now control his enthusiasm for meeting Protagoras. He chooses reasoned philosophical conversation with Socrates over seeing Protagoras as quickly as possible. As Socrates ends this section of the narrative, the auditor's attention should be directly focused on Hippocrates' change of perspective regarding Protagoras. In this way, Hippocrates' change should provide a model for the very same change that the auditor needs to undergo. Lampert notes that Socrates makes three observations about Hippocrates, "Hippocrates laughed. Then he blushed. Finally he listened."[35] These three narrative observations nicely encapsulate the change that should come over the auditor as well. It is important to see that the two descriptions that precede the philosophical receptivity implied in listening are both descriptions of emotional states.

Socrates then shifts his narrative focus abruptly:

> The doorman, a eunuch, overheard us. He must have been annoyed with all the traffic of sophists in and out of the house, because when we knocked he opened the door, took one look at us and said, "Ha! More Sophists! He's busy." Then he slammed the door in our faces with both hands as hard as he could. We knocked again and he answered through the locked door, "Didn't you hear me say he's busy?" "My good man," I said, "we haven't come to see Callias, and we are not sophists. Calm down. We want to see Protagoras.

That's why we've come. So please announce us." Eventually, he opened the door. (314c–e)

In contrast to the enthusiasm that Hippocrates and the auditor both display with respect to Protagoras, the prospect of having more sophists in the house annoys the eunuch. Thinking that Socrates and Hippocrates are sophists, he refuses to let them in. Like many people in Athens, the eunuch, who has probably overheard Socrates and Hippocrates conversing, cannot tell the difference between their philosophical conversation and the sophistical displays of Protagoras, Prodicus, and Hippias. In the public eyes of Athens, philosophers and sophists are the same.[36] Since the eunuch has been artificially made into an unerotic creature, his emotionality is not grounded in physicality. Nonetheless, the eunuch's response to them is emotional, even violent: "He slams the door in [their] faces with both hands as hard as he could" (314d). Though the quality of his emotional response to Protagoras is the opposite of Hippocrates' positive response, the eunuch's behavior mirrors Hippocrates' aggressive knocking at Socrates' door. Hippocrates is confronted with a reversed image of himself. By including this exchange with the eunuch in the narrative, Socrates presents the auditor with a negative view of the sophists to counter his own wholly positive view and by juxtaposing this image of an overly emotional eunuch with the image of a more thoughtful and patient Hippocrates, Socrates presents the auditor with the existential possibility that he, like Hippocrates, might change through extended reflection on his intellectual motivations and through ongoing association with Socrates.

Given that Socrates successfully moderates Hippocrates' unchecked enthusiasm for Protagoras, it is curious that Socrates does not report the exact content of their discussion that illustrates Hippocrates' changed perspective to the auditor. Coby suggests that this omission indicates the auditor's lack of aptitude for philosophy.[37] However, another interpretation is possible. From Socrates' narrative perspective, the sustained conversational process and the shared agreement between himself and Hippocrates are the central things to convey to the auditor because they are crucial for philosophical dialogue. Hippocrates' change in attitude is the important point. It is the basis of their shared agreement. The details of the conversation he has with Socrates are not crucial points to convey. Hippocrates' more cautious regard for Protagoras models the appropriate response the auditor should take with respect to both Socrates and the narrative Socrates tells the auditor about Protagoras. It is the end result of Hippocrates' conversion rather than the details of the conversation that Socrates wishes to convey to the auditor.

Having used Hippocrates for this purpose, Socrates seems to lose interest in Hippocrates as a narrative focal point. Socrates only mentions Hippocrates at two other junctures in the narrative. He introduces Hippocrates to Protagoras and asks what Hippocrates will learn from him (316c). Then, after Protagoras' speech, Socrates tells the auditor that "looking at Hippocrates, I barely managed to say, 'Son of Apollodorus, how grateful I am to you for suggesting that I come here'" (328d). Curiously, though Socrates describes how he himself responds to Protagoras' speech, he does not mention Hippocrates' response to the speech. After this point, Socrates does not refer to Hippocrates by name again. In some ways, the diminishing narrative focus on Hippocrates supports the view that Socrates is not all that interested in helping Hippocrates.[38] Gagarin suggests that Plato intends to present Socrates and Protagoras as equally viable educational paths and that "Any reference to Hippocrates at the end would disturb the friendly balance between the two main characters."[39] I do not think the text supports Gagarin's reading. Socrates does not completely forget about Hippocrates. He obliquely refers to Hippocrates at the end of his narrative when he concludes: "Our conversation was over, and so we left" (362a). By referring to the conversation with Protagoras as a joint endeavor between himself and Hippocrates, Socrates extends the sense of shared agreement that they reached at 314c to the end of the dialogue. When Hippocrates leaves with Socrates, it indicates that he prefers Socrates to Protagoras, even after a sustained encounter with Protagoras.[40] If this is the case, Socrates presents the auditor with a successful conversion toward, if not fully into, the philosophical life. Hippocrates takes the road that the auditor should follow, the very road that Alcibiades ultimately turns away from when he chooses public acclaim over philosophical inquiry (*Symposium*, 216a). How far the auditor travels on that road, we do not know. Nonetheless, just as a model of genuine reciprocity between Socrates and the auditor appears at the opening of the dialogue, a model of the possibility of genuine philosophical conversion occurs at the end.

B. The Sophists and Their Students

After Socrates recounts the conversation with the doorman, he vividly describes the scene at Callias' house:

> When we went in we found Protagoras walking in the portico flanked by two groups. On one side were Hipponicus and his brother on his mother's side, Paralus, son of Pericles and Charmides, son of Glaucon. On the other side were Pericles' other son Xanthippus, Philippides, son of Philomelus, and Antimoerus of Medes, Protagoras' star pupil who is studying professionally to become a sophist. Following behind and trying to listen to what was being said were a group of what seemed to be mostly foreigners, men whom Protagoras collects from the various cities he travels through. He enchants them with his voice like Orpheus, and they follow the sound of his voice in a trance. There were some locals also in this chorus, whose dance simply delighted me when I saw how beautifully they took care never to get in Protagoras' way. When he

turned around with his flanking groups, the audience to the rear would split in two in a very orderly way and then circle around to either side or form up again behind him. It was quite lovely. (315a–b)

This extended narrative description draws attention to the relationship between Protagoras and his students. Socrates describes the social group around Protagoras in more detail than he describes Protagoras himself. Prominent members of Pericles' family and numerous foreigners make up Protagoras' entourage. Members of Pericles' family lead each side and the foreigners follow behind them. Protagoras upholds this social hierarchy as he interacts with his students. He talks directly to the Athenians and the foreigners simply "try to listen to what was being said." Socrates mentions that Protagoras collects the foreigners on his travels to various cities. Indeed, the first detail he relates about Protagoras, that he walks in the portico, symbolizes the mobility of his sophistic practice. Socrates also emphasizes that he attracts his students through a process of emotional enchantment. In a single sentence, Socrates twice refers to the sound of Protagoras' voice and twice refers to its enchanting qualities: "He enchants them with his voice like Orpheus, and they follow the sound of his voice in a trance." Though the group divides into discrete units, Socrates portrays them as a well-ordered and well-orchestrated whole. He even compares their movements to a "dancing chorus" (315b). The cohesion of the group revolves around Protagoras himself; a cult of personality forms around him.[41] Socrates' observation that "they took care never to get in Protagoras' way" illustrates the central position that Protagoras holds within the group (315b).

Even though the auditor only expresses interest in Protagoras, Socrates describes the other sophists who were at Callias' house as well. After Protagoras, he turns to Hippias and his entourage:[42]

> And then I perceived (as Homer says) Hippias of Elis, on a high seat in the other side of the colonnade. Seated on benches around him were Eryximachus, son of Acoumenus, Phaedrus of Myrrhinous, and Andron, son of Androtion, a number of Eleans and a few other foreigners. They seemed to be asking Hippias questions on astronomy and physics, and he from his high seat was answering each of their questions point by point. (315c)

Socrates twice mentions that Hippias sits on a "high seat" (315c–315d). His seated position conveys his power over his followers. Socrates reinforces another social hierarchy in Hippias' group by referring to the Athenians before he refers to the foreigners. However, overall Hippias' entourage has less hierarchy and division than Protagoras' did. The Athenians, the Eleans, and the other foreigners all appear to be on an equal level, sitting on benches around Hippias. Their social group forms a circle. A circle is more conducive to philosophical discussion than the dancing chorus that follows Protagoras.

Indeed, Socrates describes them as engaged in conversation. They ask Hippias questions and he answers them directly (315c). Hippias' interaction with his students resembles Socrates' preferred mode of conversation. Protagoras' students, in contrast, were enchanted by the sound of his voice. They did not participate in conversation with Protagoras. They only listened to what was being said (315b).[43] A little later, the overall group decides to follow Callias' proposal to "make this a general session and have everyone take seats for discussion." Socrates explains that they "arranged the benches and couches over by Hippias, since that's where the benches were already" (317e). This narrative observation reinforces the fact that Hippias works in a pedagogical mode more conducive to discussion.

Socrates refers to Hippias at several other junctures in his narrative. Most of these observations portray Hippias in a favorable light. For instance, Socrates mentions Protagoras' desire to show off for Hippias, which reinforces Hippias' high social stature. After Socrates expresses his desire to leave the gathering (336e), Callias, Alcibiades, Critias, and Prodicus each attempts to keep Socrates and Protagoras engaged in conversation (336e–337d), but Hippias' intervention is the most compelling (338a). At this point, Socrates tells the auditor, "everyone there thought this was a fine idea and gave it their approval" (338b). A little later, Socrates notes, "Prodicus, Hippias and the others urged me on" to continue interpreting Simonides' poem (342a). This comment also indicates Hippias' desire for ongoing conversation with Socrates. Socrates illustrates his ongoing affinity with Hippias when he draws Hippias onto his side against Protagoras on several occasions (358a–359a).

After Socrates describes Protagoras and Hippias, he turns to Prodicus and his followers:[44]

> And not only that but I saw Tantalus too, for Prodicus of Ceos was also in town. He was in a room, which Hipponicus had formerly used for storage, but because of the number of visitors Callias had cleared it out and made it into a guest room. Prodicus was still in bed and looked to be bundled up in a pile of sheepskin fleeces and blankets. Seated on couches next to him were Pausanias from Cerames, and with Pausanias a fairly young boy, well bred I would say, and certainly good-looking. I think I heard his name is Agathon, and I wouldn't be surprised if he were Pausanias' young love. So this boy was there and the two Adeimanti, sons of Cepis and Leucolophidas, and there seemed to be some others. What they were talking about I couldn't tell from outside, even though I really wanted to hear Prodicus, a man who in my opinion is godlike in his universal knowledge. But his voice is so deep that it set up a reverberation in the room that blurred what was being said. (315d–316a)

Socrates alludes here to Homer's account of Odysseus' descent into Hades. In the preceding description of Hippias, Socrates quotes Odysseus' words "and then I perceived" to associate himself with Odysseus and Hippias with

Heracles (315c). Here, Socrates directly compares Prodicus to Tantalus. Tantalus exists in a lamentable state. He suffers insatiable thirst and hunger. He has food and drink nearby but they always escape his grasp (315c).[45] Prodicus, too, seems to be in a lamentable state. Prodicus is not in the main room with the other sophists. He is housed in a storage room that has been converted to accommodate him (315d). Whereas Protagoras walks around and Hippias sits in a high chair, Prodicus reclines in bed, covered in blankets. Lombardo and Bell suggest that Prodicus may have been ill.[46] It is also possible that he was still asleep and his snoring reverberated through the room (316a). A little later, Callias and Alcibiades get Prodicus up and bring him into the main room (317e), which does support the idea he had been asleep.[47]

Socrates also describes Prodicus' entourage. Unlike his descriptions of the other groups, Socrates mentions only the Athenians who surround him. Pausanias and Agathon, a famous pair of lovers, are mentioned prominently. The presence of these lovers and the fact that Prodicus' students sit on couches around his bed cast the scene in an erotic light. The fact that Prodicus remains in bed to teach presents a stark contrast to Socrates' behavior with Hippocrates at the beginning of the dialogue. Socrates moves out of his bedroom and into the courtyard to converse with Hippocrates. Prodicus remains inside with his students. While Socrates wanted to bring clarity to Hippocrates regarding his desire to learn from Protagoras, Prodicus' teachings seem to lack any clarity. The blankets that surround him obscure even his voice. The fact that Prodicus is known for an emphasis on linguistic precision (341b and 358b) heightens the comic irony of this description.[48]

Other aspects of Socrates' narrative commentary portray Prodicus in a more favorable light; for instance, Socrates tells the auditor that he "really wanted to hear Prodicus" (316a). Indeed, he calls Prodicus "godlike in his universal wisdom" (316a). While a certain level of irony is present in this narrative description, Socrates makes no such positive claim in his initial description of either Protagoras or Hippias either with respect to his desire to hear them or with regard to their knowledge.[49] Furthermore, Socrates includes him, along with Hippias, as someone whom Protagoras wants to impress (317d). Like Hippias, Prodicus plays an important role in keeping the conversation going when Socrates threatens to leave (337a–c). Socrates acknowledges this contribution in his narrative remarks (337d). Also, Socrates explicitly asks Prodicus for help during his interpretation of Simonides' poem (339e, 340e), and he notes that Prodicus supports his side (342a, 358b). Moreover, while Socrates teases Prodicus about his excessive concern with accurate word usage, Prodicus seems in on the joke (358b).[50]

C. Alcibiades

Even though the auditor's questions about Alcibiades arise at the beginning of their conversation (309a), Socrates does not refer to Alcibiades for some time (316c). He defers the auditor's expectation that this narrative will be about his encounter with Alcibiades. However, Socrates does not ignore the auditor's initial interest. After the lengthy description of his conversation with Hippocrates and after his descriptions of Protagoras, Hippias, Prodicus, and their followers, Socrates mentions Alcibiades for the first time in his narrative. When he does so, he refers to the auditor directly: "We had just arrived when along came Alcibiades the Beautiful (as you call him, and I am persuaded) and Critias son of Callaeschrus" (316a). He even agrees with the auditor's description of Alcibiades. By mentioning Alcibiades just after the description of the sophists, Socrates links Alcibiades directly to the sophists. Socrates wants the auditor to remember his initial query about Alcibiades in conjunction with the array of sophists he has just described. The auditor should see a connection between his curiosity about Alcibiades and his fascination with the sophists. These narrative references to Alcibiades serve an important pedagogical function; they should provoke the auditor into viewing his fascination with Alcibiades in a broader social context.

Socrates' narrative also associates Alcibiades with Critias, a prominent Athenian. In the preceding chapter, I discussed Critias and the ultimate fate that befalls him and Athens as a result of his turn to tyranny. Alcibiades' later life also has disastrous effects for Athens.[51] At the time of the dramatic events, no one present knows what the future holds for these characters. Nonetheless, Plato's placement of Alcibiades with Critias evokes recognition of their similar tragic ends, at least in the minds of his readers. This tragic irony only exists on a textual level between Plato and the reader. Unlike the *Charmides,* where, if we allow for a later date of the narrative retelling of the *Charmides*, Socrates as narrator may employ tragic irony by drawing upon the auditor's knowledge of the fate of Charmides and Critias, here such a scenario is not possible. Because the narrative retelling occurs immediately following the dramatic events, neither Socrates qua narrator nor the auditor would know the subsequent fate of Critias and Alcibiades. On the narrative level, Socrates simply presents Alcibiades associating with a prominent Athenian, Critias. Socrates' next reference to Alcibiades reinforces his association with the sophists and another prominent Athenian, Callias. Socrates tells the auditor: "We were all overjoyed at the prospect of listening to wise men, and we laid hold of the benches and couches ourselves and arranged them over by Hippias, since that's where the benches were already. Meanwhile Callias and Alcibiades had gotten Prodicus up and brought him over with his group" (317d).

Socrates' next reference to Alcibiades explains why he makes this association between Alcibiades, the sophists, and prominent Athenians for the auditor. Protagoras agrees with Socrates' assessment that he, Protagoras, claims to teach "the art of citizenship" (319a). Socrates then offers his opinion about this claim: "The truth is, Protagoras, I have never thought that this could be taught" (319b). When explaining his position, Socrates notes that the Athenians do not demand technical expertise in the domain of city management. He remarks, "anyone can speak in the Assembly on these matters" because Athenians believe that this virtue cannot be taught (319d–e). Socrates refers to Alcibiades' own family to make his point: "Take a good look at Cleinias, the younger brother of Alcibiades here. When Pericles became his guardian he was afraid that Alcibiades would corrupt him, no less. So he separated them and placed Cleinias in Ariphron's house and tried to educate him there. Six months later he gave him back to Alcibiades because he couldn't do anything with him" (320b). Socrates points out that the old family model acknowledges the impossibility of teaching virtue. In doing so, he intimates that Protagoras should acknowledge this same impossibility. Indeed, the very presence of Alcibiades suggests the impossibility of teaching virtue.

Socrates does not mention Alcibiades again for some time. Then after he again asks Protagoras to stop giving long speeches (334d), Socrates tells the auditor, "I could see he was uncomfortable with his previous answers and that he would not longer be willing to go on answering in a dialectical discussion, so I considered my work with him to be finished" (335b). Socrates then expresses his desire to leave because of his previous engagement, probably with the auditor himself (335c). By alluding to his meeting with the auditor here, Socrates calls the auditor's attention to the stark differences between himself and Protagoras. Socrates then tells the auditor, "Having had my say, I stood up as if to go, but as I was getting up, Callias took hold of my wrist with his right and grasped this cloak I'm wearing with his left" (335d). By underscoring the fact that Socrates is wearing the very same cloak he is wearing during his discussion with the auditor, Socrates draws the auditor's focus to this moment where Alcibiades will reemerge in the narrative.[52]

When Socrates explains to Callias that he cannot keep up with Protagoras' ability to give long speeches, he seems ready to leave. He gives Callias the opportunity to intercede: "So if you have your heart set on hearing me and Protagoras, you must ask him to answer my questions now as he did at the outset—briefly. If he doesn't, what turn will our dialogue take? To me, the mutual exchange of a dialogue is something quite distinct from a public address" (336b). Callias, by contrast, supports Protagoras' preference for long speeches (336b). Socrates' departure seems imminent. Socrates then reports: "Alcibiades jumped in and said, 'You're not making sense, Callias. Socrates admits that long speeches are beyond him and concedes to Protagoras on that score. But when it comes to dialectical discussion and understanding the give and take of argument, I would be surprised if he yields to anyone'" (336d). This moment refers back to Socrates' initial observation in the enacted prologue that "Alcibiades rallied to my side and said a great many things to support me" (309b). Socrates' narrative strategy here is similar to the moment where he highlights Hippocrates' change of perspective regarding Protagoras and the value of his teaching (313e). Like Hippocrates, Alcibiades appears to choose Socrates over Protagoras. Socrates, no doubt, hopes the auditor will make the same choice.

Alcibiades' support of Socrates highlights the difference between Protagoras' desire to make long speeches and Socrates' desire for mutual dialogic exchange. It suggests, further, that Alcibiades prefers Socrates' mode of philosophical engagement over Protagoras' long speeches. When Protagoras will not acquiesce to Socrates' preferred mode of discourse, Socrates wants to leave. At this juncture, Alcibiades sides with the philosopher over the sophist. He accuses Callias of "not making any sense" and asserts, "Socrates has a stronger case" (336c). Though Alcibiades supports Socrates, his motivation for siding with Socrates may not illustrate any innate love of philosophy. Critias points out, "Alcibiades as usual wants to be on the winning side of a good fight" (336e).

The conversation continues under the terms that Alcibiades dictates. Protagoras quickly refutes Socrates. To stall for time, Socrates calls on Prodicus for help (339e). A discussion of the Simonides poem ensues (340a–347b). Hippias then wants to present his interpretation of the ode (347b). When this new threat to a more philosophical style of conversation looms large, Alcibiades intervenes and tells Hippias that they must continue with the short question-and-answer method (347b). Socrates then tries to move the conversation away from the poets. He demands that they "converse directly with each other, testing the truth and our own ideas" (347e). Socrates emphasizes the importance of this moment by addressing the auditor directly:

> I went on in this vein, but Protagoras would not state clearly which alternative he preferred. So Alcibiades looked over to Callias and said, "Callias, do you think Protagoras is behaving well in not making it clear whether he will participate in the discussion or not? I certainly don't. He should either participate or say he is not going to, so we will know how he stands, and Socrates, or whoever, can start a discussion with someone else." (348c)

Socrates reinforces the rhetorical effectiveness of Alcibiades' intervention by telling the auditor: "It looked to me that Protagoras was embarrassed by Alcibiades' words, not to mention the insistence of Callias and practically the whole company. In the end, he reluctantly brought himself to resume our dialogue and indicated he was ready to be asked questions" (348b–c).

Socrates does not mention Alcibiades again in the narrative. However, the ending line, "Our conversation was over, so we left," may refer to Alcibiades (362a). Socrates' narrative implies that Alcibiades leaves along with Socrates and Hippocrates. This reading seems particularly plausible in light of the fact that Socrates tells the auditor that he "was just with him" at the beginning of their conversation (309b). If Socrates leaves only with Hippocrates, then it would not be accurate for Socrates to say that he was "just with" Alcibiades. On this occasion, Alcibiades chooses Socrates over the sophists just as Hippocrates does. Socrates wants the auditor to make the same choice: philosophy instead of sophistry.[53]

III. SOCRATES' STATE OF MIND

Socrates draws attention to his own actions throughout the opening exchange with the auditor. For example, he tells the auditor that "I was just with Alcibiades," (309b) and that he "took part in quite a long conversation with him, but there's something really strange I want to tell you about" (309b). Socrates draws more attention to himself by describing his state of mind: "I didn't pay him [Alcibiades] any mind; in fact, I forgot all about him most of the time" (309b). He conveys his opinion that superlative wisdom surpasses beauty (309c) and tells the auditor that he would "consider it a favor if you'd listen" (310a).

As the narrative unfolds, Socrates describes his own actions and inner experiences. Some observations may seem fairly mundane. For example, he tells the auditor that he recognizes Hippocrates' voice (310b) and that he sees Hippocrates blush (312a). By noting his visual and aural perceptions, Socrates emphasizes that he presents the story as it appeared to him. When he reports his initial encounter with Hippocrates, Socrates refers to his own perceptive process four times (309b, 310b, 311b, 312a). Socrates continues to underscore his perceptive process as he relates the events at Callias' house. For example, he finds the group, which he compares to a chorus, surrounding Protagoras particularly pleasing. He observes "how beautifully they took care never to get in Protagoras' way" (315b); he "perceived Hippias of Elis" (315c), and "saw" Prodicus (315d) and he tells the auditor that he and Hippocrates "went inside and spent a little more time looking at everything" (316b). Socrates does not embellish his own perceptive ability, but rather consistently calls attention to his perceptive process as a means of conveying his state of mind to the auditor.

Socrates also conveys his state of mind by describing the pedagogical motivation behind his use of *elenchus*. Socrates refers to his mode of discourse at numerous points in the dialogue.[54] For example, Socrates uses *elenchus* to test his interlocutors and reduce them to aporia (313a–b). Ultimately, Socrates hopes to reach mutual agreement with his interlocutors (314c). This agreement fosters additional conversation about the matter at hand (314c–d). This conversational style proceeds through dialectical exchange rather than through long speeches (335d). Most of these references to Socrates' preferred mode of conversation occur in Socrates' narrative commentary or shortly after a point where Socrates offers a narrative assessment of the events. For example, the refutation of Protagoras (329b–335b) occurs just after Socrates' extended narrative description of his response to Protagoras' performance. He tells the auditor, "I was entranced and just looked at him for a long time as if he were going to say more" (328e). Socrates tracks the effect that the *elenchus* has on Protagoras. For example, Socrates reports that Protagoras "assented, although very grudgingly" (333b). He notes further "at first Protagoras played it coy, claiming the argument was too hard for him to handle, but after a while he consented to answer" (333d). A little later, Socrates observes that "Protagoras was really worked up and struggling by now and that he was dead set against answering anymore" (333e), and then finally Socrates' observation that Protagoras "was uncomfortable with his previous answers and that he would no longer be willing to go on answering in a dialectical discussion" (335b). Each of these observations emphasizes Protagoras' emotional state and they occur on the narrative level. We only learn of them because Socrates chooses to report these emotional responses to the auditor.

Socrates also reports his emotional responses to the events that transpired at Callias' house. By including his emotional states in the narrative, Socrates draws the auditor's attention to the dynamics of oral performance of sophistical speechmaking.[55] Socrates' narrative emphasis on this dynamic begins when he describes the teacher-student relationships in the three sophistic clusters (315a–316a). For example, Socrates notes Protagoras' desire to show off in front of the crowd (317d) and the collective response to Callias' proposal to make a general session: "we were all overjoyed at the prospect of listening to wise men" (317d). After Protagoras and Socrates discuss Protagoras' ability to teach "*politike techne*" (318d–320c), Protagoras offers his audience a choice: "Would you rather that I explain by telling you a story, as an older man to a younger audience, or by developing an argument?" Socrates reports: "The consensus was that he should proceed in whichever way he wished" (320c). Initially, the performance context seems ideal from a philosophical perspective. Protagoras offers the audience a choice of how to proceed. The audience answers. On some minimal level, there is reciprocity between the speaker, Protagoras, and the listeners. But the rhetorical power of Protagoras' performance soon eclipses this mutual engagement in the process. Indeed, Protagoras sees the proper role of the audience in passive terms.[56]

At first Socrates appears to comply with this passive role. But then he responds actively. Consider his detailed description of his response to Protagoras' Great Speech:

> I was entranced and just looked at him for a long time as if he were going to say more. I was still eager to listen, but when I perceived that he had really stopped I pulled myself together and, looking at Hippocrates, barely managed to say: "Son of Apollodorus, how grateful I am to you for suggesting that I come here. It is marvelous to have heard from Protagoras what I have just heard." (328d–e)

In this extended response, Socrates emphasizes his visual and aural perceptions along with his emotional responses, saying that he was "entranced" and "eager to listen." A little later, Socrates reports his astonishment upon hearing Protagoras' claim about the relationship between justice and piety (331e). These moments of self-disclosure make clear that Socrates' intellectual engagement is infused with emotionality and with physicality.[57] As Socrates continues his refutation of Protagoras, his narrative commentary emphasizes his ability to perceive Protagoras' emotional state, as mentioned above. However, Socrates also reports his own ability to shape his responses accordingly. For example, after Protagoras becomes upset, Socrates "modifies the tone of his questioning" (333e) and when Protagoras is unwilling to answer further, Socrates "considers his work with him to be done" (335a).

Socrates then contrasts how he responds to Protagoras and how the others who are present respond. They applaud (334d); Protagoras' rhetorical ability evokes an uncritical, emotional response in the audience. Socrates, in contrast, questions Protagoras. He seeks to elicit an engaged, active response from him. Socrates further underscores this difference when he tells the auditor about his desire to leave when Protagoras refuses to participate in discussion with Socrates (335d–e). The other audience members, in contrast, show no sign of wanting to leave. They are content with roles as passive observers of Protagoras' display.

After Alcibiades convinces Socrates to stay, Socrates emphasizes the oral performance dynamic by including one last emotional response in his narrative commentary. After another round of Protagoras' oratory, Socrates remarks: "At first I felt as if I had been hit by a good boxer. Everything went black and I was reeling from Protagoras' oratory and the others' clamor" (339e). After this point, Socrates does not include his emotional response in his narrative again. It is as if he realizes that his own narrative performance runs the risk of becoming no different than Protagoras' long speech. He is simply lulling the auditor into passivity. To explain, within the temporality of the dramatic events, Socrates expresses his desire to engage in dialectical exchange instead of sophistic speech. However, when one takes into account the narrative performance that Socrates himself enacts, the situation is more complicated. Here, Socrates chooses to give a long speech. In this way, Socrates resembles a sophist. Berger argues that the auditor forces Socrates into this position.[58] However, Socrates seems quite willing to assume it (310a). Just as Socrates evokes Homeric themes and motifs to appeal to the auditor's enthusiasm for Homer, Socrates fashions himself as a sophist to appeal to the auditor's enthusiasm for Protagoras.

Though Socrates mimics elements of sophistic performance in his narrative performance, the mask must not fool us. Socrates does not tell this narrative to entertain the auditor, but rather to educate him about the true nature of the sophist he so admires. Socrates aims to draw the auditor away from his interest in Protagoras and toward philosophy. In telling his own great narrative speech, Socrates cultivates a different response from the auditor than Protagoras wants from his audience. Protagoras wants public acclaim and uncritical followers. Socrates wants fellow philosophers.[59] He tells narratives with this cooperative aim in mind. By telling this narrative about his encounter with Protagoras, Socrates implicitly asks the auditor to become reflective about complicity as an auditor.[60] The auditor should question his passive status as a listener to a lengthy account. If the auditor can reflect upon his experience as audience to Socrates' narrative, he will make an important step in overcoming his desire to be entertained. If he recognizes the limitations of his intellectual passivity, he can move beyond it and embrace the active exchange of ideas that the philosophical life demands.

Socrates provides the auditor with a concrete example to follow: himself. To explain, as the encounter at Callias' house draws to a close, Socrates presents the argument itself as an interlocutor: "It seems to me that our discussion has turned on us, and if it had a voice of its own, it would say, mockingly, 'Socrates and Protagoras, how ridiculous you are, both of you'" (361b). By enacting the voice of the argument, Socrates suggests what the auditor's response should be. The auditor, like the argument, should critically evaluate all that has just transpired. Furthermore, the auditor should respond like Socrates responds to "the Argument." When the Argument challenges him, Socrates admits his aporia, "we have gotten this topsy-turvy and terribly confused." Socrates then expresses his desire to continue: "I am most eager to clear it all up, and I would like us, having come this far, to continue until we come through to what virtue is in itself, and then to return to inquire about whether it can or cannot be taught" (361d). By referring to Prometheus and Epimetheus, the main characters of Protagoras' Great Speech, Socrates draws one last comparison with his philosophical desire for cooperative conversation and Protagoras' proclivity for telling long speeches. He uses Protagoras' own mythic characters to provide the auditor with a path to follow. The auditor should become like both Epimetheus and Prometheus. The auditor should emulate Epimetheus and apply afterthought, i.e., sustained, thoughtful reflection about the narrative he has just heard. He should imitate

Socrates and Prometheus in applying forethought over life as a whole (361d).[61] If the auditor responds appropriately, Socrates will succeed in teaching virtue after all. If we respond appropriately and take up the reflective life of philosophy, Plato will succeed in teaching us how to become virtuous as well.

IV. REVISITING THE INTELLECTUALIST SOCRATES

The intellectualist interpretation of Socrates can be traced back to Aristotle.[62] Patrick Coby explains that the intellectualist interpretation of Socrates arises primarily because the dialogues "[contain] a variety of propositions known as Socratic paradoxes: (1) virtue is knowledge, (2) virtue is one, (3) virtue is easy, (4) knowledge is the cause of faring well, and (5) evil is committed unwillingly. Together these paradoxes make up the doctrine of intellectualized virtue."[63] Cooper clearly states the intellectualist position when he writes that "knowledge—specifically, the single, unified, comprehensive knowledge of what is good and bad for human beings, or in a human life—is not only sufficient for, but actually constitutes virtue. To have that knowledge is what it is to be a virtuous person; it is in that knowledge that virtue consists."[64] This view is widely held and forcibly articulated by a number of prominent scholars.[65]

Scholars typically focus on the Protagoras as a prime example of Socrates' intellectualist commitments. Kahn remarks: "The *Protagoras* thus represents the extreme case of the general tendency of Socratic intellectualism to ignore the emotional and affective components of human psychology, or to reinterpret them in terms of a rational judgment as to what is good or bad."[66] In a similar vein, Nussbaum observes, "Its dry and abstract tone positively discourages the arousal of emotions and feelings."[67] Given the weight of the scholarly tradition that views Socrates as an intellectualist, it is not surprising that we tend to view the purpose of Socrates' philosophical practice, particularly as illustrated in the *Protagoras*, as an exhortation to embrace the life of reason.

Their rationalistic understanding of Socratic intellectualism shapes how the scholarly tradition views the discussion about the unity of the virtues in the dialogue as well.[68] However, the limitations of this orientation are increasingly acknowledged in the literature.[69] Several scholars argue that we must consider the dramatic context in which Socrates' argument with Protagoras occurs. When Socrates engages Protagoras, he does so on his own terms. Socrates presents himself as an intellectualist to match the intellectualism of Protagoras.[70] As Kahn aptly observes, "nowhere does Socrates claim that reason is the only force in the psyche, and hence that all desires are rational."[71] Rosyln Weiss has an excellent reading of Socratic paradoxes that calls into question whether Socrates generally held these views. She regards Socrates as making a series of ad hoc arguments against current opinions about the nature of the good life.[72] Nonetheless, we often continue to regard Socrates as the consummate rationalist who places reason above all aspects of human experience in his relentless quest to understand himself and the nature of the Good. Kahn suggests that to see Socrates as an omnipotent rationalist is to be tricked by the façade he presents to Protagoras.[73] This façade differs from the picture we get of Socrates in his narrative remarks. However, we should not discount the fact that Socrates presents an intellectual façade to Protagoras.

Why would Plato present Socrates as engaging in the construction of this façade? To answer this question, we must take into account the broader pedagogical context of the extended encounter with Hippocrates and the enacted prologue with the auditor. Socrates focuses on Hippocrates' disordered emotional state because it contributes to his unbridled enthusiasm for Protagoras. Protagoras' rationalism offers, to Hippocrates and people like him, a much-needed sense of stability. It offers a coping mechanism for controlling the existential difficulties of the life of eros, of ambiguity, of not knowing. Protagoras offers a potential cure for existential angst of this sort. Socrates models a different solution to the complexities of human situatedness. Socrates does not make a turn to hyperreason or embrace the highly technical art of measure as a cure for hyperemotionalism. Rather, Socrates' narrative presents us with a mode of practice that on the internal level includes rational self-examination and a nuanced awareness of one's emotional states. On an external level, it incorporates the emotional states of others into his ongoing philosophical inquiry. Socrates' narrative, then, models how he engages with others through emotional awareness as well as through rational discourse.

Viewed in this way, the narrative dimensions of the dialogue suggest that the unity of the virtues is a lived practice rather than an intellectual discussion. Much of the scholarly discussion of the unity of the virtues centers on the following points: what sense of predication Socrates employs when making statements such as "justice is pious" and "justice is just"; the relative value of the metaphors about seeing the relationship between the virtues as parts of a face or parts of a piece of gold; the extent to which Socrates deliberately engages in fallacious reasoning or linguistic ambiguity in his engagement with Protagoras; whether Socrates ultimately argues for equivalency, identity, similarity, or biconditionality of the virtues.[74] While these lines of inquiry help clarify what is at stake conceptually in Socrates' argument with Protagoras, they reinforce the view of Socrates as an intellectualist. While Socrates' understanding of the unity of the virtues involves his intellectual apprehension of the conceptual relationship between the virtues, his practice of virtue does not end with intellectual understanding. The cultivation of virtue demands an integration of that knowledge into the everyday realities of human experience, which are inevitably fraught with emotion and desire. Viewed in this way, caring for the self is more important than knowing the self. The care of the self provides a wider horizon within which knowledge of the self is situated and oriented.[75]

A more comprehensive representation of Socrates' understanding of the unity of the virtues lies in his narrative self-representation. Socrates' narrative self-representation to the auditor shows how this unity resides in the figure of Socrates himself and in the practical activities in which he engages. We see his courage in confronting Protagoras' sophistic displays, his temperance in his response to Hippocrates' exuberant entrance into his bedroom, his justice in his concern for how the conversation with Protagoras should proceed, his piety in regard for Hippocrates' soul and in his astonished response to Protagoras' assertion that justice and piety have only a "slight resemblance" (331e6), his wisdom in his knowledge of his own emotions and in his understanding of other people. Through this narrative self-representation, Socrates embodies a virtue that incorporates the intellectual, the emotional, and the practical dimensions of his experience. Socrates illustrates this practical dimension of his ethical inquiry through his narrative commentary. Here is the key point that arises out of careful attention to Socrates' narrative commentary. Without the narrative commentary, we would not see the practical or the emotional dimensions of his practice as clearly. To readers who do not attend to the narrative commentary, Plato's Socrates appears to be more of an intellectualist than he actually is. In sum, Socrates uses this narrative self-representation to teach the auditor how to practice philosophy holistically. Like Socrates, the auditor must move beyond a narrowly intellectualist understanding of what the virtuous life requires. Hopefully, the auditor will embrace the Socratic path of practicing virtue through sustained intellectual inquiry into the nature of virtue but also by means of the lived experience of virtuous actions and relationships with others.

Unfortunately, as Richard Rutherford aptly observes, the *Protagoras* has no final enacted conversation to match the enacted opening.[76] We do not know if the auditor will abandon his enthusiasm for Protagoras and Homer and embrace the model of Socratic virtue exemplified on the narrative level. This lack of specificity in the ending extends the pedagogical dimensions of the dialogue outward. As the audience of the dialogue proper, we must ask ourselves if we can moderate our emotional enthusiasm for Homer, Protagoras, and the equivalent manifestations in our culture, but not by choosing a hyperintellectual path offered by our own contemporary sophists and the myriad technological developments of today. We should follow the model of Socrates the narrator who teaches us how to live virtuously by cultivating an appreciation of how the emotions enhance our knowledge of what it means to be good. To the extent that we are able to do so, Plato becomes our own philosophical muse.

NOTES

1. See Genevieve Lloyd, *Man of Reason: Male and Female in Western Philosophy* (Minneapolis: University of Minnesota Press, 1984); Martha Nussbaum, *Love's Knowledge: Essays on Philosophy and Literature* (New York: Oxford University Press, 1990); Antonio Damasio, *Descartes' Error: Emotion, Reason, and the Human Brain* (New York: Avon Books, 1994); Steven Toulmin, *Return to Reason* (Cambridge: Harvard University Press, 2001); Martha Nussbaum, "Upheavals of Thought: The Intelligence of Emotions," *Graduate Faculty Philosophy Journal* 23 (2002): 235–238; Robert Solomon, "The Joy of Philosophy: Thinking Thin Versus the Passionate Life," *Review of Metaphysics* 55 (2002): 876–878; Robert Solomon, "Reasons for Love," *Journal for the Theory of Social Behavior* 32 (2002): 115–144; and Robert Roberts, *The Schooled Heart* (Cambridge: Cambridge University Press 2003).

2. See Nussbaum, *The Fragility of Goodness: Luck and Ethics in Greek Tragedy and Philosophy* (Cambridge: Cambridge University Press, 1986) and Nussbaum, *Cultivating Humanity* (Cambridge: Harvard University Press, 1997). Despite the fact that she argues strongly for the affective dimension of human experience throughout her extensive corpus, Nussbaum's view of Socrates is quite rationalistic. For a critique of Nussbaum's view of Socrates, see Michael Beaty and Anne-Marie Bowery, "Cultivating Christian Citizenship: Martha Nussbaum's Socrates, Augustine's *Confessions*, and the Modern University," *Christian Scholar's Review XXXI* (2003): 21–52; and Bruce S. Thornton, "Cultivating Sophistry," *Arion* 6 (1998): 180–204.

3. Nussbaum, "Cultivating Humanity," 17–18.

4. Charles Kahn calls this passage, "the rationalistic text." See *Plato and the Socratic Dialogue: The Philosophical Use of a Literary Form* (Cambridge: Cambridge University Press, 1996), 232.

5. T. Irwin, *Plato's Ethics* (Oxford: Oxford University Press, 1995), 80. See also Irwin, *Plato's Moral Theory* (Oxford: Oxford University Press, 1977).

6. Nehamas, "What Did Socrates Teach and to Whom Did He Teach It?" *Review of Metaphysics* 46 (1992): 280.

7. For a good overview, see D. O'Brien, "Socrates and Protagoras on Virtue," in *Oxford Studies in Ancient Philosophy* 34, ed. D. Sedley (Oxford: Oxford University Press, 2003), 59–131.

8. My thanks to Marina McCoy for reading an early draft of this chapter.

9. I have found the following sources on *Protagoras* particularly helpful: Michael Gagarin, "The Purpose of Plato's *Protagoras*," *Transactions and Proceedings of the American Philological Association* 100 (1969): 133–164; Larry Goldberg, *A Commentary on Plato's* Protagoras (New York: Peter Lang, 1983); H. Berger, "Facing Sophists: Socrates' Charismatic Bondage in *Protagoras*," *Representations* 5 (1984): 66–91; Patrick Coby, *Socrates and the Sophistic Enlightenment. A Commentary on Plato's* Protagoras (Lewisburg: Bucknell University Press, 1987); Eugenio Benitez, "Argument, Rhetoric, and Philosophic Method: Plato's *Protagoras*," *Philosophy and Rhetoric* 25 (1992): 222–252; Richard Rutherford, "Unifying the *Protagoras*," *Apeiron* 25 (1992): 135–156; Claus Scheier, "The Unity of the *Protagoras*: On the Structure and Position of a Platonic Dialogue," *Graduate Faculty Philosophy Journal* 17 (1994): 59–81; Tucker Landy, "Virtue, Art, and the Good Life in Plato's *Protagoras*," *Interpretation* 21 (1994): 287–308; Russell Bentley, "On Reading Plato's Methods, Controversies and Interpretations" *Polis* 15 (1998): 122–137; Charles Griswold, "Relying on Your Own Voice, An Unsettled Rivalry of Moral Ideals in Plato's *Protagoras*," *Review of Metaphysics* 53 (1999): 283–307; and O. Balaban, *Plato and Protagoras* (Lanham: Lexington Books, 1999).

10. Coby, "Sophistic Enlightenment"; Landy, "Good Life"; and Berger, "Facing Sophists" are helpful on the role of the auditor as is Theodor Ebert, "The Role of the Frame Dialogue in Plato's *Protagoras*," in *Plato's* Protagoras, *Proceedings of the Third Symposium Platonicum*

Pragense, eds. Ales Havlicek and Filip Karfik (Prague: OIKOYMENH, 2003), 9–20. See also Christopher Long, "Crisis of Community: The Topology of Socratic Politics in the *Protagoras*." *Epoché* 15 (2011): 361–377.

11. I use S. Lombardo and K. Bell's translation of the *Protagoras* (Indianapolis: Hackett, 1992). I also consulted Robert Bartlett, trans. Plato, *Protagoras and Meno* (Ithaca: Cornell University Press, 2004) and B. A. F. Hubbard and E. F. Karnofsky, trans. *Plato's* Protagoras (Chicago: University of Chicago Press, 1982).

12. Most scholars' assign a dramatic date of 433/432. See J. Walsh, "The Dramatic Dates of Plato's *Protagoras* and the Lesson of *Arete*," *Classical Quarterly* 34 (1984): 101–106.

13. Goldberg argues that the multiple auditors symbolize the Athenian demos. "Plato's Protagoras," 339.

14. Plato, Protagoras *and* Meno, trans. Robert Bartlett (Ithaca: Cornell University Press, 2004), viii. Coby also believes that the auditor "seems not to be close friend of Socrates." "Sophistic Enlightenment," 19.

15. Long, "Crisis of Community: The Topology of Socratic Politics in the *Protagoras*," *Epoche* 15 (2010): 362.

16. See Marina McCoy, *Plato on the Rhetoric of Philosophers and Sophists* (Cambridge: Cambridge University Press, 2011), 83.

17. Nails, "People of Plato," 11.

18. Nails, "People of Plato," 13.

19. Lampert notes this aspect of the auditor's character as well. "Philosophy Became Socratic," 25.

20. Lombardo and Bell, "Plato's Protagoras," 1, 3n.

21. See Bartlett, "Protagoras and Meno," viii.

22. Coby, "Sophistic Enlightenment,"188n4.

23. Bentley, "Reading Plato's Methods," 135–136.

24. Long, "Crisis of Community," 362.

25. Hippocrates is about twenty years old at the time of this encounter. He comes from a wealthy family, and may even be related to Pericles I. See Nails, "People of Plato," 169–170.

26. See also Berger, "Facing Sophists," 71.

27. Lampert describes Socrates' enslavement as a form of self-compulsion, "for he brings to light just what it was that force him, a private man, to go public." "Philosophy Became Socratic," 26.

28. For an excellent reading of Aristophanes through a Platonic framework, see B. Freyburg, *Philosophy and Comedy: Aristophanes, Logos, and Eros* (Indianapolis: Indiana University Press, 2008).

29. See R. Drake, "Extraneous Voices: Orphaned and Adopted Texts in the *Protagoras*," *Epoché* 10 (2005): 5–20 and F. Gonzalez, "Giving Thought to the Good Together," in *Retracing the Platonic Text*, eds. John Russon and John Sallis (Evanston: Northwestern University Press, 2000), 113–154.

30. Nussbaum notes that Hippocrates quickly returns to the domain of his physical needs and desires. "Fragility," 94.

31. Lampert suggests that social convention played no role in the timing of Hippocrates' appearance; "He restrained himself because he was tired (310c), not because it was an inappropriate time to visit either Socrates or Protagoras." "Philosophy Became Socratic," 29.

32. Socrates mentions money and payment for services ten times from 310e–311e.

33. See R. J. Mortley, "Plato and the Sophistic Heritage of Protagoras," *Eranos* 67 (1969): 24–32.

34. M. Stokes explores this notion of joint agreement in *Plato's Socratic Conversations* (Cambridge: Cambridge University Press, 1986), 386–387. See Gonzalez, "Giving Thought."

35. Lampert, "Philosophy Became Socratic," 32.

36. Berger, "Facing Sophists," 70. Protagoras' prophecy that Socrates will achieve high regard for his wisdom, i.e., for being a wise person, a sophist, enhances the irony all the more. See *Apology* 18a–20c.

37. Coby, "Sophistic Enlightenment," 188n4.

38. See Coby, "Sophistic Enlightenment" and Berger "Facing Sophists."

39. Gagarin, "Purpose," 136n11. Nussbaum notes we do not know what Hippocrates chooses. "Fragility," 120.

40. Lampert reads Socrates' last words as including Alcibiades, but not Hippocrates in that Hippocrates did not take part in the conversation. "Philosophy Became Socratic," 125.

41. On the historical Protagoras, see J. S. Morrison, "The Place of Protagoras in Athenian Public Life (360–415 B.C.)," *Classical Quarterly* 35 (1941): 1–16; W. K. C. Guthrie, *A History of Greek Philosophy*, vol. 3 (Cambridge: Cambridge University Press, 1969).

42. On the historical Hippias, see Nails, "People of Plato," 168–169.

43. It is also worth noting, that unlike Protagoras, Hippias has people from his own city in his entourage.

44. On the historical Prodicus, see Nails, "People of Plato," 254–255.

45. Coby, "Sophistic Enlightenment," 34–37. According to some sources, Tantalus stole food from the gods and gave it to mortals. Others say that he invited the gods to a feast and tried to serve them the flesh of his son, Pelops.

46. Lombardo and Bell, "Plato's Protagoras," 9, fn14.

47. I am indebted to Randy Spencer for pointing out that 317e supports this interpretation.

48. Coby, "Sophistic Enlightenment," 37.

49. See Socrates' remark at *Theaetetus* 151b where Socrates claims to learn from Prodicus. The fact that Plato mentions Prodicus in twelve different dialogues suggests that he was extensively engaged with his thought.

50. I thank Jonathan Sands-Wise for this point. See also S. Rosen, *Plato's* Symposium, 2nd ed. (New Haven: Yale University Press, 1987), 25n74.

51. On the historical Alcibiades see, Nails, "People of Plato," 10–17; W. M. Ellis, *Alcibiades* (New York: Routledge, 1989); Peter Wilson, "Leading the Tragic Khoros: Tragic Prestige in the Democratic City," in *Greek Tragedy and the Historian*, ed. Christopher Pelling (Oxford: Clarendon, 1997), 81–108.

52. This moment is strikingly similar to the opening of the *Republic* (327b) where Polemarchus' slave takes hold of Socrates' cloak and prevents him from returning to Athens. Not only is the action of the dramatic events similar, but the fact that we learn of the constraints through Socrates' narrative commentary is similar as well.

53. Lampert shares the view that Alcibiades leaves with Socrates. He observes, "But if Socrates left Callias' house with Alcibiades, the questioner is dead right: Socrates is coming directly from a successful hunt of the vernal beauty of Alcibiades." He continues, "Having just left Alcibiades, Socrates is confronted by a reminder that his hunt for Alcibiades has become a subject of public gossip." "Philosophy Became Socratic," 125.

54. See 311b, 313a, 314c, 314d, 333e, and 335b.

55. Stephen Halliwell discusses the strongly performative dimensions of the *Protagoras*. See "Between Public and Private: Tragedy and Athenian Experience of Rhetoric," in *Greek Tragedy and the Historian*, ed. Christopher Pelling (Oxford: Clarendon, 1997), 121–141. See Berger, "Facing Sophists" on this point as well.

56. M. McCoy, *Plato on the Rhetoric of Philosophers and Sophists*. (Cambridge: Cambridge University Press, 2011), 83.

57. Lampert regards these emotional disclosures as purely strategic on Socrates' part. He finds it "impossible to believe that he [Socrates] too is enchanted." "Philosophy Became Socratic," 68.

58. Berger, "Facing Sophists," 70–71.

59. These fellow philosophers would embody the cooperative values that A. W. H. Adkins explores throughout his work. See *Merit and Responsibility* (Oxford: Oxford University Press, 1960) and "*Arete, Techne*, Democracy and Sophists: *Protagoras* 316b–328d," *The Journal of Hellenic Studies* (1973): 3–12. Gonzalez argues that Socrates' understanding of virtue is precisely this cooperative undertaking. "Giving Thought," 143. See McCoy, "Philosophers and Sophists," and Long, "Crisis of Community," on this point.

60. This self-referentiality is at work in the Simonides section of the dialogue as well. See J. Cropsey, "Virtue and Knowledge"; A. Carson, "How not to Read"; T. Szelzák, *Reading Plato*, trans. Graham Zanker (New York: Routledge 1993) and Rachael Woolf, "The Written Word in Plato's *Protagoras*," *Ancient Philosophy* 19 (1999): 21–30.

61. On the Promethean and Epimethean paths, see Balaban, "Myth of Protagoras," and Landy, "Good Life."

62. Aristotle, *Nicomachean Ethics* Book VI, 1144b28–30, *Eudemian Ethics*, Book I, 1216b4–6; and *Metaphysics* 1078b23–30. On this point, see S. Rickless, "Socrates' Moral Intellectualism," *Pacific Philosophical Quarterly* 79 (1998): 355–367; and J. M. Cooper, "Plato's Theory of Human Motivation," in *Essays on Plato's Psychology*, ed. Ellen Wagner (Lanham: Lexington Books, 2001).

63. Coby, "Sophistic Enlightenment," 14.

64. Cooper, "Unity of Virtue," 263.

65. Nussbaum, "Fragility," particularly Interlude 1. Irwin succinctly describes "Socrates' view that knowledge is sufficient for virtue." "Plato's Ethics," 93. See also Irwin, "Moral Theory," 102. For reconsiderations of this view, see J. Gould, *The Development of Plato's Ethics* (New York: Russell and Russell 1972); A. Nehamas, "Socratic Intellectualism," in *Proceedings of the Boston Area Colloquium in Ancient Philosophy* 2 (1986): 275–316; A. Rorty, "Commentary on Nehamas: The Limits of Socratic Intellectualism: Did Socrates Teach Arete?" in *Proceedings of the Boston Area Colloquium in Ancient Philosophy* 2 (1986): 317–330; Yong, "Moral Habituation"; Rosyln Weiss, *The Socratic Paradox and Its Enemies* (Chicago: University of Chicago Press, 2006).

66. Kahn, "Philosophical Use," 227. Kahn himself argues against this view of Socrates.

67. Nussbaum, "Fragility,"131; Kahn, "Philosophical Use," 232. Gould calls it "the most striking statement of the 'virtue as knowledge' theory." Gould, "Plato's Ethics," 16.

68. D. Gallop, "Justice and Holiness in *Protagoras* 330–331," *Phronesis* 6 (1961): 86–93; T. Penner, "The Unity of Virtue," *Philosophical Review* 82 (1973): 35–68; P. Woodruff, "Socrates on the Parts of Virtue," *Canadian Journal of Philosophy*, supp. Vol. 2 (1976): 101–116; D. Devereux, "The Unity of the Virtues in Plato's *Protagoras* and *Laches*," *Philosophical Review* 101 (1977): 129–141; G. Vlastos, "The Unity of the Virtues in the *Protagoras*," in *Platonic Studies*, 2nd ed. (Princeton: Princeton University Press, 1981): 221–267; M. Ferejohn, "The Unity of Virtue and the Objects of Socratic Inquiry," *Journal of the History of Philosophy* 20 (1982): 1–12; R. McKirahan, "Socrates and Protagoras on Holiness and Justice (*Protagoras* 330c–332a)," *Phoenix* 39 (1985): 342–354; M. Ferejohn, "Socratic Thought-Experiments and the Unity of Virtue Paradox," *Phronesis* 29 (1984): 105–122; R. Weiss, "Courage, Confidence, and Wisdom in the *Protagoras*," *Ancient Philosophy* V (1985):11–24; J. Wakefield, "Why Justice and Holiness are Similar: *Protagoras* 330–331," *Phronesis* 32 (1987): 267–276; T. Brickhouse and N. Smith, "Socrates and the Unity of the Virtues," *Journal of Ethics* 1 (1997): 311–324; J. Cooper, "The Unity of Virtue," *Social Philosophy and Policy* 15 (1998): 233–274; D. O'Brien, "*Socrates and Protagoras on Virtue*," in *Oxford Studies in Ancient Philosophy* XXXIV, ed. D. Sedley (2003): 59–131.

69. See Patrick Yong, "Intellectualism and Moral Habituation in Plato's Earlier Dialogues," *Apeiron* 29 (1996), 49–61; Kahn, "Philosophical Use" and Weiss, "Socratic Paradox."

70. Coby notes "To a remarkable degree, Protagoras is a proponent of this doctrine [of intellectualized virtue], accepting each of its several tenets." "Sophistic Enlightenment," 14.

71. Kahn, "Philosophical Use," 247.

72. Weiss, "Socratic Paradox."

73. Kahn, Philosophical Use," 247.

74. Brickhouse and Smith, "Unity of the Virtues"; Rickless, "Moral Intellectualism"; and O'Brien, "On Virtue" all offer good overviews of the contemporary debate.

75. On the care of the self, see Michel Foucault, *The Hermeneutic of the Subject Lectures at the Collège de France 1981—1982*, trans. Michael Chase (New York: MacMillan, 2006). I explore this concept more fully in the second section of the conclusion.

76. Rutherford, "Art of Plato," 137.

Chapter Five

Evaluating Eristic in the *Euthydemus*

This chapter explores Plato's often-overlooked dialogue, the *Euthydemus*. In the *Euthydemus*, Socrates recounts his lengthy encounter with two teachers of eristic, Dionysodorus and Euthydemus, and two young Athenians, Clinias and Ctesippus. Dionysodorus and Euthydemus are brothers. They claim to be able to refute any argument presented to them and to teach virtue as a result (272b). At the beginning of the dialogue, Socrates claims to be so enamored of their teaching that he wishes to become their student (272b–d). He reiterates this point at the end of the dialogue (304b). What are we to make of Socrates' apparent admiration for these sophistic brothers? Indeed, Socrates' claim seems so implausible that scholars have regarded the dialogue as something of an extended joke. As a result, we often overlooked its serious exploration of the differences between philosophy and sophistry and the role of each in the polis. Indeed, the dialogue is relatively overlooked in the secondary literature in English. Compared to dialogues like the *Republic* and the *Protagoras* with numerous books and countless articles about them in the scholarly literature, there are a handful of articles and only a couple of book-length treatments of the *Euthydemus*.[1]

Such an omission in the scholarship is unfortunate in its own right because the *Euthydemus* adds to our understanding of the relationship between sophistry and philosophy, between politics and philosophy and the true nature of education. Beyond that, the *Euthydemus* offers an unparalleled example of Socrates' narrative activity. It is by far the most elaborate example of Socrates' narrative commentary. Socrates offers sustained and detailed analysis of the events he narrates to Crito throughout the dialogue. Unlike the other narrated dialogues, Socrates' narrative commentary does not taper off as the dialogue progresses but remains a consistent presence throughout the work. The *Euthydemus* also has the most elaborately crafted narrative frame.

Plato presents us with an extended dramatic scenario between Socrates and his auditor, Crito at the beginning of the dialogue (271a–272d). This dramatic exchange returns in the middle of Socrates' narration (290e–293b) and also at the end (304c–307c). As a result, we are given the opportunity to assess the pedagogical motives that Socrates has for telling a narrative and the effects that the narrative has on his auditor in more concrete detail than is possible in any of the other narrated dialogues. Simply put, in this dialogue, Plato carries the narrative framing mechanism to complete artistic fruition.[2] It illustrates the philosophical capacity of the rhetorical trope of Socrates as narrator that was only partially carried out in the preceding dialogues. The *Euthydemus* offers us a fertile and largely unharvested field in which to explore how the narrative framing techniques bear philosophically productive fruit. Stated briefly, the main products of this analysis are an increased awareness of the pedagogical and political function of Socrates' narrative activity. We see both of these dimensions of his narrative activity in his extended exchanges with Crito.

With these broad aims in mind, I divide my analysis of this compelling dialogue into four parts. In the first, I describe the opening dramatic setting of the *Euthydemus*. Socrates' initial exchange with Crito makes the pedagogical motivation of his narrative clear. In the second section, I follow the hermeneutic keys that Socrates' ongoing narrative commentary provides. These narrative cues draw attention to central characters: Euthydemus, Dionysodorus, Clinias, and Ctesippus. This character-driven analysis highlights crucial dramatic moments in the dialogue and underscores the ongoing contrast between the eristic practiced by the brothers and the dialectical philosophy practiced by Socrates particularly with respect to their intended effect on the souls of the youth. The eristic exchanges between the sophistic brothers, Euthydemus and Dionysodorus and the young boys are highly competitive. The verbal sparring that the brothers teach aims to humiliate and even harm those who receive its blows. In contrast, Clinias' questioning of Socrates and Socrates' questioning of Clinias illustrates the cooperative dimension of their dialectic exchange. They question each other to enhance their understanding. This notion of shared cooperation is a crucial component of engaging in philosophy as a way of life. In the third section, I analyze the ending exchange between Socrates and Crito (304c–307c). This final enacted conversation provides us with an opportunity to observe how Crito responds to Socrates' narrative provocation to take up philosophy.[3] Crito's response is complex. Indeed, he mimics Socrates' narrative practice by telling a narrative. Some dimensions of Crito's narrative suggest that he affirms the value of philosophy. Other aspects make clear that Crito fails to distinguish between genuine philosophy and its sophistic counterpart. In the fourth section, I show how Socrates' narrative remarks reveal his inner emotional states and his emotional awareness of others and how this emotional concern for self and other shapes his philosophical practice. As in the preceding dialogues, Socrates reveals aspects of his reasoning process to Crito. Socrates also describes his responses to his encounters with Euthydemus and Dionysodorus in emotional terms. Socrates' self-disclosing remarks, particularly his presentation of himself as a vanquished victim, add additional nuance to the holistic portrait of Socrates that emerges in these narrated dialogues.

I. THE OPENING FRAME AND CRITO

Like the *Protagoras*, the *Euthydemus* begins with a friend asking Socrates a question about his recent activities (271a–272d). This time, the friend is named; he is Crito. Unlike the *Protagoras*, the text makes no indication of anyone else present for Socrates' narration. Nor does it mention a specific setting. We know that this conversation between Socrates and Crito occurs the day after the events that Socrates narrates (271a). However, scholars differ with respect to the dramatic dating of this dialogue.[4]

The *Euthydemus* offers insight into Crito's character and the concerns that motivate him. This opening exchange suggests that Crito is very curious about Socrates' recent encounter at the Lyceum. Indeed, he asks six specific questions of Socrates, beginning with "Who was it, Socrates, you were talking to in the Lyceum yesterday?" Crito admits that he craned his neck to get a look over the crowd and that he couldn't hear anything clearly. He again asks, "Who was it?" (271a). Crito seems particularly curious about whom Socrates was talking to and the social context of the conversation. Though he does mention that he "wanted to listen" to the conversation, he does not ask about the content of the conversation, but rather about his conversational partners. Socrates asks Crito to clarify whom he means: "Which one are you asking about, Crito? There were not just one, but two" (271b). Socrates' response shows that Crito's characterization of the previous day's events is even more inaccurate and incomplete than he realized. Crito clarifies his question: "The person I mean was sitting next but one to you on your right—between you was Axiochus' young son" (271b). Socrates tells him, "Euthydemus is the man you mean, Crito, and the one sitting next to me on my left was his brother, Dionysodorus—he too, takes part in the discussion" (271b). Crito's questions show that he does not know the brothers. It suggests further that Crito knows all or most of the "ordinary" sophists around Athens. He concludes, "They are another new kind of sophist, I suppose." But he remains unsatisfied with his inability to classify their place in the social fabric of Athens. He inquires further, "Where do they come from, and what is their particular wisdom?" (271c).

Leo Strauss suggests that these questions are not deeply philosophical, but exist in the "sphere of gossip, of ordinary curiosity."[5] But Strauss' assessment is a bit harsh. True, Crito asks where the brothers come from, a social question, before he asks what they teach. But he does ask what they teach, indeed what their particular wisdom is, a much more philosophical question than ordinary curiosity typically demands. However, the fact that Socrates answers Crito's queries in the order he asked them suggests that Socrates realizes Crito's primary interests are social rather than philosophical. But Socrates answers Crito's social queries in such a way that they lead to more philosophical considerations. First, he tells Crito about their personal history: "By birth, I think, they are from this side, from Chios. They went out as colonists to Thurii but were exiled from there and have already spent a good many years in this region" (271c).[6] Socrates assumes that detailed information about what the brothers teach will interest Crito just as the information about their social background did. Socrates tells Crito what they teach:

> The two are absolutely omniscient, so much so that I never knew before what pancratists really were. They are both absolutely all-round fighters, not like the two battling brothers from Acarnania who could only fight with their bodies. These two are first of all completely skilled in body, being highly adept at fighting in armor and able to teach this skill to anyone else who pays them a fee; and then they are the ones best able to fight the battle of the law court and to teach other people both how to deliver and how to compose the sort of speeches suitable for the courts. Previously these were their only skills, but now they have put the finishing touch to pancratistic art. They have now mastered the one form of fighting they had previously left untried; as a result, not a single man can stand up to them, they have become so skilled in fighting in arguments and in refuting whatever may be said, no matter whether it is true or false (272a–b).[7]

Regardless of whether Crito's primary motivation is social or philosophical, Crito comes to Socrates to find out what he did not learn yesterday. He comes to receive knowledge from Socrates. On some level, Crito recognizes that he will learn from hearing Socrates' account of his conversation with Euthydemus and Dionysodorus. His insistent questioning of Socrates illustrates his desire to learn more about the sophists. In addition to illustrating Crito's curiosity about Socrates and the sophists, these questions indicate that he knows Socrates well enough to demand something of him. He tells Socrates to "explain to me what the wisdom of the two men is, to give me some idea of what we are going to learn" (272d). Unlike the auditor of the *Protagoras*, Crito does not inquire if Socrates has the leisure to narrate this conversation. Crito assumes that Socrates wants to pursue these issues and that he has the leisure to do so.

Crito clearly knows Socrates quite well. Indeed, Crito's emotional allegiance to Socrates is unrivaled by any other character in the dialogues. He has known Socrates since childhood, having grown up in the same deme. Crito exhibits his personal loyalty to Socrates throughout the dialogues. In the *Apology*, Crito offers to pay a fine on Socrates' behalf (38c). In the dialogue named after him, we learn that Crito visits him in prison each day, content to sit quietly by his side and watch him sleep (43b). Crito also arranges for his escape from prison. In the *Phaedo*, Crito attends to the details associated with Socrates' last day and death sentence.[8] Socrates even directs his last words to Crito, asking him to pay the debt he owes to Asclepius and not to forget it. Crito assures him that "it will be done" and asks him to "tell us if there is anything else." Crito's words are the last that Socrates hears. Phaedo then reports that Crito closes Socrates' mouth and eyes the moment after he dies (118a).[9]

Despite Crito's personal allegiance to Socrates and his professed willingness to learn from these sophists, a more careful examination of this opening conversation reveals an intellectual hesitancy in Crito's character. Even though Crito expresses his willingness to go along with Socrates' proposal that they study with the sophists, he then hesitates and asks Socrates to explain "what the wisdom of the two men is, to give me some idea of what we are going to learn" (272d). Crito's hesitancy is understandable and even commendable when compared to the unreflective attitude that Hippocrates and the auditor of the *Protagoras* initially display with respect to Protagoras. Nonetheless, Crito seems a bit too cautious. Crito's intellectual hesitancy also reveals itself in his apparent shock that Socrates wants to enroll in lessons with these sophists: "What's that, Socrates? Aren't you afraid that, at your age, you are already too old?" (272b).[10] Crito's shock may well be feigned, a way of showing Socrates that he sees the humor in his ironic praise of them. However, some serious concerns lurk beneath Crito's apparent jocularity. Crito expresses his own fear about learning something new. The root of his fear is unclear. Perhaps he distrusts the unfamiliar; perhaps he fears his own inadequacy in the face of acquiring new knowledge and skill. Furthermore, Crito may well fear that Socrates genuinely wants to become their student. Crito seems unable to discern whether Socrates is serious or ironic in his praise of them. Socrates' willingness to learn as a "mature age student" concerns Crito because these "late learning endeavors" were not a socially acceptable practice.[11] Crito's incredulous response to Socrates' proposal reveals another aspect of his character, namely his concern for what other people think and the social and political consequences of making unpopular choices.[12]

Socrates is not bound by these social conventions. For example, Socrates tells Crito that the social ridicule he receives when taking harp lessons with the young boys does not bother him (272c) and that he has persuaded several other older men to join in these lessons with him (272c). Socrates plans to continue this same pattern with the sophists. He intends to persuade others to join him in learning from Euthydemus and Dionysodorus (272d). Socrates asks Crito: "Why don't you come along yourself?" He presents a plan that would provide Crito with a socially acceptable ruse: "We will take your sons as bait to catch them—I feel sure that their desire to get the boys will make them give us lessons too" (272d). As in the *Charmides*, Socrates presents himself as willing to engage in social subterfuge to achieve his intellectual aims. His willingness to reveal this somewhat unsavory side of his character to Crito reinforces the intimacy of their relationship. By extending this invitation to Crito, Socrates hopes that Crito will overcome his concern for social reputation and engage in activities that will enhance his intellectual development. Socrates fashions this narrative to draw Crito out of the accustomed habits that imprison him.

Given these two dimensions of Crito's character, Plax argues that Crito is experiencing an existential crisis. He "expresses regret that he's been too busy making money to attend to the education of his sons." But at the same time Plax attributes to him "a sadness that he's wasted a great deal of his life worrying about his sons at all." Plax suggests that Crito "is experiencing ambivalence about which way of life he should have chosen. If anything, Crito's passionate 'confession' is an expression of envy of the Socratic life."[13] Socrates no doubt recognizes a sense of regret in his friend. He may well shape this entire narrative to help Crito with his personal struggles.

Several aspects of the rest of the dialogue illustrate this ongoing pedagogical concern for Crito. First, Socrates addresses Crito by name or by a friendship term twenty-three times in the dialogue.[14] These direct references indicate that Socrates tells the story with Crito very much in mind as his intended audience. Second, Crito's interruption of the narrative (290e–293b) reinforces his particular presence as the narrative audience. During this interlude, Socrates elicits a philosophical response from him as they reflect on the content of the narrated conversation.[15] Third, the final enacted conversation with Crito underscores the importance of Socrates' narrative audience (304c–307c). Crito is the only auditor, besides Echecrates in the *Phaedo*, that responds to Socrates' narration. In fact, Crito actively responds. He imitates Socrates' narrative practice by telling a mini-narrative about his encounter with the speechwriter (304d–305b). As a result, the dialogic audience can evaluate the effectiveness of Socrates' narrative pedagogy.

The opening scene between Socrates and Crito, itself of a pedagogical nature, focuses on educational practices. To explain, Crito's interest in the sophists arises because of his concern for his son, Critobulus. His concern becomes greater when he compares Critobulus to Clinias: "He seemed to me, Socrates, to have grown tremendously and to be almost of a size with our Critobulus. But Critobulus is thin, whereas this boy has come on splendidly and is extremely good looking" (271b). When Crito compares the physical appearance of the two boys, his own son, Critobulus, comes up short. Crito no doubt senses that Critobulus would fall short of Clinias in more substantial ways as well and is, hence, in need of some sort of education. We also see an emphasis on education in Socrates' detailed description of the brothers' new craft. Socrates draws upon the cultural interplay between traditional Athenian education and the new educational approaches that the sophists offer. Euthydemus and Dionysodorus previously excelled in the martial practices highly valued in a traditional Athenian context. By mastering eristic, they have aligned themselves with the newer modes of pedagogy (272a–b). However, Socrates' frequent references to warfare and violence when describing these eristic practices suggest continuity between these modes of pedagogical training. Previously, the brothers taught warfare, now they teach eristic. Given the advancing age of the brothers, perhaps they needed to find a nonphysical form of combat to practice and teach.

Several aspects of Socrates' initial description of the brothers and their technical skill indicate that his praise of them is not entirely sincere. For example, the predominance of battle metaphors suggests that Socrates regards their particular wisdom as combative. By describing their *techne* in these terms, Socrates places them in the competitive value system rather than a cooperative value system more conducive to philosophical exchange.[16] However, Crito does not note the implicit contrast even after Socrates describes his protreptic conversations with Clinias. To understand the critical nature of Socrates' comments requires a basic understanding of Socrates' commitment to dialogic exchange. It seems that Crito lacks this understanding and hence lacks the ability to ascertain Socrates' true meaning. Socrates also conveys his lack of sincerity in his praise of the brothers by mentioning that they charge a fee[17] and by making hyperbolic claims about their power. He calls their wisdom "marvelous." They are "simply all wise and no one can stand up to them" (271c). Socrates also undercuts his ostensible praise of the brothers by mentioning that the truth or falsity of the claims made against them does not matter. In contrast, Socrates consistently claims to be after the truth of the matter.[18]

Despite these seemingly dismissive comments, Socrates ends his initial description by remarking: "So that I, Crito, have a mind to hand myself over to these men, since they say that they can make any other person clever at the same things in a short time" (272a–b). Socrates invites Crito to join him in the lessons. Indeed, he suggests that they bring Crito's sons along to the sophists to use as bait (272d). In this way, Socrates links his interest in learning from the sophists with Crito's concern about Critobulus' need for education. The numerous references to pedagogy in the prologue, Socrates' invitation that Crito join him in lessons, and Crito's halting response to this invitation all contribute to the strongly educational context in which Socrates narrates this account.[19] There is even pedagogical value in Socrates' ironic descriptions of the brothers. The irony mingled in Socrates' praise is an attempt to turn Crito toward philosophical inquiry itself. To explain, Socrates senses that Crito's rejection of their teaching comes more from fear of the unknown and fear of social disapproval than from a sustained consideration of the content of their teaching. Socrates presents an ironic façade of wanting to study with the brothers to encourage Crito to engage more critically with the substance of what they offer. He wants Crito to develop better reasons for not studying with the brothers, reasons based on a genuine consideration of their intellectual worth rather than on a concern for what others think about them. Furthermore, whatever consideration Crito has engaged in prior to this point has led him to regard the brothers and Socrates as practitioners of a similar art. Though his loyalty to Socrates is strong, it does not lead him to distinguish between Socrates' practice of philosophy and the brothers' sophistic practices. Despite Socrates' commitment to truth and the brothers' patent disregard for it, Crito sees philosophy as another sort of sophistry. Unfortunately, Crito's inability to distinguish between sophistry and philosophy contributes to his unwillingness to pursue philosophy.

Socrates' desire to study with the brothers does not necessarily entail his enthusiastic support of their practices. Rather, it reflects his awareness that the intellectual environment that creates the context in which they can offer their teaching also creates the intellectual environment in which Socrates can practice philosophy. It is not their practice that Socrates affirms but the intellectual space that the Athenian polis provides to them.[20] This same civic space also gives him the space in which he practices philosophy. Socrates' recognition of this ironic symbiosis no doubt shapes his decision not to leave the city of Athens after his trial. When Crito, as a representative of the polis, questions the value of their sophistic practices, he implicitly questions the social context that allows Socrates the freedom to pursue his own practice of philosophy. By presenting himself as eager to study with the brothers and by asking Crito to join him, Socrates appeals to Crito on a personal level. This personal, albeit ironic, appeal offers Crito the occasion to ascertain what is genuine philosophy and what is not. If Crito can distinguish between sophistry and philosophy, he might value philosophy more highly because it will not be tinged with the negative connotations that sophistry has for him.

This exchange has broader political implications as well. If Crito is in some fundamental sense a representative of the city of Athens, any change Crito might exhibit with respect to his understanding of philosophy would also symbolize the possibility that the polis itself might become more accommodating to the practice of philosophy. Unfortunately, Crito accepts that Socrates is a philosopher without really understanding what the philosopher is and what the philosopher does and what the philosopher can ultimately provide for the city. In the end, he cannot distinguish philosophy from sophistry and this inability leads to the reduction of a public space for philosophy.

II. TRACING THE NARRATIVE COMMENTARY

As in the *Protagoras*, Socrates' narrative commentary is character driven. His nuanced portraits of Clinias, Ctesippus, Euthydemus, and Dionysodorus give Crito insight into their thoughts, feelings, and psychological motivations. Socrates' narrative also calls attention to the larger social context that surrounds him and his interlocutors by describing how the other people present at the Lyceum respond to the performance of the brothers. The dual emphasis on the personal and the public occurs throughout the narrative.

A. Clinias and the Brothers (273a–277d)

This concern for both public and private appears in Socrates' description of his initial encounter with Euthydemus and Dionysodorus. After Socrates' daimon prevents him from leaving the room, he tells Crito, "I sat down again, and in a moment the two of them, Euthydemus and Dionysodorus, came in, and some others with them, disciples of theirs, who seemed to me pretty numerous. When the pair came in, they walked around the cloister" (273a). Socrates draws attention to the close relationship between the brothers by using the dual case, by referring to them as a pair and by describing their joint action. They come in together and they walk around together. Though Socrates does not describe their entourage in detail as he did with the three sophistic camps in the *Protagoras*, there are some similarities between the two passages. Like Protagoras, the brothers are in motion. They walk around the cloister. Like Protagoras' and Prodicus' followers, Socrates describes a hierarchical relationship between the brothers and their students; the brothers lead, the students follow.

Socrates juxtaposes this image of the brothers and their social group with a description of Clinias and his social group: "they had not yet made two or three turns, when in came Clinias, who, as you rightly say, has grown a lot. Following him were a good many others, lovers of his, and among them, Ctesippus, a young man from Paeania" (273b). Much as he draws the auditor's attention to the appearance of Alcibiades in the *Protagoras* (316a), Socrates draws Crito's attention to Clinias by affirming his observation about Clinias' growth. Socrates also conveys the erotic context of this scene by mentioning the lovers who follow Clinias. Among them, he singles out Ctesippus and describes his nature as "exceedingly beautiful and good except for an aggressiveness he has on account of his youth" (273b). Plax suggests that Ctesippus and Critobulus may be rivals for Clinias' affections. If so, this rivalry may explain why Socrates describes Ctesippus in such detail.[21]

Socrates again mentions Clinias when he affirms Crito's initial observation about the situation: "From the doorway Clinias caught sight of me sitting alone and came straight up and sat down on my right, just as you describe it"

(273a). Socrates contrasts Clinias' eagerness to approach Socrates with the brothers' hesitancy: "When Dionysodorus and Euthydemus saw him, at first they stood talking to each other and glancing at us every so often (I was keeping a good eye on them) but after a while they came over and one of them, Euthydemus, sat down next to the boy, and his brother next to me on my left, and the rest found places where they could" (273c).

After Socrates tells Crito that he welcomed the brothers and that he had not seen them in some time, he shifts back to the temporality of the dramatic action. Socrates tells Clinias about the wisdom of the pair (273c). Socrates then returns to the temporality of the outer frame and gives Crito insight into the state of mind of Euthydemus and Dionysodorus: "They obviously thought little of me for saying these things because they laughed and looked at each other" (273d). Socrates uses his narrative commentary to reveal their disdain and lack of seriousness. Euthydemus' first words of the dialogue illustrate their lack of seriousness: "We are not any longer in earnest about these things, Socrates—we treat them as diversions" (273d). In response to Socrates' query about what they teach, Euthydemus tells him that they teach virtue and "we think we can teach it better than anyone else and more quickly" (273d). Socrates responds to their claim with great interest (273d–274b). Euthydemus concludes this exchange with Socrates by explaining that they are here "to give a demonstration, and to teach, if anyone wants to learn" (274b). Socrates insists that everyone will want their wisdom (274b). Socrates' narrative voice intervenes once more as he describes the ensuing social chaos:

> [I was] pointing to the lovers of Clinias who were already grouped around us. This had come about because Ctesippus had taken a seat a long way from Clinias, and when Euthydemus leaned forward in talking to me, he apparently obscured Ctesippus' view of Clinias who was sitting between us. So Ctesippus, who wanted to look at his beloved, as well as being interested in the discussion, sprang up first and stationed himself right in front of us. When the others saw him doing this, they gathered around too, not only Clinias' lovers but the followers of Euthydemus and Dionysodorus as well. These were the ones I pointed to when I told Euthydemus that everyone was ready to learn. Then Ctesippus agreed very eagerly and so did all the rest, and all together they besought the pair to demonstrate the power of their wisdom. (274c–d)

Several things are important to note in this extended narrative passage. First, Socrates juxtaposes Clinias' followers with the followers of the brothers. Second, Socrates emphasizes the social dynamics of the lover-beloved relationship. Just as Charmides' beauty caused chaos amongst his admirers in the Palaestra of Taureas (154b–d), Ctesippus' devotion to Clinias causes social disorder. The many admirers of Clinias have already gathered around him. When Ctesippus moves to get a better view of Clinias, all Clinias' other lovers and the followers of the sophists are caught in his wake. Socrates also notes that Ctesippus has erotic feelings for Clinias. Third, Socrates reports that Ctesippus seems interested in the conversation for its own sake (274c). Indeed, he "agrees very eagerly" to Socrates' suggestion that everyone was ready to learn (274d). Fourth, Socrates mentions the social context of public speech, specifically the pressure that the audience puts on the speaker to speak well. Socrates draws upon this performative context when he challenges Euthydemus and Dionysodorus to "do your absolute best to gratify these people and give a demonstration—and do it for my sake too" (274e).

Socrates asks them to focus on a specific aspect of their art: "to persuade this young man here that he ought to love wisdom and have a care for virtue" (275a). Socrates tells them about Clinias' personal circumstance: "He is the son of Axiochus (son of the old Alcibiades) and is cousin to the present Alcibiades—his name is Clinias. He is young, and we are anxious about him, as one naturally is about a boy of his age, for fear that somebody might get in ahead of us and turn his mind to some other interest and ruin him." He implores the brothers "to make trial of the boy and converse with him in our presence" (275b).

Socrates tells Crito: "When I had spoken, in almost these exact words, Euthydemus answered with a mixture of bravery and confidence, 'It makes no difference to us, Socrates, so long as the young man is willing to answer'" (275c). Though brief, this narrative comment draws Crito's attention to Socrates' description of Euthydemus' bold manner and his indifference to personal matters. Crito should note the stark contrast between Socrates' interest in the personal details of Clinias' circumstance and Euthydemus' lack of concern about them. Socrates responds to Euthydemus' indifference by reiterating the particular details of Clinias' situation: "As a matter of fact, he is quite used to that, I said, since these people here are always coming to ask him all sorts of questions and to converse with him. So he is pretty brave at answering" (275c).

Just before Socrates recounts Euthydemus' first refutative exchange with Clinias (275d–277d), Socrates addresses Crito by name and he frames the conversation he will soon report in a perplexing way: "As to what happened next, Crito, how shall I give you an adequate description of it? It is no small task to be able to recall such wisdom in detail, it was so great. So I ought to begin my account as the poets do, by invoking the Muses and Memory" (275d). Though Socrates previously expressed confidence in his narrative ability (272e, 275b), here he expresses doubts about his narrative ability. Even more curiously, Socrates compares his narrative activity to a poetic activity. He calls upon the Muses and their mother, Memory, just as the poets do. Socrates' undercutting of his narrative ability and his hyperbolic invocation of the Muses and Memory should cause Crito and the reader to pay careful attention to the exchange that follows.[22]

Throughout this first refutation, Socrates' narrative voice frequently intervenes on the dramatic action. His comments often describe Clinias' emotional state and how Socrates helps him. For example, after Euthydemus asks Clinias, "Which are the men who learn, the wise or the ignorant?" (275d), Socrates tells Crito, "Being confronted with this weighty question, the boy blushed and looked at me in doubt. And I, seeing that he was troubled said, 'Cheer up Clinias, and choose bravely whichever seems to you to be the right answer—he may be doing you a very great service'" (275e). Comments such as this one call attention to Socrates' concern for Clinias' emotional state and his willingness to respond to Clinias in these terms.

In addition to underscoring how Clinias and Socrates interact, Socrates' narrative comments frequently delineate the method that Euthydemus and Dionysodorus employ along with their motivation for employing it. For example, before reporting Clinias' first response to Euthydemus, Socrates' narrative voice underscores Dionysodorus' emotional state and the eristic method the brothers will employ: "Just at this moment Dionysodorus leaned a little toward me, and smiling all over his face, whispered in my ear and said, 'I may tell you beforehand, Socrates, that whichever way the boy answers he will be refuted.' While he was saying this, Clinias gave his answer, so that I had no chance to advise the boy to be careful" (275e–276a). Euthydemus does as Dionysodorus predicts and refutes Clinias (276a–c).

Also, Socrates' narrative comments often call attention to the response of the crowd. For example, Socrates observes: "When he said this, the followers of Dionysodorus and Euthydemus broke into applause and laughter, just like a chorus at a sign from their director" (276d). Here, Socrates describes the audience members' response in emotional terms. They laugh and applaud. Socrates even compares them to a chorus following the leader. This simile reinforces the performative and emotional context of the situation and suggests that they are controlled by Dionysodorus' eristic power. Socrates also describes the negative effect that the argument has on Clinias: "Before the boy could well recover his breath, Dionysodorus took up the argument and said, 'Well then, Clinias, when the writing master gave you dictation, which of the boys learned the piece, the wise or the ignorant?'" (276d). Socrates intimates that Dionysodorus acts unfairly, as if he were striking an opponent while down. The competitive rather than cooperative nature of their method is evident here.

Clinias responds that it is the wise that learn (276c) and Dionysodorus points out his mistake. Socrates describes the audience's response. It grows more intense: "Whereupon the supporters of the pair laughed and cheered very loudly indeed, in admiration of their cleverness" (276d). Socrates reinforces the enthusiasm of the audience by calling them "lovers of the men" instead of "followers in a chorus." Socrates links this emotional response in the audience with the sophistic techniques of the brothers with his explanation that the audience members "admire the brothers' cleverness." Socrates further heightens the emotional dimensions of this exchange by juxtaposing the response of Clinias and his followers with the response of the brothers and their followers: "We, on the other hand, were panic-struck and kept quiet." Socrates notes how Euthydemus observes their emotional state and tethers his response to it: "Euthydemus, recognizing our distress, and in order to confound us further, would not let the boy go but went on questioning him" (276d).

Through his narrative commentary, Socrates develops a string of metaphors that describe Euthydemus' activity: he acts as a chorus director, a wrestler who strikes an opponent while he is down. Now, Socrates likens him to "a skillful dancer [who] gave a double twist to his questions on the same point" (276d). In addition to developing these metaphorical descriptions, Socrates relates how Dionysodorus describes Euthydemus' ongoing attempts to trip up Clinias: "And Dionysodorus again whispered to me in a low voice, 'This is another, Socrates, just like the first'" (276e). Socrates tells him that the "first move seemed good enough." He observes further: "It seems to me this is why you are honored so much by your students" (276e). This conversation illustrates Euthydemus and Dionysodorus' tag-team strategy. After Euthydemus refutes Clinias once more (277a–c), Socrates reports, "Euthydemus had barely said this when Dionysodorus picked up the argument as though it were a ball and aimed it at the boy again, saying 'Euthydemus is completely deceiving you, Clinias'" (277c). Euthydemus refutes the first position that Clinias takes, regardless of what it is, and Dionysodorus then picks up the argument and refutes the opposite position that Euthydemus' argument has forced him into (277c–d).

As Socrates narrates this exchange, he adds to the string of metaphors he uses to describe their eristic strategy. He reports that Dionysodorus "picked up the argument as though it were a ball and aimed it at the boy again" (277b). Socrates compares Euthydemus' next entrance to a wrestling move: "Euthydemus was hastening to throw the young man for the third fall" (277d). These metaphors place their eristic activity within an agonistic context. These competitive practices also contain a strong undertone of violence. Socrates describes Clinias as the potential victim of some physical harm: being hit by a ball, being thrown for a fall. Through this metaphorical description of physical harm coming to Clinias as a result of his engagement with the brothers, Socrates implies that some harm may befall his soul at the same time. Socrates' next narrative intervention makes this link between Clinias' physical state and his inner state more explicit: "I, seeing that he was going down and wanting to give him a chance to breathe so that he should not turn coward and disgrace us, encouraged him" (277d).

In these brief comments about his own motivation, Socrates draws upon the pedagogical context of the opening exchange between himself and Crito.

Crito is worried that some harm may befall his own son, Critobulus. When Socrates mentions this consequence of Clinias' encounter with the brothers, he reinforces Crito's worst fears about sophists and philosophers. But Socrates' purpose in doing this is to help Crito overcome his suspicion that philosophy would be just as harmful as sophistry. Socrates clearly contrasts his own philosophical approach with the sophistical approach the brothers employ. They seek to strike Clinias down by using argumentative moves that take his breath away; Socrates gives Clinias a chance to breathe. Second, Socrates links his own action to Clinias' emotional state and his need for help. Socrates hopes to give Clinias a rest and embolden him so that he will not be a coward and disgrace them. Third, Socrates underscores the public context of this engagement by noting that Clinias has followers who support him. These narrative comments also call Crito's attention to Socrates' lengthy addresses to Clinias:

> Don't be surprised, Clinias, if these arguments seem strange to you, since perhaps you don't take in what the visitors are doing with you. They are doing exactly what people do in the Corybantic mysteries when they enthrone a person they intend to initiate. If you have been initiated you know that there is dancing and sport on these occasions; and now these two are doing nothing except dancing around you and making sportive leaps with a view to initiating you presently. So you must now imagine yourself to be hearing the first part of the sophistic mysteries. (277e)

By comparing the argumentative strategies of Euthydemus and Dionysodorus to Corybantic mysteries, Socrates places all the previous metaphors that he has used to describe their behavior in a different light. The images of a wrestling match (271c, 277d), a skillful dance (276d), and being struck by a ball (277b) now become part of this larger metaphor which compares the sophists and their arguments to a Corybantic initiation.[23] This larger metaphor reinforces Socrates' implicit suggestion that harm will come to Clinias' soul. Mystery religions, such as Corybantic initiation, typically sought to purify the soul of the initiate through a variety of physical practices.[24] In contrast, these sophistic mysteries, which Socrates compares to a variety of physical practices, seek not to purify but to destroy. They have no regard for Clinias' soul.

Socrates tells Clinias where he went wrong: "In the first place, as Prodicus says, you must learn about the correct use of words; and our two visitors are pointing out this very thing" (278a). Socrates explains how Euthydemus and Dionysodorus exploit Clinias' linguistic carelessness (278a–278b) and offers his assessment of their practices:

> These things are the frivolous part of study which is why I also tell you that the men are jesting; and I call these things "frivolity" because even if a man were

to learn many or even all such things, he would be none the wiser as to how matters stand but would only be able to make fun of people, tripping them up and overturning them by means of the distinctions in words, just like the people who pull the chair out from under a man who is going to sit down and then laugh gleefully when they see him sprawling on his back. So you must think of their performance as having been mere play. (278b–c)

Socrates refers to their practice as either frivolous or a matter of jest or play six times. Socrates even compares their activity to slapstick humor: tripping people and pulling chairs out from underneath them. These practices appeal to the comic dimensions of human experience. However, to laugh and derive joy from such occasions, as the brothers and their followers do, suggests a callousness, and perhaps even violence within them. To explain, these linguistic practices place people in danger just as surely as tripping someone and causing them to fall does. Socrates recognizes the danger in their practice. He commands Euthydemus and Dionysodorus to "stop joking" and tells them: "I think we've had enough of it" (278d). However, Socrates apparently recognizes that this request alone will not change how they proceed. He decides to "give you two a demonstration of the way in which I conceive the undertaking and of the sort of thing I want to hear" (278d). Socrates tells them how to respond to his demonstration: "And if I seem to you to be doing this in an unprofessional and ridiculous way, don't laugh at me—it is out of a desire to hear your wisdom that I have the audacity to improvise in front of you. Therefore, you and your disciples restrain yourselves and listen without laughing" (278d–e).[25] By directly addressing both the brothers and their disciples, Socrates circumvents the normal performative context for a public speech of this sort. Rather than laughing at the discomfort of a person who cannot respond to an argumentative move, they should restrain themselves. They should learn to listen to what transpires in a public exchange of ideas without laughing. Socrates asks them to develop a different conceptual framework as they observe what follows. Socrates himself models a different framework in his exchange with Clinias. Socrates does not seek eristic entertainment but philosophical protreptic.[26]

B. Socrates and Clinias (278e–282e)

Socrates tells Clinias to answer him and starts his demonstration (278e). Throughout this exchange, Socrates reports Clinias' response to the argument and his own observations about Clinias' behavior and character in careful detail. Whereas Euthydemus admitted that the details of Clinias' personal history and circumstance did not matter to him, Socrates makes nuanced comments about Clinias at several junctures. For instance, he notes that Clinias "was amazed" and explains to Crito that "he is still so young and guileless" (279d). Socrates "notices his surprise" as he continues the conversation (279e). This attention to Clinias' character contributes to Socrates' apparent success in exhorting him to take up the practice of philosophy. The exchange ends with Clinias exclaiming that he will pursue the love of wisdom as best as he can (282d).

In the preceding section, Socrates' commentary drew out the combative and competitive dimensions of the exchange between Clinias and the brothers in order to illustrate these aspects of sophistic practice. Here, Socrates emphasizes shared agreement, affirmation, and cooperation as he reports his conversation with Clinias. For example, Clinias' first five responses express either affirmation or agreement with Socrates' position: "There is no such person" (278e6), "he agreed" (279a4), "Very much so" (279a6), "he agreed" (279b2), "he agreed" (279b3). In fact, Socrates mentions Clinias' affirmation or agreement over twenty times in this exchange.[27] However, Clinias does not simply affirm whatever Socrates says. He asks questions of Socrates as well (279c8, 279d2, 279d4, 279e). Clinias' willingness to question Socrates illustrates the cooperative dimension of their exchange. Socrates does not simply impart information to Clinias. Rather, they question each other. Their questioning enhances both Socrates' ability to teach and Clinias' ability to learn. This notion of shared cooperation is a crucial component of engaging in philosophy as a way of life. The reciprocity in their relationship contrasts with the one-sided exchanges that Euthydemus and Dionysodorus try to force Clinias into accepting.

Euthydemus and Dionysodorus demanded that Clinias answer in carefully delineated terms; Socrates, in contrast, asks him open-ended questions such as "What kinds of existing things are good for us?" (279a) and "How does it seem to you?" (279b). Socrates also creates a more open space for Clinias to answer freely by consistently referring to this inquiry as a joint endeavor. He asks Clinias: "Whether you think we will be putting these in the right place if we class them as goods or if we refuse to do so? Perhaps someone might quarrel with us on this point" (279b). He cautions Clinias that "we are in danger of leaving out the greatest good of all [good fortune]" (279c) and tells him "you and I have nearly made ourselves ridiculous in front of our visitors" (279d). Socrates refers to this shared inquiry when he tells Crito: "We finally agreed (I don't know quite how) that, in sum, the situation was this: if a man had wisdom, he had no need of any good fortune in addition. When we had settled this point, I went back and asked him how our former statements might be affected. We decided, I said, that if we had many good things, we should be happy and do well" (280b). As Socrates relates their conversation, he notes Clinias' agreement and affirmation (280c–282b). Socrates then tells Clinias that the agreement they have obtained, namely that "every man should prepare himself by every means to become as wise as possible" (282a), depends upon the possibility of wisdom being taught (282c). Socrates acknowledges, "this point still remains for us to investigate and is not yet settled between you and me" (282c).

Socrates draws Crito's attention to Clinias' affirmation of this point saying, "I was pleased." After Clinias affirms his willingness to love wisdom, Socrates tells Crito: "When I heard this I was delighted" (282d). Socrates concludes his demonstration of how he exhorts Clinias to care for virtue. He addresses the brothers by saying: "There, Dionysodorus and Euthydemus is my example of what I want a hortatory argument to be, though amateurish, perhaps, and expressed at length and with some difficulty" (282e). Just as Socrates set the parameters for how the brothers and their followers should behave as an audience to his conversation with Clinias, Socrates dictates how their subsequent conversation should unfold. He remarks: "Now let either of you who wishes give us a demonstration of the same thing in a professional manner. Or if you do not wish to do that, then start where I left off and show the boy what follows next" (282e). Socrates reminds Euthydemus and Dionysodorus that Clinias' improvement matters a great deal to Socrates and those who care about him (282e). In doing so, Socrates contrasts his personal regard for Clinias' soul and their ongoing indifference to its welfare. As was the case in the preceding dialogues, Socrates illustrates an ongoing care for the souls of his interlocutors. This care provides the context within which knowledge and wisdom are sought. Crito seems not to notice this larger context in which Socrates' philosophy practice takes place and as a result, he cannot readily distinguish between sophistry and philosophy. He sees both as potentially harmful to the city and its citizens.

C. Socrates, Ctesippus,[28] and the Brothers (283a–288d)

At this point, Socrates addresses Crito directly:

> This is what I said, Crito, and I paid particular attention to what should come next and watched to see just how they would pick up the argument and where they would start persuading the young man to practice wisdom and virtue. The elder of the two, Dionysodorus, took up the argument first and we all gazed at him in expectation of hearing some wonderful words immediately. And this is just what happened, since the man began an argument, which was certainly wonderful, in a way, Crito, and worth your while to hear, since it was an incitement to virtue. (283a)

Socrates' narrative interruption draws Crito's attention to this important juncture in several ways. He addresses Crito by name twice (283a and b). He tells Crito that the conversation is "worth his while to hear" and that he himself "paid very careful attention." Socrates also reminds Crito of the performative context of this exchange. Everyone present "gazes in expectation at the pair and in the hope of immediately hearing some exceedingly wondrous arguments" (283a). In addition, Socrates' narrative interruption calls attention to the fact that Dionysodorus, rather than Euthydemus, responds first. Previously, Euthydemus took the lead in engaging Clinias; Dionysodorus typically explained their strategy to Socrates and then picked up the second half of the refutation after Euthydemus revealed the inadequacy in Clinias' first answer. As Dionysodorus takes a more active role, the conversation becomes increasingly violent.

Dionysodorus responds to Socrates' request that they be serious: "Tell me, Socrates, and all you others who say you want this young man to become wise—are you saying this as a joke or do you want it truly and in earnest?" (283b). Socrates notes that "he paid particular attention to what should come next" (283b). However, Dionysodorus' tactics do not change even when he claims to become serious. He simply turns his rhetorical arsenal on Socrates. He warns Socrates that he is about to be refuted (283c). Socrates insists otherwise, but Dionysodorus manages to refute Socrates. Socrates relates this moment to Crito observing that "when I heard this, I was thrown into confusion" (283d). Socrates tells Crito that Dionysodorus "broke in upon me while I was in this confusion." Socrates' previous metaphorical descriptions of their argumentative strategies contained an undertone of violence. The violence now becomes explicit as Dionysodorus draws out the violent implications of Socrates' desire for Clinias to grow and change. This desire entails the death and destruction of Clinias as he currently is: "since you wish him no longer to be what he is now, you apparently wish for nothing else but his death. Such friends and lovers must be worth a lot who desire above all things that their beloved should utterly perish" (283d).[29] Dionysodorus' reference to death is likely to unsettle Crito who very much values societal order. Indeed, when Dionysodorus attributes the desire for Clinias' death to Socrates himself it is difficult not to think of Socrates' death at the hands of the Athenian populace. Socrates faced death because he challenged the youth of Athens to think beyond the confines of their socially defined circumstance. The rest of this exchange that Socrates reports continues to draw attention to these disruptive elements.

Socrates tells Crito: "When Ctesippus heard this he became angry on his favorite's account. Ctesippus interjects: "Thurian stranger, if it were not a rather rude remark, I would say, 'Perish yourself' for taking it into your head to tell such a lie about me and the rest, which I think is a wicked thing to say—that I could wish this person die!" (283e). These words are the first that Ctesippus speaks in the dialogue. Earlier, Socrates already called Crito's attention to Ctesippus' emotional attachment to Clinias and how it disrupts the social order (274c). Here also, Socrates mentions Ctesippus' emotional state and his attachment to Clinias: "He is angry on behalf of his beloved" (283e). Once the conversation turns explicitly violent, Ctesippus recognizes the threat to his beloved and Ctesippus defends him. Ctesippus' response escalates the level of violence in the conversation when he implies that Dionysodorus himself should perish (283e). Euthydemus takes up the argument now that Dionysodorus is under direct attack and returns to his original strategy of forcing the interlocutor into ridiculous contradictions. Euthydemus engages Ctesippus in a refutation about whether it is possible to lie (283e–284d). However, Ctesippus, unlike Clinias, understands the linguistic ambiguity that this argument plays upon and is not undone by it. He points out that Dionysodorus "speaks things that are only in a certain way and not as really is the case (284d)." When Ctesippus challenges Euthydemus so boldly, Dionysodorus takes up the argument (284d).

During Ctesippus' and Socrates' encounter with the brothers, Socrates' narrative voice intervenes at three junctures. The first instance occurs after Dionysodorus tells Ctesippus "you are being abusive, very abusive indeed" (284e). Ctesippus holds his ground. He replies: "I am certainly doing no such thing, Dionysodorus, since like you, I am merely giving you a piece of friendly advice and endeavoring to persuade you never to say, so rudely and to my face, that I want my most cherished friends to die" (285a). Socrates remarks: "Since they seemed to be getting pretty rough with each other, I started to joke with Ctesippus" (285e). The second narrative comment occurs when Euthydemus manages to refute Ctesippus about the existence of contradiction. Socrates tells Crito, "Ctesippus fell silent at this and I was astonished at the argument." The third narrative interruption occurs after Ctesippus tells Euthydemus and Dionysodorus that nothing matters to them since they "speak complete nonsense." Socrates continues, "I was worried in case there might be hard words, and started to pacify Ctesippus once again" (288b–c). In each of these passages, Socrates shows his sensitivity to Ctesippus' emotional state and his willingness to intervene in response to the escalating levels of anger and violence in the exchange. Socrates tells the brothers:

> I think we ought to accept what the strangers tell us, if they are willing to be generous, and not to quarrel over a word. If they really know how to destroy men so as to make good and sensible people out of bad and stupid ones, and the two of them have either found out for themselves or learned from someone else a kind of ruin or destruction by which they do away with a bad man and render him good, if, as I say, they know how to do this—well, they clearly do, since they specifically claimed that the art they had recently discovered was that of making good men out of bad ones—then let us concede them the point and permit them to destroy the boy for us and make him wise—and do the same to the rest of us as well. And if you young men are afraid, let them "try it on the Carian," as they say, I will take the risk. Being elderly, I am ready to run the risk and I surrender myself to Dionysodorus here just as I might to Medea of Colchis. Let him destroy me, or if he likes boil me, or do whatever else he wants, but he must make me good. (285a–c)

Violent words and images occur throughout this passage. Socrates mentions "destruction" or "ruin" six times and refers to "fear" or "running a risk" three times. Socrates' culminating comparison of Dionysodorus to Medea who kills her own children intensifies the violent imagery. Ctesippus mimics and even intensifies Socrates' violent imagery: "I too, Socrates, am ready to hand myself over to the visitors; and I give them permission to skin me even more thoroughly than they are now skinning me so long as my hide will in the end become not a wineskin (which is what happened to Marsyas), but a piece of virtue" (285d). In addition to mimicking Socrates' behavior here, Ctesippus resembles Socrates in his ability to sense the emotional state of his interlocutor. For example, he remarks: "Dionysodorus here thinks I am cross with him" (285d).

Dionysodorus does not respond directly to the violent characterization of his practice. Instead, Dionysodorus latches onto the distinction Ctesippus upholds between abuse and contradiction (285e). Dionysodorus confounds Ctesippus. Socrates intervenes on his behalf (285e–286b). Here, Socrates elaborates the violent dimensions of Dionysodorus' practice by comparing it to Protagoras' arguments: "The followers of Protagoras made considerable use of it, and so did some still earlier. It always seems to me to have a wonderful way of upsetting not just other arguments, but itself as well" (286c). Socrates debates the brothers about this claim (286c–288b). He finally concludes: "it looks as if this argument has made no progress and still has the old trouble of falling down itself in the process of knocking down others. And your art has not discovered how to prevent this from happening in spite of your wonderful display of precision in words" (288b).

Socrates' final narrative intervention in this section reinforces the violent feelings between Ctesippus and the brothers: "I was worried in case there might be hard words, and started to pacify Ctesippus once again" (288c). He pacifies Ctesippus by making light of their antics: "It's just that the two of them are unwilling to give us a serious demonstration, but are putting on conjuring tricks in imitation of that Egyptian sophist, Proteus" (288c). Socrates wants the brothers to reveal their serious side. To elicit this response from the brothers, Socrates gives them another model of serious protreptic as he turns to talk with Clinias.

D. Socrates and Clinias Again (288d–290e)

Socrates continues his narrative. He reports that he and Clinias "finally agreed that it was necessary to love wisdom" (288d). Socrates and Clinias consider a number of arts: "Knowledge of how to make men immortal (288b), knowledge which combines making and knowing how to use the things which it makes" (289c), the art of flute playing (289c), the art of speechwriting (289d), and the art of generalship (290c–d). On the surface, it appears that Socrates recounts their conversation without significant narrative interruption other than the markers to indicate change in speaker. However, more careful attention to Socrates' description of Clinias' responses to him reveals Clinias' philosophical growth and independence of thought. For example, during the first part of the conversation, Socrates reports Clinias' affirmation and agreement with him eight times.[30] When the conversation turns to "the art of writing speeches," Clinias disagrees with Socrates (289c). Socrates asks him to explain and he does so with admirable insight. Socrates affirms his insight and compares it to "the enchanters' art, but slightly inferior to it" (290e). Socrates adds generalship to the list after Clinias admits his aporia about which art to consider next (290a). Clinias argues against this observation calling it "a kind of man hunting" because speechwriters "have no idea of how to use their prey but only to hunt it." As a result, the sensible ones "hand over the task of using their discoveries to the dialecticians" (290c–d). Clinias explains that the art of generalship is limited because generals "hand over the things they capture to the statesman." Clinias concludes, "if we are in need of that art which will itself know how to use what it acquires through making or capturing, and if it is an art of this sort which will make us happy, [...] we must look for some other art besides that of generalship" (290d). Clinias seems to flourish in this cooperative intellectual context. He exhibits an ability to think through the limitations of their previous examples of the art that will best produce the love of wisdom. Even as he does so, he acknowledges that this search is a cooperative endeavor. He sees it as something he and Socrates must do together. In this way, Clinias models a successful conversion to the philosophical life. Unlike many of Socrates' young interlocutors, Clinias both understands and embraces the cooperative dialogical exchange that Socrates offers. Clinias seems quite comfortable with the ongoing nature of this Socratic inquiry into the nature of the good.

E. Socrates and Crito (290e–293b)

After Socrates reports Clinias' impressive performance, Crito interrupts Socrates' account. A similar narrative interruption occurs when Echecrates interrupts Phaedo after he recounts Simmias' and Socrates' discussion about the fate of the soul (*Phaedo*, 88d). However, this occasion marks the only time that an auditor interrupts one of Socrates' own narratives. Crito and Socrates have a lengthy conversation before Socrates resumes his narrative (290e–293b). This unique exchange demands careful scrutiny because it offers us the opportunity to see how an auditor responds to Socrates' narrative. Unlike the other dialogues, where we have little if any indication of how the auditor responds, here we are presented with a detailed presentation of how Socrates' narrative affects the auditor.

Crito expresses his incredulity: "What do you mean, Socrates? Did that boy utter all this?" (290e). Socrates asks him in turn: "You're not convinced of it, Crito?" (290e). Crito explains his surprise: "In my opinion, if he spoke like that, he needs no education, either from Euthydemus or anyone else" (290e). Socrates responds in an ambiguous way. On the one hand, he implicitly affirms Crito's observation: "Dear me, then perhaps after all it was Ctesippus who said this, and I am getting absent-minded" (290e). On the other hand, Socrates undercuts his previous display of narrative confidence (272e) by alluding to his possible absentmindedness. In doing so, Socrates forces Crito into a reflective mode. Crito must acknowledge that his knowledge of these events depends upon Socrates' narrative reliability. As a result, Crito needs to be reflective not only about the events that are told but also about the speaker who transmits those events. He should question whether he can trust Socrates' ability to recall the events accurately. These questions should force Crito to take a more active role as auditor to Socrates' narration.

Indeed, Crito seems to do just that. He questions Socrates' suggestion that Ctesippus spoke these words (291a). Crito's incredulity forces Socrates to be more specific about what he does remember: "I'm sure of one thing at least, that it was neither Euthydemus nor Dionysodorus who said it." Socrates asks Crito, "Do you suppose, my good Crito, that some superior being was there and uttered these things—because I am positive I heard them?" (291a). What are we to make of this curious remark? First, Socrates refers to Crito as "daimonic Crito," which calls to mind the earlier appearance of his daimon (272e). The appearance of Socrates' daimon occasioned his meeting with the brothers and Socrates started his narrative by referring to the appearance of the daimon. When Socrates calls Crito "daimonic," he reminds Crito of the narrative situation itself. Crito must recognize his dependence on Socrates for knowledge of these events. By making such a strange claim, Socrates provokes Crito into questioning Socrates' narrative authority. One could argue that Crito fails to sense Socrates' intent here because his response seems to convey that he finds Socrates' alternative suggestion acceptable: "Yes, by heaven, Socrates, I certainly think it was some superior being, very much so!" (291a). However, after making this claim, Crito immediately resumes his questioning of Socrates: "But after this did you still go on looking for the art? And did you find the one you were looking for or not?" (291a).[31] This quick return to the subject under discussion suggests that he does not take Socrates' suggestion all that seriously.

Socrates continues: "Find it, my dear man—I should think not! We were really quite ridiculous—just like children running after crested larks; we kept thinking we were about to catch each one of the knowledges, but they always got away. So why should I recount the whole story?" (291b). Several things are interesting to point out about Socrates' response to Crito. First, he describes himself and Clinias as "entirely ridiculous." This self-description suggests that Socrates' attempt to engage Clinias in a serious conversation fails to a significant degree. Socrates uses other metaphors that convey this failure to Crito. Socrates describes himself and Clinias as "children running after crested larks." Socrates compares the knowledges themselves to birds that fly away. Also, the fact that Socrates sees no point in recounting the whole story indicates his sense of its futility. This emphasis on the ridiculousness of their conversation also offers insight into how we might more adequately interpret Socrates' claim that some great being appeared in their midst and spoke the words he initially attributed to Clinias. In making that claim, Socrates extends the "ridiculousness" of the dramatic events to his conversation with Crito. He wants Crito to experience the futility of their attempts to find the kingly art. Socrates wants Crito to experience the very same aporia that he does at this juncture.

Socrates reports some of their conversation about the kingly art: "When we got to the kingly art and were giving it a thorough inspection to see whether it might be the one which both provided and created happiness, just there we got into a sort of labyrinth: when we thought we had come to the end, we turned round again and reappeared practically at the beginning of our search in just as much trouble as when we started out" (291b). The labyrinth analogy suggests that they ended in an aporia about the kingly art. It also continues the string of monstrous metaphors that Socrates has been developing by drawing upon Theseus' slaying of the Minotaur, which ends the Athenian sacrificing of human life. At this point, Crito asks three specific questions of Socrates: "How did it come about, Socrates?" (291c3), "And then what?" (291c6), and "And wasn't your idea a good one, Socrates?" (291d4). Crito's curiosity about how the conversation about the kingly art turns out suggests he has at least some philosophical interest in the conversation. Socrates seems to acknowledge that Crito's interest in the conversation is genuine because he tells him: "You will form an opinion, Crito, if you like to hear what happened to us next" (291d). For all his faults, Crito does not utterly fail to distinguish between true philosophizing and eristic games. In this section of the dialogue, he at least notes the superiority of Clinias' analysis (that is to say, the analysis Socrates tentatively attributes to Clinias). Crito dismisses the possibility that the brothers were responsible for that analysis.

Socrates begins his report: "We took up the question once again in somewhat this fashion: 'Well, does the kingly art, which rules everything, produce some result for us, or not? Certainly it does, we said to each other.'" Then, Socrates pauses and directly asks Crito his opinion: "Wouldn't you say so too, Crito?" (291e). Prior to this point, Socrates has recounted his conversations with the brothers and the boys and, from time to time, offered his assessment of the events and how the characters responded to each other. Socrates now recounts the story in such a way that he engages Crito in the refutation rather than simply reporting the refutation to Crito. He pushes Crito out of his spectator role and into a new role: active philosophical participant.[32] Though Socrates must initiate Crito's increased involvement, Crito, for his part, seems willing to follow where Socrates leads him. Socrates and Crito continue this exchange for some time (291e–292e). Crito's direct involvement in the conversation continues until Socrates reports the moment that they reached aporia: "It is altogether a case of the proverbial 'Corinthus, son of Zeus,' and, as I was saying, we are in just as great difficulties as ever, or even worse when it comes to finding out what that knowledge is which will make us happy" (292e).

Though Crito affirms that they arrived at "a great aporia" (292e), he does not include himself in the aporia that the characters in the narrative experience. It is their great aporia, not his great aporia. At this point, Crito stops participating in the recounted conversation and returns to his role as passive auditor. Crito's unwillingness to experience the aporetic outcome of the refutation suggests that his commitment to philosophy is minimal. While Crito likes to hear about philosophy, he does not want to experience its intellectual difficulties. Like Pentheus, he would rather watch things unfold from a distance. Nonetheless, Socrates conveys the experience of aporia to Crito by describing how he felt in some detail:

> As far as I was concerned, Crito, when I had fallen into this difficulty, I began to exclaim at the top of my lungs and to call upon the two strangers as though they were the Heavenly Twins to rescue both myself and the boy from the third wave of the argument and to endeavor in every conceivable way to make plain what this knowledge can be which we ought to have if we are going to spend the remainder of our lives in the right way. (293e)

Crito wants a way out of the aporia. He wants to hear Euthydemus' answer: "And what about it? Was Euthydemus willing to reveal anything to you?" (293a). After this point, Socrates no longer draws Crito into the conversation. Socrates gives up on his attempt to engage Crito on a more deeply philosophical level. He returns to reporting the conversation for him.[33] Crito seems content to return to his role as passive auditor because he does not interrupt Socrates' narrative again. Crito's passivity suggests that he is unwilling or unable to engage Socrates as an equal partner. As is the case in the *Crito* and the *Phaedo*, Crito's personal regard for Socrates does not extend to the philosophical domain. He remains a friend to Socrates but not a friend of philosophy. It is up to us, the readers of the dialogue, to become the true friends of philosophy. We must take up the invitation that Crito refuses.

F. Socrates, Ctesippus, and the Brothers Again (293b–304b)

As Socrates recounts this last part of his encounter with the brothers, he continues to describe their emotions and motivations. Socrates also uses vivid metaphors to describe the brothers' argumentative strategies and the crowd's responses to them. Socrates' self-disclosing comments also increase during this final part of the narrative. Socrates recounts Euthydemus' demonstration that he already possesses knowledge of the art that he seeks and his claim that "you also know everything if you really know even one thing" (294a). Socrates responds with incredulity and asks them if their knowledge of absolutely everything includes "carpentry and shoe making, cobbling, the ability to tell the number of the stars and of the sands" (294b). Dionysodorus answers: "Of course. Do you think we would not agree to that?" (294b). At this point, Socrates tells Crito, "Ctesippus interrupted." Ctesippus demands proof for their extravagant claims. He challenges Dionysodorus to "say how many teeth Euthydemus has and for Euthydemus to do the same" (293c).

After Ctesippus' interruption, Socrates addresses Crito at length:

> Well, they weren't willing to do it, since they thought they were being laughed at, but they claimed to know every single thing they were questioned about by Ctesippus. And there was practically nothing Ctesippus did not ask them about in the end, inquiring shamelessly whether they knew the most disgraceful things. The two of them faced his questions very manfully, claiming to know in each case, just like boars when they are driven up to the attack. The result was that even I myself, Crito, was finally compelled, out of sheer disbelief, to ask whether Dionysodorus even knew how to dance, to which he replied that he certainly did. (294d–e)

Socrates' observation gives Crito insight into the brothers' state of mind. They are unwilling to answer Ctesippus because they believe they are being laughed at. Socrates' observation reveals the pretense behind their rhetorical playfulness. They are not merely being playful. They seek to make others into an object of ridicule while remaining untouched by ridicule.

At first, Socrates describes them as holding up "very manfully" under Ctesippus' attack, but he undercuts that description by comparing them to wild boars being driven to attack. The brothers are not manly and courageous, but animalistic. Socrates picks up Ctesippus' assault and extends it. Socrates asks them if they know to dance, if they turn somersaults over swords and if they know how to be turned about on a wheel (294e). The phrase, "turning somersaults over swords," combines the metaphors of playfulness (somersaults) and violence (swords). Socrates presses them further, asking if they were born with this knowledge. Socrates calls attention to the incredulity of their claim by telling Crito: "They both answered yes at the same moment" and "the thing struck us as unbelievable" (295a). When Euthydemus senses that Socrates does not believe him, he harshly questions Socrates. Socrates then tells Crito:

> I realized he was angry with me for making distinctions in his phrases, because he wanted to surround me with words and so hunt me down. Then I remembered that Connus, too, is vexed with me whenever I don't give in to him, and that as a result, he takes fewer pains with me because he thinks I am stupid. And since I had made up my mind to attend this man's classes too, I thought I had better give in for fear he might think me too uncouth to be his pupil. (295d)

The metaphors that Socrates uses to describe Euthydemus' argumentative strategy contain strong undertones of violence. Euthydemus wants to hunt him down and surround him like one would an animal before killing it. By using these violent metaphors, Socrates offers Crito insight into Euthydemus' agitated emotional state. He is angry because Socrates has thwarted this plan of attack. Despite his claim to conform to Euthydemus' desired style of argument, Socrates continues to "add on something to the question" that Euthydemus poses (296a). Socrates pits his belief that he does not know everything against their claims of omniscience (296a–e). Finally, he succeeds in trapping them in a contradiction about the good being unjust (297a). Socrates underscores his rhetorical success by observing that Dionysodorus blushes (297b). Euthydemus and Dionysodorus counter back and accuse Socrates of running away from the argument (297b–298b).

Socrates tells Crito "Ctesippus took up the argument" (297b). Ctesippus delights in playing the sophists' game. Previously, Socrates had indicated Ctesippus' enthusiasm for their linguistic practice by telling Crito that "there was practically nothing Ctesippus did not ask them about in the end, inquiring shamelessly whether they knew the most disgraceful things" (294e). Here, Dionysodorus recognizes what a worthy opponent Ctesippus has become: "Dionysodorus cut in quickly to keep Ctesippus from making some reply first and said, 'Just answer me one more small question: Do you beat this dog of yours?'" (298e). Socrates focuses on Ctesippus' emotional response to Dionysodorus and links it to his desire to inflict violence on Dionysodorus: "Ctesippus laughed and said, 'Heavens yes, since I can't beat you'" (298e). Ctesippus continues the argument (299a–e). Socrates notes that Euthydemus was silent, but Dionysodorus went back to the answer that Ctesippus had given earlier and asked, "And what about gold, then? In your opinion is it a good thing to have?" (299d). They continue on discussing gold and wood and stones and pieces of iron, the capability of sight and the silence of speaking (300c). Socrates also reports: "I had the notion that Ctesippus was very much keyed up on account of his favorite being there" (300c).

A little later, Socrates tells Crito: "Ctesippus gave one of his tremendous laughs and said, 'Euthydemus, your brother has made the argument sit on both sides of the fence and it is ruined and done for!'" (300d). Socrates describes how Clinias responds to Ctesippus' performance: "Clinias was very pleased and laughed too, which made Ctesippus swell to ten times his normal size" (300d). Socrates then offers Crito his assessment of Ctesippus' character: "It is my opinion that Ctesippus, who is a bit of a rogue, had picked up these very things by overhearing these very men, because there is no wisdom of a comparable sort among any other persons of the present day" (300e). Socrates' use of the word πανοεργω for "rogue" is intriguing. Typically, it refers to a knavish or villainous person, but it can simply mean someone who is cunning, crafty or clever. The ambiguity in this word forces Crito to make his own judgment about Ctesippus' nature. Does his affinity for the brothers' craft arise out of his intellectual ability or because he shares an underlying tendency toward inflicting violence with them?

At this point, Socrates attempts to bring Clinias back into the conversation by asking him why he is "laughing at such serious and beautiful things" (300e). Dionysodorus circumvents Clinias' answer. The argument between Dionysodorus and Socrates continues for some time (301b–302b). Socrates tells Crito: "I had a suspicion (a correct one as it turned out) of the way in which the argument would end, and I began to make a desperate effort to escape, twisting about as though I were already caught in the net" (302b). Socrates uses one more violent metaphor to describe the argumentative strategy. Dionysodorus' argument has "caught him in a net" like a fish or an animal or perhaps like Hephaestus catching Aphrodite and Ares in his net.[34] Socrates tells Dionysodorus to "mind his tongue" (302c). He warns him not to give a "lecture which is prematurely harsh" (302c). Socrates senses that Dionysodorus has nearly trapped him into admitting he has impious views about the gods. Socrates tells Dionysodorus that he has altars and shrines to the gods "just like the other Athenians" (302c). Dionysodorus pushes Socrates into admitting he has "the right to sell them [the gods] or give them [the gods] away or treat them in any way you like, as you do with other living creatures" (303a). Just as Socrates is about to acknowledge that he must actually believe this blasphemous statement, Socrates addresses Crito directly and emphasizes the violent effect of the argument: "I, Crito, lay speechless, just as if the argument had struck me a blow" (303a). He then reports, "Ctesippus ran to my aid, saying, 'Bravo, Heracles, what a fine argument!'" And Dionysodorus pushes his use of linguistic equivocation to absurdity by responding, "Is Heracles a bravo or is a bravo Heracles?" And Ctesippus responds in turn, "By Poseidon, what marvelous arguments! I give up—the pair are unbeatable" (303a). This last reference to Ctesippus places him in a favorable light. He runs to Socrates' aid and shares in defeat with him.

Socrates describes the response to their defeat:

> Whereupon, my dear Crito, there was no one there who did not praise to the skies the argument and the two men, laughing and applauding and exulting until they were nearly exhausted. In the case of each and every one of the previous arguments, it was only the admirers of Euthydemus who made such an enthusiastic uproar; but now it almost seemed as if the pillars of the Lyceum applauded the pair and took pleasure in their success. Even I myself was so affected by it as to declare that I had never in my life seen such wise men; and I was so absolutely captivated by their wisdom that I began to praise and extol them. (303b–c)

This narrative remark focuses Crito's attention on the performative context of the argument. The audience praises the brothers as the winners. They laugh and applaud wildly. The effect of the argumentative display expands. At first, it was just the followers of Euthydemus who laugh wildly and applaud but now everyone responds in this highly emotional manner. Socrates even claims that the building itself was affected. Socrates describes a chaotic, Dionysian scene of excess and revelry.

Socrates' effusive description calls Crito's attention to Socrates' final response to Euthydemus and Dionysodorus (303c–304b). Socrates exclaims, "O happy pair, what miraculous endowments you possess to have brought such a thing to perfection in so short a time!" Socrates now reveals a profound understanding of their inner motivations: "Among the many other fine things which belong to your arguments, Euthydemus and Dionysodorus, there is one which is the most magnificent of all, that you care nothing for the many or in fact for men of consequence or reputation, but only for persons of your own sort" (303c). Socrates also predicts how others will respond to them: "I am convinced that there are very few men like you who would appreciate these arguments, but that the majority understand them so little that I feel sure they would be more ashamed to refute others with arguments of this sort than to be refuted by them" (303d).

Socrates uses another violent metaphor to describe the nature and effect of their refutation: "There is this other public-spirited and kindly aspect of your performance; whenever you deny that there is anything beautiful or good or white, and that the different is in any way different, you do in fact completely stitch up men's mouths, as you say" (303e). Socrates delivers his final refutation of their practices by pointing out how the strategy turns upon itself: "But since you would appear to stitch up your own as well, you are behaving in a charming fashion and the harshness of your words is quite removed" (303e). Though they reduce others to aporia, they reduce themselves as well. On this point, Chance notes that "The architects of that inescapable maze in which all its victims perish are the brothers themselves.... That prison without doors is the eristic mind itself."[35] Socrates continues his assessment as follows:

> But the greatest thing of all is that your skill is such, and is so skillfully contrived, that anyone can master it in a very short time. I myself found this out by watching Ctesippus and seeing how quickly he was able to imitate you on the spur of the moment. This ability of your technique to be picked up rapidly is a fine thing, but not something which lends itself well to public performance. If you will take my advice, be careful not to talk in front of a large group; the listeners are likely to master it right away and give you no credit. Better just to talk to each other in private, or, if you must have an audience, then let no one come unless he gives you money. And if you are sensible you will give your disciples the same advice, never to argue with anyone but yourselves and each other. For it is the rare thing, Euthydemus, which is the precious one, and water is cheapest, even though, as Pindar said, it is the best. But come, said I, and see to admitting Clinias and me to your classes. (304a–b)

Despite all his warnings, Socrates wants to arrange classes with them for both himself and Clinias. Socrates makes no mention of Ctesippus taking the lessons with them. Ctesippus has so quickly picked up the art that he has no need of further lessons.[36] At this point, Socrates addresses Crito by name: "After saying these things, Crito, and making a few other brief remarks, we separated" (304c). Socrates indicates that he has not reported all that he said to them and he offers no final account of how Euthydemus and Dionysodorus responded to his plea for further instruction. He ends the narrative by saying "we separated," not "we made plans to meet the following day." However, Socrates' next remark to Crito suggests that he and Clinias have already made plans to study with the brothers. Socrates turns his attention to Crito directly: "Now figure out a way to join us in attending their classes, since they claim to be able to instruct anyone who is willing to pay, and say that neither age nor lack of ability prevents anyone whatsoever from learning their wisdom easily. And, what is specially relevant for you to hear, they say that their art is in no way a hindrance to the making of money" (304c). Socrates ends his narrative in such a way that it demands a concrete response from Crito. Will Crito join them in the lessons or will he distance himself from Socrates' enthusiasm for learning?

III. THE ENDING EXCHANGE WITH CRITO (304C–307C)

Like the *Protagoras*, the *Euthydemus* explicitly returns to the temporality of the external frame as it ends. Unlike the *Protagoras*, the *Euthydemus* offers the reader the opportunity to see precisely how the auditor responds to Socrates' narrative. The *Euthydemus* ends with an extended conversation between Crito and Socrates. This enacted ending, which parallels the enacted beginning, is the only such occurrence in the entire Platonic corpus.[37] This enacted conversation allows the audience of the entire dialogue to see how Crito responds to Socrates' narrative provocation, a response that is quite complex. Crito does exhibit self-knowledge as he responds to Socrates' invitation. He describes himself as someone who "loves to listen," a characteristic he has just illustrated by listening to Socrates' lengthy account. Furthermore, Crito claims that he would be "glad to learn something" (304c). However, Crito places that desire to learn beneath his love of listening. This ordering of his desires illustrates his intellectual passivity. In addition, Crito is reluctant to join Socrates in his plans to take lessons from Euthydemus and Dionysodorus. Crito separates himself from Socrates' enthusiasm for Euthydemus' teaching: "I am one of those people you mentioned who would rather be refuted by arguments of this kind than use them to refute" (304d).

Crito's response to Socrates' invitation does not end with this emphatic refusal. He tells Socrates a narrative of his own. Crito tells Socrates about his encounter with an unnamed speechwriter, "someone who has a high opinion of himself for wisdom" (304d). The speechwriter confronts Crito about his relationship with the brothers. Crito denies any association quite emphatically. "'Heavens no,' I said—there was such a crowd that I was unable to hear, even though I stood quite close" (304e). The speechwriter sees Socrates as one and the same as the sophists. Crito tries to defend Socrates as he exclaims, "'But, surely,' I said, 'philosophy is a charming thing'" (304e). The speechwriter voices strong disagreement: "Charming, my innocent friend." He said, "Why it is of no value whatsoever!" (305a). The speechwriter tells Crito "And if you had been present, I think you would have been embarrassed on your friend's account, he acted so strangely in his willingness to put himself at the disposal of men who care nothing about what they say, but just snatched at every word. And these men, as I was just saying, are among the most influential people of the present day. But the fact is, Crito, he said, that both the activity and the men who engage in it are worthless and ridiculous" (305b). Crito ends his narrative with this negative assessment of philosophy. He then addresses Socrates directly, "Now as far as I am concerned, Socrates, the man is wrong to criticize the activity and so is anyone else who does so. But to be willing to argue with such people in front of a large crowd does seem to me worthy of reproach" (304d–305c). With this observation, Crito reveals that his primary allegiance is to his reputation in the polis, not to philosophy.

Clearly, Crito has heard Socrates tell many stories over the course of their long association. He knows Socrates' narrative style well enough to employ many of the tropes Socrates uses in his own narratives. For example, just as Socrates begins the *Lysis* and *Protagoras* by mentioning that his interlocutors happen upon him as he is walking, Crito does so as well. In addition, Crito offers meta-narrative comments that provide details about the story he tells. For example, he describes his interlocutor as "someone who has a high opinion of himself for wisdom and is one of those clever people who write speeches for the law courts." He also makes qualifying remarks such as, "This is pretty much what he said." Crito even gives Socrates insight into his state of mind as he narrates. For example, it seems to him ridiculous to offer Socrates advice (304d) and he thinks people should not criticize philosophy (305b).

Crito imitates Socrates' pedagogical use of narrative as well. He hopes that Socrates will listen to the narrative, recognize some limitation within himself or some negative consequence of his actions as a result of hearing the narrative, and change his behavior according to that recognition. More specifically, Crito believes that Socrates' unwillingness to take into account how other people regard the practice of philosophy will cause him great harm. Crito tells this narrative in the hope that Socrates will start to care about the public perception of his philosophical practice. To facilitate this process, Crito presents Socrates with the image of the speechwriter who in many ways resembles himself. Like Socrates, the speechwriter begins a conversation by addressing Crito by name and asking him a question about his interest in the sophists (304c).

Later, he refers to Crito as a *makarie*, a blessed one (305a), just like Socrates himself does on several occasions in the narrative. Like Socrates, the speechwriter says that the brothers' display was "worth hearing" (304d). However, he undercuts this apparently positive judgment by describing them as "speaking silliness," giving "undeserved seriousness to things that don't matter" (304e), and "caring nothing about what they say" (305a). These assessments match many of Socrates' own observations about their practice. The speechwriter tells Crito that he should be embarrassed for Socrates who acted so strangely by putting himself in the company of these men.

When Crito tells this narrative, we must reassess the way in which Crito initially presented himself to Socrates. Crito said nothing about this encounter when he first asked Socrates about his conversation the previous day. He said nothing about having already heard a report of the conversation. In fact, Crito creates a very different context for asking Socrates about the conversation: namely an interest in Critobulus' education. We must now ask ourselves if Crito's actual motivation was to find a way to warn Socrates about the potential harm to his reputation that will come if he studies with Euthydemus and Dionysodorus more than an earnest desire to find a teacher for Critobulus. The rhetorical strategies the brothers employ clearly discourage Crito from turning to them as possible educators for his son. Their ridiculous argument also threatens to turn Crito and others like him, i.e., the speechwriter, into misologists.[38] Perhaps people like the speechwriter already had a dismissive attitude towards philosophers, but the association of philosophy with people like Euthydemus and Dionysodorus makes the situation worse. Though they operate in the social context that also makes Socratic philosophy possible, they also make it more difficult for philosophy (already held in suspicion or thought merely useless) to make its distinctive voice heard.

Just as Crito responds to Socrates' narrative, Socrates responds to Crito's: "Crito, men like these are very strange. Still, I don't yet know what to say in return." In doing so, Socrates models the response of an ideal auditor. First, he admits the limitations of his ability to respond adequately. Then, he asks numerous questions to further his understanding: "What sort of man was this who came up and attacked philosophy? Was he one of those clever persons who contend in the law courts, an orator? Or was he one of those who equip such men for battle, a writer of speeches, which the orators use?" (305b). This questioning on the part of the auditor should cause the narrator to provide more information or to engage in conversation about the narrative. Crito does both. He clarifies the sort of person the speechwriter is: "He was certainly not an orator, no indeed. Nor do I think he has ever appeared in court. But they say he understands the business—very much so—and that he is a clever man and can compose clever speeches" (305c).[39] Then, he and Socrates continue their conversation (305c–307c).

Socrates' request for additional information solves his initial perplexity: "Now I understand—it was about this sort of person that I was just going to speak myself" (305e). Several things are important to note about the way that Socrates describes Crito's interlocutor. Socrates uses Prodicus' metaphor of a boundary zone to place him between the philosopher and the statesman. The use of the boundary zone, or no-mans' land, subtly continues the battle imagery that Socrates has used to describe the brothers and their activity throughout his narration. Though he distinguishes between this speechwriter and the sophist, the speechwriter and the sophist are both at odds with the philosopher and the speechwriter is also at odds with the sophist. Socrates explains that the philosophers are the only ones who hinder the "universal esteem" that speechwriters want for their wisdom. As a result, they make the philosopher "seem to be worth nothing" so that they will be "undisputed" in their victory in the contest for the reputation for wisdom. Speechwriters are also at odds with the sophists like Euthydemus who employ *elenchus* and "cut them short in private conversation." Socrates describes the peculiar position of the speechwriters:

> It is no easy matter to persuade them that a man or anything else which is between two things and partakes of both is worse than one and better than the other in the case where one of the things is good and the other evil; and that in the case where it partakes of two distinct goods, it is worse than either of them with respect to the end for which each of the two (of which it is composed is useful). It is only in the case where the things in the middle partake of two distinct evils that it is better than either of those of which it has a share. (306b)

Throughout this passage, Socrates emphasizes the inner motivation of the speechwriters. They "think themselves wisest of all men." They desire public acclaim. They avoid risk and conflict. They seek to accrue the public benefits of wisdom (305e). After hearing Socrates' lengthy assessment, Crito asks, "Do you think there is anything in what they say? For surely it can't be denied that their argument has a certain plausibility" (305e). Socrates upholds the distinction he has made between the magnificent appearance of their wisdom and its lack of grounding in truth, "Plausibility is just what it does have, Crito, rather than truth" (306b). Despite this lack of concern for truth, Socrates tells Crito: "We ought to forgive them their ambition and not feel angry, although we still ought to see these men for what they are" (306d).

At this point, Crito senses that Socrates has no intention of abandoning his plan to study with Euthydemus and Dionysodorus. He returns the conversation to his personal dilemma about what to do with Critobulus. However, just as Crito is unsuccessful in his attempt to dissuade Socrates from studying with Euthydemus and Dionysodorus, he remains unsuccessful in his attempt to find appropriate educators for Critobulus. Crito confesses his confusion to Socrates. He laments, "Whenever I take a look at any of those persons who set up to educate men, I am amazed; and every last one of them strikes me as utterly grotesque, to speak frankly between ourselves. So the result is that I cannot see how I am to persuade the boy to take up philosophy" (306d–307a). Though Crito agrees that the appropriate education is important, he finds himself uncompelled by any of those who set themselves up as educators in the polis. He cannot see that Socrates offers a different alternative than the sophists. As a result, he remains at a loss with respect to how to educate Critobulus.

Socrates attempts to lead Crito out of his aporia one last time: "My dear Crito, don't you realize that in every pursuit most of the practitioners are paltry and of no account whereas the serious men are few and beyond price?"(307a). Crito agrees. Socrates presses the point about the laughable nature of most practitioners of any art. Crito confirms the truth of this observation. Socrates asks him, "Do you intend to run away from all these pursuits and entrust your son to none of them?" (307c). Curiously, in the *Crito*, Crito attempts to persuade Socrates to run away from the city and his personal obligations (45d). Here, though, Crito admits it would be unreasonable to run away from the obligations that bind us to others. Socrates concludes the dialogue with the following exhortation: "Don't do what you ought not to, Crito, but pay no attention to the practitioners of philosophy, whether good or bad. Rather give serious consideration to the thing itself: if it seems to you negligible, then turn everyone from it, not just your sons. But if it seems to you to be what I think it is, then take heart, pursue it, practice it, both you and yours, as the proverb says" (307c). As we read Socrates' particular exhortation to Crito, we come to see it as our own. We should consider philosophy for ourselves and take it to heart, pursue it, and practice it. Socrates' narrative practice of philosophy offers one concrete model of how we can cultivate the practice of philosophy in our lives.

IV. SOCRATES' SELF-DISCLOSING NARRATIVE COMMENTARY

Socrates makes numerous comments about his own mental and emotional states. In his self-disclosing narrative commentary, he integrates his emotional awareness in his philosophical engagement with others and in his presentation of his own self-understanding. The emotional dimensions of Socrates' self-disclosing remarks call into question the intellectualist interpretation of Socrates' practice of philosophy.

Socrates first mentions his inner state of mind in the opening exchange with Crito. He tells Crito, "I have it in mind to hand myself over to these men since they say that they can make any other person clever at the same things in a short time" (272b). Socrates does not just describe his thought process in intellectual terms but uses emotional language to describe his intentions. When Crito asks him if he is afraid of being too old to learn from Euthydemus and Dionysodorus, Socrates responds, "Not in the least, Crito. I have enough example and encouragement to keep me from being afraid." Nonetheless, Socrates does acknowledge that he "fears disgracing them as a student" (272c).[40] Socrates also reveals his state of mind when he tells Crito that he "will attempt to persuade some others for this project" and he "knows that their desire for Crito's sons will make them teach us too" (272c).

Socrates begins by describing his state of mind:

> For I am not able to say that I did not pay close attention to the two of them, but paid entirely close attention and I remember and I will try to narrate everything from the beginning. As good luck would have it, I was sitting by myself in the undressing room just where you saw me and was already thinking of leaving.[41] But when I got up, my customary divine sign put in an appearance. So I sat down again, and in a moment the two of them, Euthydemus and Dionysodorus, came in, and some others with them, disciples of theirs, who seemed to me pretty numerous. (272e–273a)

This episode is the only explicit reference Socrates makes to his daimon in any of the dialogues that he narrates. This appearance of the daimon accords well with Socrates' description of it in the *Apology*. There, he explains: "It is a voice, and whenever it speaks it turns me away from something I am about to do, but it never encourages me to do anything" (31d). Socrates believes that the divine sign keeps harm from coming to him, that he would have "died long ago and benefited neither you nor myself" had he entered into public affairs (31d).[42] By mentioning the appearance of the daimon, Socrates emphasizes the peculiarity of his inner life and his willingness to listen to aspects of his experience that exist beyond the strictly rational domain. Also, Socrates' reporting of the daimon encounter illustrates his adaptability to circumstance. As in the *Lysis*, the *Charmides*, and the *Protagoras*, Socrates is involved in a particular course of action, but his emotional awareness often alerts him to a new situation when it arises and he changes his plans to meet its demands.[43] This adaptability enables him to find interlocutors and opportunities for philosophical conversation wherever they appear. For example, when the brothers appear, Socrates conveys his interest in Euthydemus and Dionysodorus by telling Crito, "I was keeping a good eye on them" (273b). He reports: "Since I hadn't seen the two for quite a time, I gave them a good welcome" (273c). This remark indicates that Socrates has some previous familiarity with the brothers, whereas Crito did not even know who they were. Indeed, Socrates knows them well enough to remark: "they obviously thought little of me for saying this" (273d).[44] When Socrates reveals his prior acquaintance with the brothers, we realize that Crito, despite his personal allegiance to Socrates, does not know everything about Socrates' acquaintances and activities. Nothing in Crito's original questioning suggests that he knows of Socrates' prior acquaintance with the brothers. Socrates underscores how closely he paid attention to the brothers later in his narrative: "I paid particular attention to what should come next and watched to see just how they would pick up the argument and where they would start persuading the young man to practice wisdom and virtue" (283a).

Socrates refers to his intellectual thought process throughout the narrative. Some of Socrates' descriptions about his engagement with Euthydemus, Dionysodorus, Clinias, and Ctesippus are fairly mundane. At times, he makes simple comments like: "When I had spoken in almost these exact words" (275b), "I had no chance to warn the boy to be careful" (276a), and "We agreed with each other on all points of this sort" (281d).[45] Other times, his description is more elaborate. For example, before recounting Euthydemus' refutation of Clinias, Socrates reflects upon the difficulty of the task before him: "It is no small task to be able to recall such wisdom in detail, it was so great." If we take Socrates' statement at face value, it illustrates Socrates' intellectual humility. He is honest about his limitations. If we read it as tinged with irony that is directed toward the sophists, Socrates suggests to Crito that their wisdom was not very great at all. Both levels of meaning can certainly exist at the same time. Socrates presents his awareness of the limits of his knowledge as a corrective to the brothers' unwillingness to acknowledge any limitations to theirs.

Socrates' next remark reinforces his intellectual humility in a different way. Socrates characterizes his narrative activity by comparing it to poetic activity: "So I ought to begin my account as the poets do, by invoking the

Muses and Memory" (275d). Given his dismissive remarks about narrative poetry in the *Republic*, it seems strange that he would present his own practice in a similar light. Nonetheless, it is important to see that Socrates characterizes his narrative honestly, as an account laden with emotionality, like poetry. By making this comparison, Socrates suggests to Crito that the account he will hear is not a simple report of the argument, but an account meant to evoke an emotional response in the audience. As readers of the dialogue, we are forced to confront the puzzling fact that Socrates engages in the same sort of poetic activity that he criticizes in the *Republic*. This passage is a good example of Miriam Byrd's idea of a summoner, an intentional contradiction in the text that alert the reader to Plato's intention. Passages such as this one suggest that Plato's view of poetry and the role it can play in the philosophical life is substantially at odds with a literal reading of the critique of poetry found in the *Republic*.[46]

Socrates again demonstrates his intellectual humility when he tells Crito: "This gave me the idea that they must have thought we were joking earlier when we asked them to talk to the boy, and that this was why they made a joke of it and failed to take it seriously. When this idea occurred to me, I insisted all the more that we were in dead earnest" (283b).[47] When Socrates tells Crito that he himself misunderstood the twins' intentions, he acknowledges his fallibility. Socrates also reveals his awareness of how his mistaken thought process influences the behaviors of those around him. Despite the initial misunderstanding, Socrates reassesses the situation and gives the brothers another chance to be serious.

In addition to giving insight into his intellectual thought process, Socrates also includes numerous references to his emotional states in his narrative commentary. At times, Socrates conveys his own emotional states by including himself in the response of the whole group. For example, he remarks, "We were panic-struck and kept quiet." He continues describing the situation; "Euthydemus, observing our distress and in order to confound us further, would not let the boy go" (276d). Later, he tells Crito, "We all gazed at him in expectation of hearing some wonderful words immediately" (283a). Socrates characterizes his response to the boys and the brothers in emotional terms. For example, he is "pleased" (282c) and "delighted" (282d) with Clinias' response to the question of whether wisdom can be taught. Similarly, when Euthydemus tells Socrates that they see their previous pastimes as diversions, Socrates responds, "I was astonished and said, 'Your serious occupation must certainly be splendid if you have important things like these for your diversions'" (273d). Later, after Ctesippus falls silent in the face of the brothers' assault, Socrates tells Crito, "I was astonished at the argument and said, 'How do you mean this Dionysodorus?'" (286c).

While we often associate wonder with positive feelings, like the awe we experience in the presence of great beauty, some of Socrates' emotional responses are more unpleasant. He tells Crito, "When I heard this I was thrown into confusion, and he broke in upon my confusion" (283d). Socrates also mentions that he is "worried in case there might be hard words" (288c). At numerous junctures, Socrates presents himself as being overwhelmed by the sophists and their reasoning. "Then I, Crito, lay speechless, just as if the argument had struck me a blow" (303a). Socrates even goes so far as to say, "I was in every way enslaved by their wisdom" (303c). Several of Socrates' most vivid narrative descriptions focus on the aporetic impasses in the argument. He laments, "We were really quite ridiculous—just like children running after crested larks; we kept thinking we were about to catch each one of the knowledges, but they always got away" (291b). A little later, he remarks that "We are in just as great difficulties as ever, or even worse, when it comes to finding out what that knowledge is which will make us happy" (292e). Socrates does not describe this aporia simply as an intellectual impasse of thought, but rather a moment filled with emotionality:

> As far as I was concerned, Crito, when I had fallen into this difficulty, I began to exclaim at the top of my lungs and to call upon the two strangers as though they were the Heavenly Twins to rescue both myself and the boy from the third wave of the argument and to endeavor in every conceivable way to make plain what this knowledge can be which we ought to have if we are going to spend the remainder of our lives in the right way. (293e)

Socrates links his aporetic state to his emotions: "This put me in a terrible fix, which I thought I deserved for my grumbling" (301e). Another emotionally laden characterization of aporia occurs as his narrative draws to a close: "I had a suspicion, a correct one as it turned out, of the way in which the argument would end, and I began to make a desperate effort to escape, twisting about as though I were already caught in the net" (302b). Socrates' inclusion of these moments of extreme emotionality in the narrative illustrates the level of the intimacy in his friendship with Crito. In this intimate context, he can present himself in a vulnerable light. However, given that Socrates describes himself as captured animal or wounded victim, it seems unlikely that Socrates sees these emotional states as ideal. Indeed, they seem almost dehumanizing. Nonetheless, Socrates does not try to minimize the effects of these emotions or expunge them from his narrative. Socrates tells the story of his philosophical conversations in such a way that he draws attention to both his rational thought process and his emotional responses to events. He does not tell this story of his encounter with the brothers as the victory of reason over emotion. Socrates' self-disclosing narrative commentary show that his emotions shape his interpretation of events, that they play a role in directing the course of his philosophical conversations, and that they are an integral part of his self-knowledge. By including observations about his reasoning process and his emotional process, Socrates provides Crito a realistic portrait of what it means to have self-knowledge. Self-knowledge facilitates the ability to care for one's own soul as well as the souls of others. In this way, Socratic self-knowledge is a deeply communal endeavor.

By presenting himself as eager to study with the brothers and by asking Crito to join him, Socrates appeals to Crito on a personal level. This personal, albeit ironic, appeal offers Crito the occasion to ascertain what is genuine philosophy and what is not. If Crito can distinguish between sophistry and philosophy, he is more likely to recognize the value in philosophy because it will not be tinged with the negative connotations that sophistry has for him. Once Crito sees philosophy and sophistry as distinct practices, he will be more able to solve his own dilemma about how best to educate Critobulus. To the extent that Crito can decide how to educate Critobulus, Crito begins to philosophize for himself and for others. This sort of philosophizing is necessary if philosophy is ever going to have a genuine role in the affairs of the city. A cooperative understanding of philosophical engagement stands as an ongoing corrective to the competitive tendencies within all of us that lead to various manifestations of tyrannical behavior as illustrated by figures like Charmides and Critias. As was the case in the *Charmides* and the *Protagoras*, Socrates' narrative commentary presents a model of philosophy that asks us to regard the other as a vital partner in our attempts to achieve the good life. Philosophical exchange can unite citizens of polis together. This insight will be important to keep in mind as we examine Plato's *Republic*.

NOTES

1. I have found the following studies particularly helpful: L. Strauss, "On the *Euthydemus*," *Interpretation* 1 (1970): 1–20; D. Roochnik, "The Serious Play of Plato's *Euthydemus*," *Interpretation* 18 (1990): 211–232; R. Jackson, "Socrates' Iolaos: Myth and Eristic in Plato's *Euthydemus*," *Classical Quarterly* 40 (1990): 378–395; T. Chance, *Plato's* Euthydemus (Berkeley: University of California Press, 1992); T. Landy, "Philosophy, Statesmanship, and Pragmatism in Plato's *Euthydemus*," *Interpretation* 25 (1998): 181–200; M. McCabe Smith, "Silencing the Sophists: The Drama of the *Euthydemus*," *Proceedings of the Boston Area Colloquium in Ancient Philosophy* 15 (1999): 139–168; M. Plax, "Crito in Plato's *Euthydemus*: The Lover of Family and of Money," *Polis* 17 (2000): 35–59; C. Gill, "Protreptic and Dialectic in Plato's *Euthydemus*," in *Plato:* Euthydemus, Charmides. *Proceedings of the V Symposium Platonicum. Selected Papers*, vol. 13., eds. Tom Robinson and Luc Brisson (Sankt Augustin: Academia Verlag, 2000), 133–143; H. Tarrant, "Plato's *Euthydemus* and a Platonist Education Program," *Dionysius* 21 (2003): 7–22; and R. Parry, "The Craft of Ruling in Plato's *Euthydemus* and *Republic*," *Phronesis* 48 (2003): 1–28.

2. Strauss, "*Euthydemus*"; Chance, *Plato's* Euthydemus; Rutherford, *Art of Plato*; Landy, "Philosophy, Statesmanship"; and Plax, "Lover of Family" are particularly sensitive to the narrative dimensions of the dialogue.

3. This protreptic use of narrative is particularly apparent in the intervening exchange between Socrates and Crito (290e–293).

4. Opinions range from 430–420 BCE to closer to Socrates' trial. Nails suggest around 407 as she outlines the scholarly debate. *People of Plato*, 318.

5. Nonetheless, they illustrate Crito's curiosity about Socrates and his activities. Furthermore, as the dialogue unfolds, Crito demonstrates more interest in philosophy than Strauss

suggests. Plax sees Crito's view of philosophy as largely Protagorean. "Lover of Family," 56–58.

6. On the significance of Thurii, see Plax, " Lover of Family," 48–50.

7. I use Rosamond Kent Sprague's translation in *Plato, Collected Works*, ed. John Cooper (Indianapolis: Hackett, 1997), 708–745.

8. 60b, 63d, 115b–118a.

9. On the historical Crito, see Nails, *People of Plato*, 114–116. On Crito's character in the *Euthydemus*, see Chance, *Plato's* Euthydemus; Landy, "Philosophy, Statesmanship"; Plax, "Lover of Family"; and S. Kato, "The Crito–Socrates Scenes in the *Euthydemus:* A Point of View for a Reading of the Dialogue," in *Plato:* Euthydemus, Charmides. *Proceedings of the V Symposium Platonicum. Selected Papers*, vol. 13, eds. Tom Robinson and Luc Brisson, 123–132: 2000.

10. Whether Crito understands Socrates' irony is a contested matter in the secondary literature. Strauss, on the one hand, sees him as "impervious to Socrates' irony." "*Euthydemus*," 1. Plax sees him as "not unaware of it" (42) and, at times, employing it himself. "Lover of Family," 51 and 53.

11. H. Tarrant, "Plato, Prejudice, and the Mature-Age Student in Antiquity," *Dialogues with Plato*, ed. E. Benetiz, *Apeiron* 29 (1996): 105–20. The mature-age student, a comedic trope employed by Aristophanes, provides a subtle thematic link between the opening of the *Protagoras* and the opening of the *Euthydemus*.

12. See *Crito*, 43c.

13. Plax, " Lover of Family," 41.

14. In each of his responses to Crito in the enacted prologue (271a–272c), Socrates addresses Crito by name (271a, 271b, 271c, 272b, and 272c). As Socrates tells the narrative, he addresses Crito by name or by friendship term six times (275c, 283a, 294e, 303a, 303b my dear Crito, 304c). In the intervening exchange (290e–293b), Socrates' references to Crito occur at 290e, 291a, 291b, 291d, 291e, 292a, 293a, and 293b. In the ending exchange (304c–307b), he calls Crito by name five times (305b, 395b, 306a, 307a, 307c).

15. Strauss notes a similarity to the *Crito* where "the performed conversation with Kriton surrounds the quasi-conversation, evoked by Socrates, between Socrates and the Laws of Athens." "*Euthydemus*," 1.

16. See Adkins, *Merit and Responsibility*.

17. The fact that Socrates does not charge money for his services is one of the primary ways that Socrates distinguishes himself from the sophists. *Apology*, 19e.

18. *Apology*, 17c; and *Symposium*, 201c.

19. Landy remarks, "Socrates is not being entirely straightforward with Crito. What he needs most of all from him is tuition money." "Philosophy, Statesmanship,"199n7.

20. Though Landy convincingly argues for the deeply apolitical nature of philosophy, he does point out that without society there can be no philosophy. "Philosophy, Statesmanship,"184.

21. Plax, "Lover of Family," 43.

22. I discuss the implications of this remark more fully in section IV.

23. On the Corybantic allusions in Plato, see M. Linforth, "The Corybantic Rites in Plato," *University of California Publications in Classical Philology* 13 (1998): 121–162.

24. On mystery religions, see W. Burkert, *Ancient Mystery Cults* (Cambridge: Harvard University Press, 1987); P. Kingsley, *Ancient Philosophy, Mystery, and Magic: Empedocles and the Pythagorean Tradition* (Cambridge: Cambridge University Press, 1995); and R. G. Edmonds, *Myths of the Underworld Journey: Plato, Aristophanes and the 'Orphic' Gold Tablets* (Cambridge: Cambridge University Press, 2004).

25. This remark echoes Socrates' own remarks in the *Apology* (17b) where he tells the crowd not to make a disturbance.

26. On the importance of serious play metaphors, see Roochnik, "Serious Play."

27. 279c, 279e1, 279e3, 279e6, 280a, 280b, 280c, 280d1, 280d3, 280d8, 281a1, 281a4, 281a6, 281b4, 281c3, 281c8, 281d1, 281e1, 281e5, 282a7, 282b7.

28. On the role of Ctesippus, see Jackson, "Socrates' Iolaos."

29. Plax notes that this is, in fact, what Crito wishes for Critobulus. "Lover of Family," 44.

30. 288d6, 288d8, 288e2, 289a3, 289a8, 289b3–4, 289c4, 289c7.

31. Chance suggests that Crito "cannot recognize that he has just witnessed Kleinias bridge the gap between learning and knowing by 'coming to know' through a cooperative process." *Plato's Euthydemus*, 123.

32. Strauss, "*Euthydemus,*"15.

33. Landy remarks that this intervening conversation illustrates "the extent to which Socrates has transcended the concerns of the demotic man." "Philosophy, Statesmanship,"194.

34. If the allusion is to Ares and Aphrodite, it further underscores the erotic/emotional dimensions of the exchange.

35. Chance, *Plato's* Euthydemus, 129.

36. Jackson suggests that "Ctesippus emerges as an ambivalent figure, whose partiality for the sophists' art makes him a Socratic ally of dubious value." "Socrates' Iolaos," 382.

37. The *Phaedo, Symposium,* and *Protagoras* end with the narrator's voice giving the final word but there is no extended final conversation in the external frame of any other dialogue.

38. See *Phaedo*, 89d on the dangers of misology.

39. On the role of the speechwriter, see Chance, *Plato's* Euthydemus, 194–209.

40. See also Strauss, "Euthydemus," 295e.

41. Though Sprague's translation obscures it, Socrates describes the intercession of the daimon as "a matter of chance according to the god" (273a).

42. Plax argues that the daimon has failed him in this instance and has allowed harm to come to him by talking with the brothers and being forced to admit a lack of belief in the gods and incurring the enmity of people like the speechwriter as a result. Plax even suggests "Socrates also may have actually engaged in an unjust action, by revealing to the young men who were listening his final 'admission' regarding the ability of men to control the gods." Plax, "Lover of Family," 55.

43. See *Lysis*, 203a; *Charmides*, 155b; *Protagoras*, 310b; and *Republic*, 327b.

44. D. Hitchcock argues that "on the basis of the structure of the conversational practice of the two brothers in Plato's dialogue, and of other evidence, that the ultimate origin of their practice of eristic is none other than the historical Socrates." "The Origin of Professional Eristic," in *Plato:* Euthydemus, Charmides. *Proceedings of the V Symposium Platonicum, Selected Papers,* vol. 13, eds. Tom Robinson and Luc Brisson (Sankt Augustin: Academia Verlag 2000): 59.

45. See also 277d, 279e, 289b, 291d, 292b.

46. See M. Byrd, "Summoner Approach," *Journal of the History of Philosophy* 47 (2007): 365-381.

47. See Strauss, "*Euthydemus,*" 280b.

Chapter Six

Self-Mastery and Harmony in Plato's *Republic*

This chapter takes a different approach from the preceding chapters. Rather than beginning with Socrates' narrative commentary itself, I describe two models of virtue cultivation that are present throughout the *Republic*: the self-mastery model and the harmony model. I define the self-mastery model and outline some practical and conceptual limitations of it. I then explore the many references that Socrates makes to justice as harmony throughout the *Republic*.[1] With this conceptual framework in mind, in section two, I offer an analysis of Socrates' narrative commentary in Books I, II, and V. As is the case in the preceding dialogues, Socrates' narrative description of his primary interlocutors, along with the dramatic action of the dialogue, draws attention to important aspects of each interlocutor's character. The narrative commentary in the *Republic* shows how Cephalus, Polemarchus, Thrasymachus, Glaucon, and Adeimantus each grapple with different aspects of the self-mastery as a means of virtue cultivation. Each of these characters illustrates at least one practical limitation of the self-mastery model.

I. TWO MODELS OF VIRTUE CULTIVATION

A. The Self-Mastery Model

The self-mastery model of virtue requires that the *logistikon*, the rational part of the soul, rule over the *epithumetikon* with the help of the *thumetikon*. In this model, the appetites and emotions hinder our ability to be virtuous. The *logistikon* must therefore master these strong influences and work to diminish them as much as possible. This model depends upon the tripartite conception of the soul found in Book IV of the *Republic*. Given the importance of this model for my narrative analysis of the dialogue, it is worth examining where this view of the soul arises in the context of the *Republic*. After completing his vision of the luxurious city in speech, Socrates exhorts Adeimantus to "get yourself an adequate light somewhere; and look yourself—and call in your brother and Polemarchus and the others—whether we can somehow see where the justice might be and where the injustice, in what they differ from one another, and which the man who's going to be happy must possess" (427d). Under Socrates' guidance, Glaucon, Adeimantus, and the others look first for wisdom, then courage and moderation with the hopes of finding justice in the remainder (427d–434c). Socrates finally suggests that justice is "the having and doing of one's own and what belongs to oneself would be agreed to be justice" (434a). Glaucon affirms this view and Socrates returns to using the city as soul analogy as a means of testing this definition of justice (434d–435a).

At this point, Socrates presents the famous tripartite account of the human soul. Before he describes the parts of the soul, Socrates qualifies his confidence in their ability to "get a precise grasp of it on the basis of procedures such as we're now using in argument" (435d) and explains the difficulty of separating out the parts of the soul from each other (436b–437a).[2] Nonetheless, Socrates proceeds with his analysis (437b). He first discusses the *epithumetikon*. It is the seat of our appetites, desires, and the emotions associated with satisfying our appetites and desires. I regard appetites, desires, and emotions as somewhat different aspects of the *epithumetikon*. For example, appetites are drives that are directed toward satisfying a physical need for food, drink, or sex. Clearly, we often refer to these appetites as desires, particularly in the case of sexual desires. However, we can also desire things that do not directly satisfy a physical need. For example, we often desire a material object because of its aesthetic qualities or we want time to pursue our hobbies and intellectual endeavors for their own sake. The satisfaction of an appetite or a desire leads to a particular emotional response, typically contentment or pleasure, satisfaction or excitement. Our inability to satisfy an appetite often leads to another set of emotional responses, typically impatience, irritation, frustration, or even anger. While some emotions are connected to the satisfaction of a particular appetite, other emotions like fear, pity, happiness, and joy, for example, are not necessarily associated with the satisfaction of an appetite but arise in response to a variety of human situations. A fight with a loved one can produce anger. Getting lost can produce frustration. An unexpected windfall elicits thankfulness. The misfortune of a friend results in sympathy and sadness. Further, sometimes emotions themselves produce other desires and emotions. For example, anger at a betrayal produces desire for revenge. Love produces joy and also pain when those we love suffer. Our unhappiness can result in greater compassion for the misfortunes of others. The interrelationship of emotions accords well with David Konstan's argument that the Greeks typically understood emotions as "a reaction rather than an inner state to be disclosed."[3] Clearly, the philosophical exploration of how the Greeks understood the emotions is a complex task and beyond the scope of my current investigation.[4]

In this particular section of the *Republic*, however, Socrates defines the *epithumetikon* in rather reductive terms. Simply put, the *epithumetikon* is the lowest part of the soul. Socrates describes its scope as "being thirsty and hungry, and generally the desires, and further, willing and wanting" (437b). It presents numerous obstacles to our intellectual endeavors because it constantly keeps us oriented toward the satisfaction of our appetites and desires. The *epithumetikon* also motivates our desire to acquire money. The drive to make money fits well within the appetitive domain because money provides a direct means by which we satisfy many of our material and physical desires. Lorenz remarks, "The satisfaction of such desires through money also establishes, reinforces, and sustains patterns and habits of attention, response, and attachment, both at an individual and at a communal level."[5] The association with the *epithumetikon* and money highlights Socrates' concern with *pleonexia*, the insatiable desires for more, as the resulting psychic condition when the *epithumetikon* is allowed full reign. Socrates regards *pleonexia* as a primary disruptor of justice in the city and the soul. Socrates' concern with the vice of *pleonexia* helps explain why he is so critical of the *epithumetikon* in the self-mastery model.

This negative view of the *epithumetikon* is also found in Socrates' numerous complaints about Homeric poetry. This extended criticism of Homer and the poets begins at the end of Book II, just after Socrates and his interlocutors have constructed the feverish city and continues in Book X of the *Republic* with some important qualifications that allow for the return of poetry to the city. I will consider the critique of Homer at length in section three. Here, I will just note that Socrates' critique of Homer draws upon the self-mastery model of virtue cultivation, specifically the negative assessment of the appetitive part of the soul. Poetry is harmful because it cultivates the appetitive, desiring part of our soul. (390b). Within the self-mastery model, it can never truly be conducive to the cultivation of virtue. In fact, it will work against the cultivation of virtue. This point arises again in the reconsideration of poetry in Book X. Socrates asserts that those who listen to Homer will cultivate an "irritable and various disposition" (605a). Homeric poetry "awakens this part of the soul and nourishes it, and by making it strong, destroys the calculating part" (605b). Socrates asserts that this negative effect arises "when even the best of us hear Homer" (605d). Homeric poetry creates a context for people to "give themselves over" to the emotional aspects of poetry (600d). We "enjoy" the suffering of heroes and we "praise as a good poet the man who most puts us in this state" (600d). Unfortunately, even though it is natural to feel the emotional response that poetry cultivates within us, the appetitive aspects of soul take over the other parts of the soul. Socrates explains how this transfer of control to the *epithumetikon* occurs, "what is by nature best in us, because it hasn't been adequately educated by argument or habit, relaxes its guard" (606a). As a result, poetry encourages the "mournful part" (606a), the pitying part (606b), the laughing part (606c), the sexual part, and the spirited part to grow stronger (606d). Socrates uses self-mastery language here to explain the result of this situation. The emotions "set themselves up as rulers in us when they ought to be ruled" (606d). Within the context of the self-mastery model, the *logistikon* should rule over the emotions and Homeric poetry promotes the opposite situation, where the emotions rule over the *logistikon*.

After Socrates describes the *epithumetikon*, he discusses the *logistikon*. This part of the soul is responsible for our ability to reason and reflect. It participates in all pursuits related to learning and acquiring knowledge. It contemplates and philosophizes. Simply put, the *logistikon* is the seat of the highest human activity. Socrates articulates the activity of the *logistikon* at length in Book VI. However, at least in his initial presentation of it, Socrates describes its purpose as largely negative and constraining. Socrates asks Glaucon, "if ever something draws it [the *epithumetikon*] back when it's thirsting, wouldn't that be something different in it from that which thirsts and leads it like a beast to drink?" (439b). Socrates asks again, "isn't there something in their soul bidding them to drink and something forbidding them to do so, something different that masters that which bids?" (439c). Socrates presents the *logistikon* and the *epithumetikon* as opposing forces. Our appetites demand satisfaction. Our reason forbids their satisfaction. Viewed in this way, these parts of the soul cannot help but be in conflict with each other. Socrates describes them as two warring political factions (440b). Given that the *logistikon* is the highest part of the soul and the *epithumetikon* the lowest, if justice is to arise in the soul, the *logistikon* must not only win the war with the *epithumetikon*. It must continually subdue the *epithumetikon* for justice in the soul to flourish.

The third part of the soul contains spirit [*thumos*]. Socrates explains that *thumos* is that "with which we are spirited" (439e). Socrates notes that the spirited part of the soul produces ferocity and courage when properly balanced, however, if "raised to a higher pitch than it ought to have, it would be likely to become cruel and harsh" (410e).[6] Socrates conveys some doubt as to whether the thumetic part of the soul is really a distinct third part of the soul. He clearly states that the other two parts have been distinguished from each other, but asks if it has the same nature as either of the other two (439e). Socrates asks Glaucon if the *thumetikon* is more like the *epithumetikon* or the *logistikon*. Glaucon initially regards it as more like the *epithumetikon*. Socrates tells the story of Leontinus to show that the *thumetikon* can be at war with the *epithumetikon* just as the *logistikon* is. Leontinus had a strong desire to look at the corpses along the North Wall of the city. Even though he tries to overcome the desire, eventually his desire overpowers the internal disgust that he feels at having this desire. Leontinus "opened his eyes wide, ran toward the corpses and said, 'Look, you damned wretches, take your fill of the fair sight'" (440a). Socrates tells this story to illustrate that the thumetic part of the soul has a self-reflective function. It is the part of us that gets angry when we do the wrong thing, when our desires get the better of us, when we fail to follow the lead of the *logistikon*. If we did not get angry with ourselves for doing the wrong thing, we would have no motivation to do the right thing in the future. As a result of this self-reflective capacity, the *thumetikon* is "by nature an auxiliary to the calculating part if it is not corrupted by bad rearing" (441a).

As should be clear from the preceding analysis, within this conceptual understanding of the soul, justice occurs through self-mastery. It is also important to remember that this understanding of the soul is meant to explain the state of souls of those who live in a city that is sick, sick because it allows for the satisfaction of unnecessary appetites and desires (372c). In this political context, individual justice can only arise when the *epithumetikon* is mastered and subordinated to the rule of the *logistikon* within that same soul. Socrates ask Glaucon, "Isn't it proper for the calculating part to rule, since it is wise and has forethought about all of the soul, and for the spirited part to be obedient to it and its ally?" (441e). Glaucon responds enthusiastically. The self-mastery model accords with the traditional understanding of Socratic intellectualism, which "seems to identify virtue with knowledge and therefore appears to consider the affective side of our nature irrelevant to our virtue, to what counts as a good life."[7] The self-mastery model prioritizes reason as the means by which we become good and dismisses the role the other parts of the soul can play in the process of becoming good. Indeed, under this view the appetites present distracting and, at times, even dangerous obstacles that we must overcome in our pursuit of justice in the soul.[8] In many ways, the image of the sea god, Glaucus, illustrates this aspect of the self-mastery model quite well. Prior to beginning the Myth of Er, Socrates and Glaucon discuss the immortality of the soul. Socrates claims that they must see the soul as it truly is, "not maimed by community with the body and other evils" (611c). He claims further that they must examine the nature of this purified soul by "calculation." At that point, they will be able to discern the nature of justice and injustice more easily (611c). Socrates uses the image of Glaucus to illustrate their current predicament with respect to understanding the soul. We cannot see the true divine nature of Glaucus because his body is broken and destroyed by his time in the ocean and covered over by "shells, seaweed, and rocks." As a result, he appears as a beast and not a god (611b). So too, we cannot see the nature of the soul because of these "countless evils" (611c). Just as the shells, seaweed, and rocks obscure the vision of the true nature of the soul, the self-mastery model itself obscures our ability to regard the emotions in positive terms, as potential helpmates for the philosophical life.

B. Some Conceptual Limitations of the Self-Mastery Model

Though Socrates employs the self-mastery model throughout the *Republic*, several aspects of dialogue also illustrate the limitations of the model as a means of understanding justice in the soul. First, the self-mastery model emerges in the context of the "feverish" city, not the city of necessity. After Socrates presents his vision of the city of necessity, he asks where justice and injustice would be found in the city (371e). Adeimantus responds, "I can't think, Socrates, unless it's somewhere in some need these men have of one another" (372a). When Adeimantus answers, he does not define justice as mastery. No one part of the city controls or dominates another part. Another sense of justice is at work here, one that is better captured with the metaphor of harmony, than mastery. Each part of the city needs the other parts. The farmer needs the builder, the builder needs the farmer, and the shoemaker needs the weaver and the weaver the shoemaker. Each part of the city plays a valuable role in the creation of justice. This harmonious sense of justice as interdependence recognizes that the appetitive aspects of soul require satisfaction, not suppression. Socrates specifically mentions that they feast and drink. The citizens also sing hymns to the gods.[9] They "delight" in each other's company (372b).[10] Though many things, like the practice of philosophy, are missing from this original city, Socrates provisionally approves of Adeimantus' formulation of justice as harmonious interrelationship. Socrates responds, "Perhaps what you say is fine. It really must be considered and we mustn't back away" (372a). Glaucon, in contrast to Adeimantus, rejects this city as not even suitable for pigs (372d). In doing so, he rejects a different understanding of justice at work within it. After Glaucon rejects this healthy city, Socrates clarifies his understanding of the situation. They are looking for justice in the "luxurious city." He also describes this city as "feverish" (372e). The tripartite view of the soul and the self-mastery model emerge within the confines of this second city: the feverish city. Self-mastery is initially presented as a cure that restores health to unhealthy citizens in an unhealthy city, not as a model that one should adopt as the ideal model for human behavior. Perhaps, if we are not born in the right sort of city, the self-mastery model is necessary to achieve justice in the city and in the soul, but it should not be taken as the only model by which we order our cities and ourselves.

Second, Socrates himself raises a conceptual problem with the self-mastery model when discussing temperance. He remarks, "Isn't the phrase 'stronger than himself' ridiculous [*geloion*] though? For, of course, the one who's stronger than himself would also be weaker than himself, and the weaker stronger. The same 'himself' is referred to in all of them" (430e). Socrates calls self-mastery "ridiculous" because it involves a logical contradiction. We cannot be both stronger and weaker than ourselves. Socrates explains what he thinks people mean by this perplexing and ridiculous concept:

> This speech looks to me as if it wants to say that, concerning the soul, in the same human being there is something better and something worse. The phrase "stronger than himself" is used when that which is better by nature is master over that which is worse. At least, it's praise. (431a)

This answer does not address a basic conceptual problem with the self-mastery model. The conceptual problem emerges when the appetitive part of the soul becomes master over the rational part of the soul. Socrates explores this dynamic at length in Books VIII and IX. Many of the challenges that the tyrannical soul confronts result from the fact that the lower part of the soul rules the higher part. Under the viewpoint of self-mastery, that situation would improve if the *logistikon* were in control. However, here Socrates observes that the dynamic of mastery and enslavement is itself philosophically problematic. It is worth noting that Socrates also casts mastery over others in a negative light. For example, if the guardians were allowed to satisfy their desire through the acquisition of private property, they would "become masters and enemies of their fellow citizens instead of allies" (417b). This enslavement of one part to another diminishes the intrinsic value of the constituent parts of the soul. If one of the parts does not have the ability to exercise freedom, ultimately, it is not conducive to freedom of the whole.

When Socrates uses the word "ridiculous [*geloion*]," he links this conceptual problem with self-mastery to the discussion of the three waves of political regulation in Book V, each one more "ridiculous" than the one preceding it. Taken together, the repeated references to comedy and laughter and the use of the word, "ridiculous [*geloion*]," suggest that these recommendations, though having a serious intent, are not meant as literal recommendations for the proper ordering of civic life.[11] In making this suggestion, I am not arguing that the self-mastery model is an elaborate farce any more than that the recommendations in Book V should be dismissed without regard to their serious intent. However, the repeated use of the word, "ridiculous," should cause us to examine the model of self-mastery with the same careful regard that we bring to the political regulations of Book V. On a related point, Rosen notes "Socrates makes it quite clear that whereas the philosophers must rule, philosophy is something distinct from ruling."[12] This observation gives some indication of why self-mastery is ultimately inadequate. Virtue is not about ruling over ourselves any more than philosophy is about ruling over others. Virtue, like philosophy, ultimately resides in another domain, the domain of freedom. The virtues that arise out of either an externally or an internally imposed self-control are not the highest form of virtues. Rather, the highest forms of virtue should arise harmoniously out of an appropriate interweaving of all the parts of the soul.[13] I will explore this alternative model in the following section.

The self-mastery model also necessitates a divided view of the self. In the self-mastery model, the parts of the soul relate to each other through a mechanism of submission and control. In the self-mastery model, the *logistikon* rules over the other parts of the soul. That the *logistikon* rules is not, in and of itself, problematic. The problem arises more out of the negative view of the *epithumetikon* that is generally associated with the self-mastery model. Since the emotions are viewed in negative terms, part of the role of the *logistikon* is to diminish their presence. Rosen explains, "Socrates conceives of human beings as divided against themselves, not merely as between the body and the soul but also within the soul itself. To be human is to suffer from what Hegel once called *innere Zerissenheit*, 'inner tornness.'"[14] Adeimantus exhibits this inner tornness. Because of his distrust of the appetitive domain, Adeimantus makes ongoing negative judgments about himself. Adeimantus resembles the guardian that Socrates describes, one who "never communes with a Muse" (411d). Such a man becomes a misologist and unmusical. He lives ignorantly and awkwardly. He exists without rhythm or grace (411e). As a result, he is at odds with himself and with the world.

This negative view of the appetitive obscures the emotional dimensions of philosophical experience itself. Socrates uses highly emotional, often erotic, language to describe the philosophical activity of the soul. Immediately after characterizing philosophy as accord with reason, Socrates defines philosophy as having "intercourse with this divine order." Through this divine intercourse, the philosopher "becomes well ordered and divine, to the extent that is possible for a human being" (500d). Elsewhere, Socrates describes the genuine philosopher in emotional terms. Philosophers are "those who delight in and love that on which knowledge depends." They "delight in each thing that is itself" (480a). Furthermore, they "hate" falsehood and desire the truth. Socrates even compares the philosopher's love of truth to a relationship of a lover and a beloved. The lover loves everything related to the object of his love (485c). Much like the lover of young boys who loves all sorts of boys and the wine lover who "delight[s] in every kind of wine, and on every pretext" (475a), philosophers are lovers of all sorts of wisdom.

Socrates uses erotic terminology to describe this love:

> It is the nature of the real lover of learning to strive for what is . . . he does not lose the keenness of his passionate love or cease from it before he grasps the

nature itself of each thing which is with the part of the soul fit to grasp a thing of that sort: and it is the part akin to it that is fit. And once near it and coupled with what really is, having begotten intelligence and truth, he knows and lives truly, is nourished and so ceases from his labor pains, but not before. (490b)

The part of the soul most suited to grasp this highest truth is the *logistikon*. However, erotic language surrounds the description of this experience. The *logistikon* has "intercourse" with true being. It is nourished by this erotic contact.[15] With these descriptions, Socrates links the highest level of philosophical activity to the appetitive dimensions of human experience. The pleasure associated with the philosophical life provides a place for the appetites and emotions in philosophical experience. While one might argue that these are intellectual pleasures, not pleasures we associate with the appetites and emotions, it is nonetheless striking that Socrates uses such erotic language to describe them. Socrates' use of this language suggests there is another model of virtue cultivation at work in the *Republic* as well, what I term, the harmony model.

C. The Harmony Model

As a means of elucidating the harmony model, consider the image of the sea god, Glaucus, in this light of the erotic dimensions of philosophical pursuit. Scholars frequently regard this passage as an example of a purely rational image of the soul. In many ways, it does seem to support an understanding of the soul in keeping with the self-mastery model. The body and its associated appetites appear to harm the soul. They obscure our ability to see its rational nature through calculation. However, Socrates does not end his account here. Socrates tells Glaucon that we have to look beyond this image to see the true nature of the soul. He leaves the description of the soul's true nature suggestively open to interpreting it according to an understanding of the harmony model. When Glaucon asks Socrates where they must look to see the true nature of the soul, Socrates implores him to consider its "love of wisdom" (611e). Socrates says they must examine the longings and desires of the soul to see its nature. Socrates describes the soul, albeit in its embodied state, as having longings and desires. He tells Glaucon that they must "recognize what it lays hold of and with what sort of things it longs to keep company on the grounds that it is akin to the divine and immortal" (611e). The soul wants "to give itself over entirely to this longing" (612a). This "impulse" draws the soul out of Glaucus' barnacle-filled oceanic state. Although one might argue that the point of this image suggests that we understand the true longing of the soul as oriented beyond all these emotional concerns, it is striking that Socrates advocates that we look to these appetitive dimensions of the soul's activity to see its "true nature." These impulses, not just the *logistikon's* calculative capacity, help us understand the true nature of the soul. Beyond that, Socrates does not say precisely what that true nature of soul is. He certainly does not define it as pure rationality, devoid of all emotionality and spiritedness. Indeed, we do not know "whether it is many-formed or single-formed, or in what way it is and how" (612a). It could very well include all the parts that the soul has in its embodied state: the *logistikon,* the *thumetikon,* and the *epithumetikon*. Socrates describes justice "with respect to what is within, with respect to what truly concerns him and his own," in precisely these terms (443d). Socrates explains, "he doesn't let each part in him mind other people's business or the three classes in the soul meddle with each other, but really sets his own house in good order and rules himself. He arranges himself, becomes his own friend, and harmonizes the three parts, exactly like three notes in a harmonic scale, lowest, highest and middle" (443d).

What, then, would an understanding of justice based on a harmonious interrelationship of the three parts of the soul rather than self-mastery entail? Unlike the self-mastery model, the harmony model allows the *epithumetikon* to have a voice. It provides necessary notes on the scale of internal justice (443d). The harmony model should not be understood as a means of replacing the rule of the *logistikon* with the rule of the *epithumetikon*, but rather as a call to recognize the importance of the appetites and the emotions in the process of understanding justice in the soul.[16] One might argue that something still has to put the harmonious parts in order to create justice and that is true. So what replaces the rule of the *logisitkon* in the harmony model? Consider the metaphor of a composer. A composer exerts control over the players of the musical ensemble, but also necessarily gives each part a voice. Indeed, if all the voices are not heard, the performance of the musical piece is not complete. If we take the analogy to the soul, it might well be that each part of the soul has the ability to serve as composer when necessary. At times, the *logistikon* leads the way, at other times the *thumetikon*, at still other times the *epithumetikon*. True harmony of soul requires this flexibility and adaptability; the same adaptability to circumstance that Socrates exhibits on both the narrative and the dramatic level. Take the analogy to the level of the polis. If the self-mastery model applied at the level of the city, the city would be a tyrannical one, one of the lowest forms of government that Socrates outlines in Book VIII.

Throughout the *Republic*, Socrates employs images of harmony to describe the nature of justice in both the city and the soul. For example, early in the *Republic*, Socrates refutes Thrasymachus' view that justice is nothing other than the interest of the stronger. He remarks that justice produces "unanimity and friendship" amongst people (351d). In a just city, people live in harmony with each other. One faction of the population does not rule over another faction.[17] Another instance of the harmony model on the level of the city occurs after Socrates presents the image of the sun, the line, and the cave. Socrates explains how they will ensure the establishment of justice in the city by "compelling" those with the best natures to rule (519d). Glaucon objects: "Are we to do them an injustice, and make them live a worse life when a better is possible for them?" (519e). Socrates employs a harmony metaphor to address Glaucon's concern. They are not concerned with a particular person or class of people doing well, but "the city as a whole, harmoniously uniting citizens by persuasion and necessity, causing them to share with each other the benefit each is able to bring to the commonwealth" (520a). A just city functions according to the principles of harmony, not the principles of mastery. Similarly, each part of the soul, like each part of the city, constitutes a good and provides a benefit for the whole.[18]

Although there are occasions in the text where Socrates intermingles references to self-mastery with references to harmony, generally the references to harmony win out. For example, in his discussion of political virtue of the city, he refers to the act of "ruling" or "governing" seven times in this brief passage (431a–431e). However, after all of these references, Socrates abandons the mastery language and claims, "we divined pretty accurately a while ago that moderation is like a kind of harmony" (431e). Socrates also employs metaphors of disharmony when discussing injustice in the city. In his initial exchange with Thrasymachus, Socrates notes that injustice "produces factions, hatreds, and quarrels" (351d). The citizens cannot live in harmony with each other. They fight against each other instead of working for the good of the city together.[19] Other examples of disharmony metaphors occur when Socrates explains that the regimes devolve because guardians fail to pay attention to the geometric and astronomical attunements that should properly govern the generation of offspring (546b–e). When people breed "out of season, children will have neither good natures nor good luck" (546d). Indiscriminate breeding results in "unlikeness" and inharmonious irregularity. The children from these ill-formed unions will become increasingly "unmusical" (546e). In other words, they lack appropriate poetical and musical education. Within the context of a self-mastery model, this holistic education will be more difficult to achieve because of the negative regard for the emotions.

II. FIVE INTERLOCUTORS AND THE SELF-MASTERY MODEL

A. Cephalus and the Limits of His Self-Mastery

Of the dialogues narrated by Socrates, the *Republic* is the one most frequently recognized as being narrated by him. The dialogue famously begins with Socrates reporting to an unknown auditor, "I went down yesterday to the Piraeus with Glaucon" (327a). Though there is widespread awareness of the narrated status of this dialogue and numerous references to its narrated dimensions, there is to date no sustained attempt to interpret the dialogue in these terms, much less to read it in concert with all the other dialogues narrated by Socrates.[20] The remainder of this chapter along with the following chapter approach the *Republic* in this manner. As his narrative unfolds, Socrates draws attention to the emotional dimensions of his interactions with these interlocutors and how the interlocutors comport themselves with respect to their emotional states. The self-mastery model provides a useful framework for understanding these detailed character portraits. I will consider Socrates' five primary interlocutors in these terms and show how each of them illustrates some problematic dimension of self-mastery as a mode of virtue cultivation.

Socrates first mentions Cephalus after reporting that he and Glaucon returned to Polemarchus' house. He observes that Cephalus "seemed very old to me, for I had not seen him in some time. He was seated on a sort of cushioned stool and was crowned with a wreath, for he had just performed a sacrifice in the courtyard" (328c). Cephalus' description of the path of old age conforms well to the self-mastery model. He characterizes his physical appetites and desires in negative terms. He quotes Sophocles who refers to sexual desire as a "frenzied and savage master" (329c). Cephalus can now master his sexual appetites rather than having them master him because he lacks the physical capacity to indulge them. The "mad masters" (329d) of his appetites no longer rule him. In contrast to many of his friends, who find old age difficult to bear, Cephalus regards the matter differently. He describes his release from the lure of the senses and his forced retirement from the pursuit of physical pleasures in positive terms. It promotes inner tranquility. Cephalus now experiences "great peace and freedom from such things" (329c). As a result, he pursues pleasure in other domains. For example, he enjoys listening to speeches (328d). However, he does not find pleasure in sustained engagement in philosophical dialogue. He also spends a great deal of time offering sacrifices (328b and 331d). His pursuit of pleasure is directed toward a different understanding of what will benefit him, i.e., placating the gods to overlook his past transgressions.

If Socrates were working wholly within the self-mastery model, one would expect him to applaud Cephalus' current situation, particularly if Cephalus had actually mastered his emotions and channeled them toward philosophical pursuits. While Socrates responds enthusiastically to the possibility of conversation with Cephalus, he does not explicitly affirm the path of renunciation itself (328e). In fact, Socrates senses that Cephalus is still quite engaged with his appetites. He challenges Cephalus to describe his views more fully by appealing to his emotions and by referring to his wealth. He remarks, "I stirred him up saying, 'Cephalus, when you say these things, I suppose that the many do not accept them from you but believe rather that it is not due to character that you bear old age so easily but due to possessing great substance. They say that for the rich there are many consolations'" (329e). Socrates' provocation is successful. Cephalus responds at some length to Socrates' query about whether or not he inherited his wealth or created it. Cephalus recognizes that the lack of money leads one to commit unjust actions and that money is a safeguard, which makes it possible to avoid committing injustices against others. Cephalus sees the benefit of his wealth in its ability to help him atone for past injustices. His wealth enables him to perform elaborate rituals to placate the gods (330a–331b).

As he explains his views about the value of money, Cephalus reveals his underlying motivation for his virtuous actions: he fears what will happen to him in the afterlife if he is held accountable for his past injustices (330b). In his younger days, Cephalus' desire to gratify his appetites led him to engage in many unjust actions. As did his particular line of work. On this dimension of Cephalus' activities, Gifford writes, "In operating his very lucrative shield factory for thirty years in the Piraeus, the metic Cephalus abetted the war machine of the Athenian democrats in its ethically unbalanced drive to subjugate and economically exploit virtually the whole of the Greek world."[21] Having mastered his physical desire, at least on some level, he finds his behavior governed by another set of emotional concerns. His fear of the afterlife motivates his action instead of his desire for physical satisfaction. Cephalus describes this fear in stark terms. He is "full of suspicion and terror." He "wakes from his sleep in a fright as children do, and lives in anticipation of evil" (330e). He is primarily concerned that he "not depart for that other place frightened" (331b). Cephalus attempts to master his emotions, but in the end he remains controlled by them. Cephalus' failure, here, suggests that the self-mastery model itself is not sufficient to the task of controlling the power of the *epithumetikon*. His fear in the face of death stands in stark contrast to Socrates' own equanimity with respect to what fate waits for him in the afterlife.[22]

At times, Cephalus seems to recognize that a different mode of existence is possible. For example, he admits that the character of a person will determine how well they will deal with the vicissitudes of age (329d) and that money will benefit "the decent and orderly" person more than someone who has an unsavory character (331b). However, Cephalus himself cannot attain this orderly contentment of soul. Socrates uses this emotionally charged moment to draw out the first definition of justice that emerges in the dialogue: "speaking the truth and giving back what one takes" (331d). Once the conversation moves in this philosophical direction, Cephalus does not participate further. Cephalus' departure suggests that the pleasure he experiences when listening to speeches is not all that great.[23] He is more interested in placating his fears about the fate that awaits him in the afterlife than in participating in a philosophical conversation about justice. When he rejects further philosophical discussion, he reveals how the *epithumetikon* rules his soul. He prefers to placate his emotions rather than cultivate his intellect further. The last image of Cephalus illustrates how the emotions rule him. When Polemarchus, probably in jest, expresses some insecurity about being Cephalus' heir, Socrates notes that Cephalus "laughed and with that he went away to the sacrifices" (331d). Cephalus leaves laughing, but still ruled by his fear.

B. Polemarchus: Self-Mastery through Mastery over Others

After Cephalus hands over the argument to Polemarchus, Socrates and Polemarchus redefine justice as "doing good to friends and harm to enemies" (332d). Since Socrates does not offer any narrative commentary during their subsequent conversation (332d–336a), it is helpful to return to Socrates' narrative description of his initial encounter with Polemarchus to understand Polemarchus' reasons for presenting this definition of justice. While Cephalus tries to control his future fate by paying recompense for his past indiscretions, Polemarchus tries to control his present social circumstance directly.[24] He compels others to satisfy his own desires. Socrates' first narrative reference to Polemarchus illustrates this tendency.

Socrates reports:

> Catching sight of us from afar as we were pressing homewards, Polemarchus, son of Cephalus, ordered his slave boy to run after us and order us to wait for him. The boy took hold of my cloak from behind and said, "Polemarchus orders you to wait." And I turned around and asked him where his master was. "He is coming up behind," he said. "Just wait." (327b)

Socrates draws the auditor's attention to Polemarchus' desire for social control in several ways. First, Socrates describes many of the characters in terms of their relationship to Polemarchus. These descriptions convey the strong social control Polemarchus exerts in this social situation. For example, Socrates calls Cephalus Polemarchus' father (325b). He mentions that Polemarchus' slave stops them (327b). Adeimantus and the others come with Polemarchus (327c). They go to Polemarchus' house (328b). Second, he uses a form of the verb κελεύω, meaning "to order" or "to command," three times in his opening description of his encounter with Polemarchus' slave boy (327b). Polemarchus' slave boy takes hold of Socrates' cloak and physically restrains him (327b). The external constraint on Socrates' physical body symbolizes the social constraint that Polemarchus employs.

Polemarchus' declaration that he "won't listen" to Socrates' attempts to persuade him shows Polemarchus' unwillingness to engage with other people on their terms (327c). He wants to dictate the terms of social engagement. Polemarchus does not just order people around; he even threatens them. He tells Socrates and Glaucon to "either prove stronger than these men or stay here" (327c). Some scholars have suggested that Polemarchus makes this threat largely in jest.[25] However, even if his threat is meant as playful banter, his casual use of threatening language is not without serious import. In fact, it is probably more illustrative of his true character since he defaults to this aggressive mode of discourse when he is at ease.

Polemarchus also engages in more subtle forms of social control to achieve his ends. For example, after Adeimantus mentions the torchlight horseback race (328a), Polemarchus realizes that Socrates may be more receptive to this mode of persuasion. He immediately answers Socrates saying, "That's it, and besides they'll put on an all-night festival that will be worth seeing. We'll get up after dinner and go to see it" (328a). Polemarchus cajoles Socrates into staying by promising, "there we'll be together with many of the young men and we'll talk" (328b).

Polemarchus' desire to control the social situation reemerges at the beginning of Book V. Socrates reports:

> And I was going to speak of them in the order that each [form of badness in the soul] appeared to me to pass from one to the other. But Polemarchus—he was sitting at a little distance from Adeimantus—stretched out his hand and took hold of his cloak from above by the shoulder, began to draw him toward himself, and, as he stooped over, said some things in his ear, of which we overheard nothing other than his saying, "Shall we let it go or what shall we do?" (449a–b)

As in the opening scene, Socrates intends to go in one direction, but Polemarchus detains him for his own purposes. The narrative and dramatic details of the dialogue make clear that Polemarchus goes to great lengths to control his social circumstance. The text does not explicitly tell us why he does so. We must ask ourselves what psychological need his desire for social control fulfills. One possible way of understanding Polemarchus' motivation would be seeing that he needs to control his external circumstances precisely because he cannot control his inner experience. Polemarchus does not want to acknowledge the disappointments and frustrations that will emerge for him if his fears overwhelm him and if his various appetites are not satisfied. Polemarchus' query to Cephalus, "Am I not the heir of all that belongs to you?" indicates this fear of uncertainty and loss of control that lurks beneath the surface of his desire for control (331d). Like his father Cephalus, Polemarchus' *epithumetikon* rules when it ought to be ruled. Because it is master over him, he attempts to master others so that they will satisfy his desires.[26] Another similar example of the practical limits of suppressing the appetitive domain because of its potentially disruptive power occurs in the *Symposium*. At the beginning of Agathon's party, Eryximachus banishes excessive alcohol consumption along with the flute girls (177a). In doing so, he banishes the outlets for satisfying the desire for food and sexual pleasure. However, Aristophanes' hiccups suggest he has continued to drink all along (185d) despite Eryximachus' admonitions against excessive consumption (176e). When Alcibiades arrives, the party embraces these banished pleasures without question (*Symposium*, 213b). Indeed, they welcome him with enthusiasm.

With this awareness in mind, let us return to the definition of justice that Polemarchus and Socrates explore together, namely "doing good to friends and harm to enemies" (332d). This view of justice allows Polemarchus to control the dispensation of justice. This view of justice also has an underlying emotional motivation. It is based on a preference for one's friends and a disdain for one's enemies. Socrates draws out many limitations of this definition and ends his refutation of Polemarchus by pointing out that one can easily be mistaken about who one's friends and enemies are (334c). Socrates presses Polemarchus further and forces him to agree, "it is never just to harm anyone" (335e). Polemarchus, at this point, appears ready to be Socrates' "partner in battle" against anyone who claims otherwise (336a). If so, Polemarchus must recognize that his attempts to attain self-mastery by controlling those around him lead to his engagement in unjust actions. He must also stand ready to look for another mode of social engagement. Socrates reinforces a possible alliance between them by suggesting they will "do battle as partners, you and I" (335e) and also by describing their shared emotional response to Thrasymachus' outburst, "then both Polemarchus and I got all in a flutter from fright" (336c). Thrasymachus' outburst presents Polemarchus with an immediate challenge. At this point, Thrasymachus seems to be an enemy, not a friend. One might well expect that Polemarchus would attempt to gain control of the situation by commanding the others to control Thrasymachus or by attempting to harm him in some way. Polemarchus' fear may arise because he does not know how to respond in a manner appropriate to his new understanding of what justice is.

Socrates' expressed emotional affinity with Polemarchus undercuts the seriousness of any level of discord that may have existed between them at the beginning of the dialogue. While it is certainly possible that Socrates is being ironic when he expresses this affinity with Polemarchus, the irony is not directed at Polemarchus himself within the dramatic events. Polemarchus does not hear these comments that Socrates makes to the auditor. Polemarchus would simply feel Socrates' social support of him against Thrasymachus' onslaught and have little reason to question it. He stands firmly in his friendship with Socrates.

C. Thrasymachus and the Practical Limits of Suppressing the Emotions

After Socrates secures Polemarchus' agreement that it is never just to harm anyone, Thrasymachus bursts into the conversation. Socrates describes the moment in these terms:

Now Thrasymachus had many times started out to take over the argument in the midst of our discussion, he had been restrained by the men sitting near him, who wanted to hear the argument. But when we paused and I said this, he could no longer keep quiet; hunched up like a wild beast, he flung himself at us as if to tear us to pieces. Then both Polemarchus and I got all in a flutter from fright and he shouted out into our midst and said, "What is this nonsense that has possessed you for so long, Socrates?" (336b–c)

Socrates' initial description of Thrasymachus accords well with the self-mastery model of justice because he presents Thrasymachus' emotional outburst in negative terms. This passage illustrates the harmful effects that the emotions can have on both the individual and the communal level. On the individual level, Thrasymachus' emotions are so extreme that he becomes beastlike. His uncontrolled emotional outburst diminishes his humanity. On the communal level, when Thrasymachus attempts to take over the conversation, the others must restrain him so the discussion can continue. They prevent Thrasymachus from disrupting the conversation temporarily, but not permanently. Once Thrasymachus overcomes his external restraint, he interrupts the conversation quite forcefully (336c).

Socrates' other narrative descriptions of Thrasymachus focus on the negative aspects of his emotional volatility. For example, Socrates describes Thrasymachus' initial response to his request for leniency for himself and Polemarchus as one of "scornful laughter" (337a). Thrasymachus swears at Socrates, "Heracles! Here is that habitual irony of Socrates. I knew it, and I predicted to these fellows that you wouldn't be willing to answer, that you would be ironic and do anything rather than answer if someone asked you something" (337a). Socrates proves Thrasymachus' observation to be correct. He goads Thrasymachus into presenting his definition of justice to the group rather than providing one himself. Socrates commands Thrasymachus: "Do as I say; gratify me by answering and don't begrudge your teaching to Glaucon here and the others" (338a). Socrates describes the emotional undertones of the situation, "After I said this, Glaucon and the others begged him to do as I said. And Thrasymachus evidently desired to speak so that he could win a good reputation, since he believed he had a very fine answer. But he kept up the pretense of wanting to prevail on me to do the answering. Finally, however, he conceded" (338b).

Like Polemarchus, Thrasymachus defines justice in emotional terms. Justice is that which serves the needs, desires, and wishes of the stronger. Socrates prevails in his argument with Thrasymachus by forcing him to admit that the most powerful people make mistakes about what is in their best interest (339b–342d). Socrates underscores Thrasymachus' defeat in argument saying, "He finally agreed to this, too, although he tried to put up a fight about it" (342d). Socrates notes, "He assented with resistance" (342e). Socrates draws the auditor's attention to Thrasymachus' increasing volatility saying,

"When we came to this point in the argument and it was evident to everyone that the argument about the just had turned around in the opposite direction, Thrasymachus, instead of answering, said, 'Tell me, Socrates, do you have a wet nurse?'" (343a). Thrasymachus abandons any pretense of arguing with Socrates. He ignores the force of Socrates' argument against him and simply reiterates his claim that "justice and the just are really someone else's good, the advantage of the man who is stronger and rules, and personal harm to the man who obeys and serves" (343d).

Once again, Thrasymachus' emotional response causes him to lose autonomy. He cannot control himself, so others must control him. Socrates compares him to a "bathman, after having poured a great shower of speech into our ears all at once. But those present didn't let him and forced him to stay put and present an argument for what had been said" (344d). Socrates' narrative descriptions culminate in this remark, "Now, Thrasymachus did not agree to all of this so easily as I tell it now, but he dragged his feet and resisted, and he produced a wonderful quantity of sweat, for it was summer. And then I saw what I had not yet seen before—Thrasymachus blushing" (350d). Thrasymachus' blush, an emotional response, signifies his intellectual defeat. Socrates emphasizes this point saying, "we had come to complete agreement about justice being virtue and wisdom, and injustice being both vice and lack of learning" (350e). However, Thrasymachus does not give up. He tries to escape Socrates' attempt to confine him a strict *elenchus* (350e). He goads Socrates by comparing his own forced responses to Socrates' argument to how he would respond to an "old wives tale" (350e). Despite Socrates' call for an orderly discussion (350e), many potentially disruptive emotional undertones remain in their conversation. For example, Thrasymachus will not let Socrates forget that he would prefer to speak in another manner. He tells Socrates he is "gratifying him" with his short answers (351c). Socrates responds in kind (351c–354a).

Given this presentation of Thrasymachus, one might well assume that the correct response to the emotions is to suppress them so that they exert as little influence as possible on our philosophical endeavors. At the same time, however, Socrates' encounter with Thrasymachus and his narrative description of the encounter point to the limitations of the self-mastery model. Socrates' narrative descriptions of Thrasymachus show how Thrasymachus' own attempt to control his emotions by forceful constraint and the attempts of the others both meet with limited success. The fact that Thrasymachus does not completely give up and remains abusive in his interactions with Socrates points to the practical limitations of the self-mastery model. Both internal and external attempts to suppress the presence of strong emotions and appetites are not an adequate response to their potentially disruptive power.

The willpower needed to sustain this suppression of natural appetites typically cannot be sustained over a long period of time, particularly in situations of high stress. Socrates himself underscores the limits of self-restraint by comparing his part in the preceding argument to an act of gluttony, "I am just like the gluttons who grab at whatever is set before them to get a taste of it, before they have in proper measure enjoyed what went before." Socrates laments that he could not "restrain himself" from following the wrong argument, "so that now as a result of the discussion I know nothing. So long as I do not know what the just is, I shall hardly know whether it is a virtue or not and whether the one who has it is unhappy or happy" (354c). Socrates' admission of aporia points to the limitations of self-mastery as a mode of self-control just as the aporia points to the limits of what they achieved in argument. Perhaps if Thrasymachus had been able to "restrain himself," he would have followed the correct argument, but his inability to restrain himself suggests that the path of restraint is not foolproof. Other methods are needed to lead us to the correct argument.[27]

D. Glaucon and the Inadequacy of Self-Mastery

In many ways, Glaucon is Socrates' primary interlocutor throughout the *Republic*. It is not surprising that throughout the dialogue, Socrates makes several narrative comments that provide insight into Glaucon's character. He describes Glaucon as "most courageous in everything" (357a). He tells the auditor that he has always been "filled with wonder about his nature" (367e). He twice mentions that Glaucon laughs (398d, 451d) and notes that Glaucon encourages him to continue on with the philosophical argument (357a, 368c). Unfortunately, these narrative observations are quite brief. The dramatic action of the dialogue offers more insight into Glaucon's character. In sum, Glaucon is a high-spirited and exuberant interlocutor. His interest in erotic matters illustrates his strong association with the appetitive domain. He also has both an interest in and an aptitude for philosophy. Within the confines of the self-mastery model, these aspects of Glaucon's character conflict with each other. I will examine several passages that demonstrate Glaucon's strong association with the appetitive domain and several passages that illustrate his aptitude for philosophy.

Glaucon's appetitive orientation emerges at the very beginning of the *Republic*. Socrates associates the trip to Piraeus with Glaucon; he tells the auditor that he "goes down to Piraeus with Glaucon." They pray and look at things together. They head homeward together (327a). However, Glaucon's first spoken words suggest they are not of one mind. It is Glaucon, not Socrates, who answers, "Of course we'll wait," in response to the slave boy's demand (327b). After Socrates asks about "persuading" Polemarchus and the others that they be allowed to leave (327c), Glaucon answers for Socrates saying there is "no way" they can persuade Polemarchus if he "won't listen" (328a). Unlike Socrates, Glaucon wants to stay and take part in the other pleasurable activities associated with the festival. After hearing Adeimantus and Polemarchus describe the evening activities, Glaucon remarks, "it seems we must stay" (328b). Ferrari notes that Glaucon comes regularly to Piraeus. His presence in Cephalus' house is in no way out of the ordinary.[28] Glaucon's regular presence underlies the difference between himself as a regular visitor and Socrates as only a sporadic one.

Another example that illustrates Glaucon's appetitive drive occurs when he rejects Socrates' first description of the city of necessity. Socrates reports that Glaucon "interrupted saying, 'you seem to make these men have their feast without relishes'" (372c). This subtle intrusion of Socrates' narrative voice underscores Glaucon's dissatisfied response to the city. Glaucon finds the city unacceptable because it does not provide sufficient means for satisfying his appetites. There is no room for relishes, desserts, and other luxuries. Fittingly, Socrates characterizes Glaucon's response as "an interruption." His affinity for the appetitive domain disrupts the articulation of the harmonious city. To placate Glaucon's desire, Socrates describes the luxurious city, which he also characterizes as the sick, feverish city (372e). In this feverish city, the self-mastery model keeps the appetites and desires in check.[29]

Glaucon's interest in erotic matters also illustrates his appetitive orientation. Examples of this interest arise at numerous junctures. Socrates makes clear that he has erotic relationships with other men (368a and 402e). Glaucon supports Polemarchus and Adeimantus in their demand that Socrates address the sharing of women and children in common (450a). He suggests that the guardians of the city be allowed to kiss whomever they desire (468a). Glaucon acknowledges that he, like most lovers, behaves quite indiscriminately while pursuing young boys (474d).

At the same time, Glaucon shows both an interest in and an aptitude for philosophy. Rosen notes that Glaucon "is erotic, spirited or brave, as well as highly intelligent."[30] As Socrates' primary interlocutor, he illustrates this philosophical capacity throughout the dialogue. Glaucon implores Socrates to continue the conversation at numerous junctures.[31] Roochnik describes Glaucon's central role in the dialogue in these terms, "Glaucon is responsible for the forward momentum of the *Republic*. His energy, his passion for the conversation, his forcefulness, and his crucial insights are necessary goads for an otherwise reluctant Socrates."[32] Glaucon wants to be persuaded of the intrinsic value of a just life, a life oriented toward philosophy. He tells Socrates that he wants to hear the just life "extolled all by itself" (358d). His desire to be convinced expresses itself at numerous junctures. Many of these exhortations to Socrates are interlaced with emotionality. For example, after Socrates makes note of Glaucon's laughter, Glaucon's subsequent exhortation alludes to their possible emotional response to the argument. He assures

Socrates, "Your audience won't be hard-hearted, or distrustful or ill-willed" (450d). Glaucon placates him further saying, "if we are affected in some discordant way by the argument, we'll release you like a man who is guiltless of murder and you won't be our deceiver." He exhorts Socrates to "be bold and speak" (451b).

However, Socrates seems to sense that if Glaucon is to see the philosophical life as viable for him, he needs to find a way to integrate his appetitive experience into his practice of philosophy. An understanding of philosophy divorced from these concerns would strike Glaucon as unappealing. Much as he objects to Socrates' insistence that the philosophers return to the cave instead of pursuing what they truly enjoy (519d), Glaucon would object to a practice of philosophy that does not allow a place for the appetites and emotions (519d). Indeed, his objections about the intrinsic rewards of living a just life center on the inability to satisfy the appetites under such constraints. Glaucon, speaking on behalf of the opinion of the many, remarks "it seems to belong to the form of drudgery, which should be practiced for the sake of wages and the reputation that comes from opinion, but all by itself it should be fled from as something hard" (358a). The path of virtue is difficult and most will choose an easier path.

Glaucon's account of Gyges' ancestor makes this point most starkly. Once rendered invisible, the first act that Gyges' ancestor commits is adultery. He then kills the king in order to obtain the power necessary to satisfy all his desires (360b). Glaucon asserts that if the just man were to put on such a ring, he would not continue to be just. He, like the unjust man, would engage in whatever activity enabled him to satisfy his appetites, "having the license to take what he wanted from the market without fear, and to go into houses and have intercourse with whomever he wanted" (360c). This story makes clear that Glaucon cannot see the benefits of justice because he cannot conceptualize justice in a way that allows for the satisfaction of desire. Under the self-mastery model, one might simply regard Glaucon as flawed because his soul is disordered and that he allows the *epithumetikon* to rule when it ought to be ruled. But the model has no resources to offer him as a way out of this dilemma. In the battle between the *epithumetikon* and the *logistikon*, Glaucon believes the *epithumetikon* will prevail. Because the self-mastery model assumes that the appetites are in conflict with the higher parts of the soul, it cannot offer Glaucon a way of conceptualizing philosophy that he could wholeheartedly follow. Philosophy, for him, must address the appetitive domain in a more inclusive way.

E. Adeimantus and the Regulation of Emotion

The narrative references to Adeimantus are not particularly robust. In fact, he is almost always mentioned as being in the company of another character.

Socrates even refers to him simply as "Glaucon's brother" at one point (376d).[33] Given the lack of narrative description of Adeimantus himself, it is helpful to focus on the dramatic interactions that Adeimantus has with the other characters as a means of ascertaining his character. In many ways, Adeimantus is similar to his brother, Glaucon. They are products of the same cultural upbringing; they share the same value system. Both exhibit an aptitude for philosophy and both are favorably disposed toward Socrates. Adeimantus shares Glaucon's desire to be truly convinced that the just life is best (362d–367e). The main difference between them resides in the appetitive domain. Adeimantus is significantly less exuberant than Glaucon. He is keenly aware of the potential negative effects of the appetites and emotions. Throughout the *Republic*, Adeimantus exhibits a mistrust of the emotional dimensions of experience. This aspect of his character is most apparent in conversations with Socrates about the city of necessity, in his willingness to censor poetry in the feverish city, and in his interest in the various regulations of Eros in Book V. I will explore each of these passages in turn.

After Glaucon presents Socrates with the Ring of Gyges story, Adeimantus marshals his own challenge to Socrates, "You surely don't believe, Socrates, that the argument has been adequately stated?" (362d). Adeimantus expresses his concern that justice, in and of itself, is not praised sufficiently. He suggests that the good reputation of being a just person is what people really desire because they are primarily motivated by their love of pleasurable experiences (363a). Adeimantus blames the poets for presenting the moderate and just life as "hard and full of drudgery" (364a) and the unjust life as one that provides many enjoyable rewards to satisfy the appetitive domain. He is concerned about the corruptive effect of appetitive rewards on the young. He asks, "What do we suppose they do to the souls of the young men who hear them?" (365a). Socrates emphasizes the importance of Adeimantus' challenge by narrating his response to it, "I listened, and although I had always been full of wonder at the nature of Glaucon and Adeimantus, at this time I was particularly delighted" (368a). As a result, Socrates agrees to come to the aid of justice to the best of his ability.

Socrates presents the city and soul analogy (368e). He also describes the vision of justice in the first city of necessity (368e–372a). During this exchange, Adeimantus is the primary interlocutor. In fact, he affirms each of Socrates' recommendations about how to structure the city of necessity. The only qualified response he offers is at the very end of Socrates' account. When Socrates asks him if the city has "already grown to completeness," Adeimantus answers with some hesitation. He simply says "perhaps" (371e). He responds to Socrates' query about where justice arises, quite readily, by saying "in the need these men have of one another" (372a). Adeimantus' general affirmation of the city of necessity stands in stark contrast to Glaucon's dissatisfaction with what it provides. Adeimantus does not mind a life without relishes and other delights for the appetites.

Adeimantus' distrust of the emotions arises in his exchange with Socrates about the regulations of poetry in the city. Once the discussion turns to how to educate the young, Adeimantus takes over as Socrates' primary interlocutor (376d). At times, however, Adeimantus seems unable to follow Socrates' line of reasoning. For example, he asks which sort of tales must be thrown out (377c). He does not know what Socrates means by "the greater tales" (377d) nor does he immediately understand what Socrates finds blameworthy in them (377d–e). However, as Socrates explains the harmful effects that this portrayal of the gods has on the young, Adeimantus agrees with Socrates enthusiastically. As Socrates explains that the gods must be presented as entirely good and not responsible for evil events, Adeimantus' affirmative responses culminate with his pledge to "give my vote to you in support of this law" (380c). He exclaims that this regulation "pleases me" (380c).

As Socrates explains the problems inherent in presenting the gods as changeable or participating in lies and illusions, Adeimantus asserts, "I am in complete agreement with these models and would use them as laws" (383c). Likewise Adeimantus agrees with Socrates' proposed regulations against the descriptions of Hades (387b), his regulations against the "laments and wailings of famous men" (387d), and his concern about poetry making people lovers of laughter (389e). Adeimantus also agrees that the presentation of the gods engaging in licentious and violent actions works against the cultivation of moderation (390a–e). Adeimantus affirms those regulations that conform to his preconceived notions of appropriate behavior, those defined by the self-mastery model. Within the confines of the self-mastery model, there is nothing particularly troubling about Adeimantus' negative view of the emotions. However, Adeimantus has taken self-regulation so far that there is little place at all for the emotions in his life or in the life that he envisions as best for others. Rosen senses this limitation of Adeimantus, calling him "the representative or, better still, the symbol of justice as temperance. But his defense of temperance is so to speak intemperate, and this is because one cannot defend the temperance of the body without restricting the poetic power to persuade."[34] Rosen puts the point even more starkly; "The austerity of Adeimantus must be channeled into something higher than moral outrage by the Eros of Glaucon."[35] Adeimantus' distrust of the emotions leads to an impoverished sense of justice in the soul. He needs some measure of the eros that his brother so abundantly manifests. In many ways, Adeimantus and Glaucon illustrate the polar dangers of a self-mastery model of virtue cultivation. Adeimantus represents the undesirable extreme of a life without proper regard for the *epithumetikon* and Glaucon represents the danger of the opposite extreme. I consider these two most extended character portraits of the *Republic* in light of Socrates' critique of Homeric poetry in the next chapter.

NOTES

1. The secondary literature on the *Republic* is immense. I have limited my use of the secondary literature to works that illuminate the dramatic and narrative aspects of the dialogue and those that directly bear upon the self-mastery and harmony models. I have found the following sources particularly helpful for enhancing my understanding of how the dramatic dimensions of the *Republic* interweave with the narrative dimensions: M. Gifford, "Dramatic Dialectic in *Republic* Book 1," in *Oxford Studies in Ancient Philosophy* 20, ed. D. Sedley (Oxford: Oxford University Press, 2001), 35–106; C. Rowe, *Plato and the Art of Philosophical Writing* (Cambridge: Cambridge University Press, 2007); S. Rosen, *Plato's* Republic. *A Study* (New Haven: Yale University Press, 2008); D. Roochnik, *Beautiful City* (Ithaca: Cornell University Press, 2003); L. Craig, *The War Lover* (Toronto: University of Toronto Press, 1996); G. R. R. Ferrari, *City and Soul in Plato's* Republic (Chicago: University of Chicago Press, 1999); R. Blondell, *The Play of Character in Plato's Dialogues* (Cambridge: Cambridge University Press, 2002); C. Zuckert, *Plato's Philosophers* (Chicago: University of Chicago Press, 2009); and L. Lampert, *How Philosophy Became Socratic* (Chicago: University of Chicago Press, 2010). I have found the following studies most helpful with respect to my consideration of the self-mastery and harmony models: H. Lorenz, *The Brute Within: Appetitive Desire in Plato and Aristotle* (Oxford: Clarendon Press, 2006) and "The Analysis of the Soul in Plato's *Republic*," in *The Blackwell Guide to Plato's* Republic, ed. Gerasmios Santas (Malden: Blackwell, 2006), 146–165; D. Konstan, *The Emotions of the Ancient Greeks* (Toronto: University of Toronto Press, 2006); J. M. Cooper, *Reason and Emotion. Essays on Ancient Moral Psychology and Ethical Theory* (Princeton: Princeton University Press, 1999); D. Rice, "Plato on Force: The Conflict Between His Psychology and Political Sociology and His Definition of Temperance in the *Republic*," *History of Political Thought* 10 (1989): 565–576; S. Rickless, "Socrates' Moral Intellectualism," *Pacific Philosophical Quarterly* 79 (1998): 355–367; J. Lear, "Inside and Outside the *Republic*," in *Plato's* Republic *Critical Essays*, ed. Richard Kraut (Lanham: Rowman and Littlefield, 1997), 61–94; L. Gerson, *Knowing Persons* (Oxford: Oxford University Press, 2003).

2. On the provisional nature of the tripartite account, see Roochnik, *Beautiful City*, 17–19; and Rosen, "Plato's *Republic*," 151–156.

3. Konstan, *The Emotions*, 31.

4. For those interested in the Greeks and the emotions, see note one of this chapter. For current state of research into the emotions, I refer them to chapt. 1 of Konstan, *The Emotions*.

5. Lorenz, *Brute Within*, 47. See also H. P. P. Lotter, "The Significance of Poverty and Wealth in Plato's *Republic*," *South African Journal of Philosophy* 22 (2003): 189–206, and P. Gooch, "Plato on Philosophy and Money," *Philosophy in the Contemporary World* 4 (2000): 13–20.

6. This is a musical reference to the strings of a lyre. On musical imagery in Plato's work, see Eva Brann, *The Music of the* Republic (Philadelphia: Paul Dry Books, 2004).

7. Alexander Nehamas, "What Did Socrates Teach and to Whom Did He Teach It?" *Review of Metaphysics* 46 (1992): 280.

8. Socrates allows for some positive therapeutic function for certain forms of poetry in early education. It seems there, at least, the proper formation of the lowest part does allow it to play some role in becoming good, or welcoming the good when one sees it. Cf. *Republic*, 401d–402a.

9. Socrates twice refers his prayers to the goddess at the beginning of his narrative. *Republic*, 327a.

10. As Allan Bloom puts it, they have "sweet intercourse" with each other." *Republic*, 372b.

11. See Rosen, "Plato's *Republic*"; Bloom, "Interpretive Essay"; and Roochnik, *Beautiful City*.

12. Rosen, "Plato's *Republic*," 103.

13. Socrates' discussion on this point prefigures Aristotle's discussion of temperance and self-indulgence in *Ethics* III, 10–12. Perhaps the best one can get out of the self-mastery model is continence, not authentic temperance.

14. Rosen, "Plato's *Republic*," 350.

15. The erotic metaphors of the philosophical ascent also occur in *Symposium* (210a–212c) and *Phaedrus* (246a–257c). Jill Gordon's recent book, *Plato's Erotic World: From Cosmic Origins to Human Death* (Cambridge: Cambridge University Press, 2012) offers a detailed account of how the fundamental nature of the soul and its activities are deeply erotic.

16. See also *Republic*, 441a.

17. On this point, see Patrick Coby, "Minding Your Own Business: The Trouble with Justice in Plato's *Republic*," *Interpretation* 31 (2004): 37–58.

18. Socrates uses metaphors of harmony to describe the structure of the cosmos. *Republic* 531d and 617b. A just soul mirrors the harmonious ordering of the cosmos.

19. See *Republic*, 547a.

20. Zuckert mentions it as one of the narrated dialogues and Lampert reads it in concert with the *Protagoras* and the *Charmides*, though the narrative dimensions of those dialogues are not his primary focus.

21. Gifford, "Dramatic Dialectic," 76.

22. See *Apology*, 29a, 40d–42a and *Phaedo*, 67d, 115a–188a.

23. Cephalus receives rather negative treatment in the secondary literature. Patrick McKee offers a good summary and offers a much more favorable reading of Cephalus and his motivations in "Surprise Endings: Cephalus and the Indispensable Teacher of *Republic* X," *Philosophical Investigations* 31 (2008): 68–82. Lewis Pearson offers a sustained revaluation of Cephalus as both a pivotal and positive figure in his dissertation, "Force and Persuasion in Plato's *Republic*," (doctoral dissertation, Baylor University, 2009).

24. In fact, Polemarchus exhibits a similar tyrannical desire for social control that Critias exhibited in the *Charmides*. Rosen notes both Polemarchus and Cephalus share this tendency toward tyranny. "Plato's *Republic*," 27.

25. Bloom, *Republic*, 310.

26. Socrates discusses the tyrannical soul and the tyrannical regime more fully in bk. IX (571a–592b).

27. Lampert has a compelling interpretation of the exchange between Socrates and Thrasymachus. He argues that Thrasymachus is not angry at all but that he feigns anger to provoke Socrates into engaging with him on a deeper and more profound level. Lampert argues further that Socrates knows this and intentionally misrepresents Thrasymachus' anger to his narrative audience in order to evoke their anger at Thrasymachus. Lampert argues that Socrates betrays Thrasymachus in doing so. Socrates' narrative is a betrayal because it makes a private conversation public. See chap. 3, sec. I and II, in *How Philosophy Became Socratic* (Chicago: Chicago University Press, 2010).

28. Ferrari, *City and Soul*, 12.

29. Rosen, "Plato's *Republic*," 12.

30. Rosen, "Plato's *Republic*," 12. Rosen notes further, "he lacks the austerity of his brother Adeimantus that is the necessary restraint upon erotic madness." "Plato's *Republic*," 12.

31. 357a, 450c, 450d, 451d, 457d. On this point, Rosen observes, "As usual, it is Glaucon who insists that Socrates pursue the most difficult issues. His enthusiasm is more effective than Adeimantus' questions." "Plato's *Republic*," 253.

32. Roochnik, *Beautiful City*, 56. Roochnik lists Glaucon's important insights and interventions in the *Republic*.

33. Narrative references occur at 327c, 338a, 362c, 368a, 368c, 376f, 378c, 419a, and 449b.

34. Rosen, "Plato's *Republic*," 72.

35. Rosen, "Plato's *Republic*," 72.

Chapter Seven

Musing on the *Republic*

Its Homeric, Socratic, and Platonic Narratives

In this chapter, I use the self-mastery and the harmony model to discuss the numerous ways that narrative serves as a thematic inquiry that undergirds the structure of the *Republic*. First, I consider Socrates' critique of Homeric poetry in light of the self-mastery model. Socrates' critique of Homer takes place within the confines of the self-mastery model. I also explore how the sustained critique of Homer adds additional levels of nuances to our understanding of Glaucon's and Adeimantus' characters. In the second section, I examine Socrates' narrative self-description. Socrates' narrative self-description presents his philosophical practice as more in keeping with the harmony model than with the self-mastery model. These narrative comments reveal how Socrates incorporates emotions into his philosophical practice. He does so in three primary ways: (1) He discloses his own emotional states to the auditor; (2) He describes his willingness to adapt his philosophic practice to the emotions and desires of his interlocutors; (3) He describes his experience of aporia and his willingness to reassess various arguments in emotional terms. In the final section, I consider two central narratives that Socrates tells as a character within his own narrative: the Allegory of the Cave and the Myth of Er. These narratives, along with the self-reflective dimensions of Socrates' narrative commentary, provide another philosophical corrective to Homeric discourse. Socrates offers an alternative to the Homeric narratives that he criticizes. Socrates uses narrative to cultivate critical awareness and self-reflection in his interlocutors. This pedagogical dimension of Socratic narrative helps make sense of Plato's seemingly incongruous rhetorical decision to cast Socrates as a narrator of the *Republic*. He offers us a new philosophic hero, Socrates the narrator, as a philosophical corrective to the Homeric heroes and the narratives told about them.[1]

I. SOCRATES' CRITIQUE OF HOMERIC POETRY

Socrates offers an extended critique of Homer and the poets just after he and his interlocutors discuss the nature of education in the feverish city. Socrates claims they must "supervise the makers of tales" and "persuade nurses and mothers to tell the approved tales to their children" (377c). Socrates criticizes Greek poetry—the stories told by Hesiod and Homer and others—both in terms of its content and in terms of its style. First, I consider his criticism of the content of the poetry. The first objection Socrates raises concerns the presentation of violent and unjust deeds amongst the gods themselves and in their treatment of human beings (378a). Socrates argues that this traditional depiction of the gods cannot provide appropriate models for human behavior (378d). For example, consider the famous tales about Zeus killing his father Cronos and Cronos killing his father, Ouranos. They do not promote harmony in a well-ordered city (378a). Similarly, no citizen should take Ares' adulterous liaison with Aphrodite as license for his own adulterous desires (389c). Given the limitations of these models, other depictions of the gods are required. Socrates suggests that there must be a presentation of God as really good (379b). Socrates explains further that a god should be presented as "altogether simple and true in deed and speech, and he doesn't himself change or deceive others by illusions, speeches, or the sending of signs either in waking or dreaming" (382e). Socrates suggests that this presentation is required "if our guardians are going to be god-revering and divine insofar as a human being can possibly be" (383c).

Socrates also criticizes Homer's presentation of the heroes. Like the gods, the heroes should function as positive models for the guardians. However, if the heroes are presented as fearing death or acting in a cowardly manner, they cannot serve as appropriate models needed to instill courage in the guardians (386a–b). Socrates recommends that Homer "take out the laments and wailings of famous men" (387d). A hero should be presented as "most of all sufficient unto himself for living well and, in contrast to others, has least need of another" (387d). He further suggests that the heroes "shouldn't be lovers of laughter either. For when a man lets himself go and laughs mightily, he also seeks a mighty change to accompany his condition" (389a). Socrates makes several references to Glaucon's laughter after this remark, which suggests that he is aware of the limitations of these recommendations. In summary, Socrates criticizes the fact that the heroes are ruled by their emotions. They cannot function as appropriate models unless they have their emotions under strict control by the *logistikon*. Indeed, many of the specific stories that Socrates recommends include excising displays of excessive emotionality. These stories also illustrate the negative consequences of acting from extreme emotional distress. For example, Achilles is so overcome by rage that he slays Hector and drags his corpse around Patroclus' tomb (391b). Socrates also mentions the story of Theseus and Perithous (391d), a story fraught with emotional overtones. The Athenian Theseus and the Thessalian Perithous went to the underworld together to try to get Persephone as a bride for Perithous. Hades trapped them in the underworld; Heracles rescued them. Several tragedians staged a Perithous in Hades. An Athenian audience wouldn't have cared too much for seeing their Athenian hero Theseus grieving over Perithous being left in the underworld.[2]

Before turning to Socrates' consideration of the style of Homeric discourse, I would like to emphasize one point about the content which should be clear from the above analysis. Though the content of Homeric poetry is problematic, Socrates focuses more on the effect of this content on the Homeric audience. For example, though the presentation of the gods is "false," the inaccurate portrayal of the gods is not the problem in and of itself. The problem with presenting the gods as engaging in immoral activities is that it promotes the same immorality in humans. Similarly, the presentation of the heroes is not problematic in and of itself. Rather, it requires censure because it promotes an overly emotional response in the audience. The two references to Glaucon's laughter that Socrates makes as he outlines these regulations illustrate the very emotional response that Socrates describes as harmful to the cultivation of the citizens of the city.[3]

This same concern with the effect of Homeric discourse arises in Socrates' critique of its style.[4] Socrates turns from his critique of the content of Homeric poems to a consideration of the "style." He explains, "then we'll have made a complete consideration of what must be said and how it must be said" (392c). When Socrates turns his criticism to the subject of style, Adeimantus has difficulty following Socrates' point. He admits quite candidly, "I don't understand what you mean." Socrates responds, "But you just have to. Perhaps you'll grasp it better in this way" (392d). Socrates asks Adeimantus, "Isn't everything that's said by tellers of tales or poets a narrative of what has come to pass, what is, or what is going to be?" (392d). Adeimantus answers, "What else could it be?" (392d). Socrates then distinguishes between simple, imitative and mixed narrative styles (392c). Adeimantus still does not understand, "I need a still clearer explanation of this as well" (392d). Socrates tries again, "I seem to be a ridiculous teacher, and an unclear one" (392e–393a). Socratic irony aside, the central issue is not Socrates' inability to be clear but rather Adeimantus' inability to see these basic distinctions in formal structure. He cannot discern where the poet speaks in his own voice and where he imitates a character. Despite his familiarity with the content of Homer, he cannot analyze its form. Socrates knows that Adeimantus, like any educated

Greek, knows the content of verses. To make his point, Socrates appeals to Adeimantus' knowledge of Homer, "the first things of the *Iliad*" (392e). Adeimantus knows the lines, as his affirmative response indicates, but he has never reflected on how they are spoken. Socrates explains for him:

> Then you know that up to these lines, "And he entreated all the Achaeans, but especially Atreus' two sons, the marshallers of the host," the poet himself speaks and doesn't attempt to turn our thoughts elsewhere, as though someone other than he were speaking. But, in what follows, he speaks as though he himself were Chryses and tries as hard as he can to make it seem to us that it's not Homer speaking, but the priest, an old man. (393b)

After being presented with this extended example, Adeimantus responds enthusiastically; he "most certainly" understands now (393b). Socrates asks another question, "Isn't it narrative when he gives all the speeches and also what comes between the speeches?" (393b). Adeimantus agrees, but does not elaborate (393b). Socrates must sense that Adeimantus needs further clarification, so he asks, "But, when he gives a speech as though he were someone else, won't we say that he then likens his own style as much as possible to that of the man he has announced as the speaker?" (393c). Adeimantus agrees, but says nothing concrete to illustrate his understanding (393c). Socrates then recites the opening lines of the *Iliad* without imitating the characters, but simply reporting what happens (393c–394b). Finally, Adeimantus grasps the distinction Socrates is trying to make about different narrative styles. He responds, "I understand" (394b). He even applies that knowledge when he acknowledges that tragedies are wholly imitative (394b). Socrates characterizes his understanding as "most correct" (394b). Socrates asserts that he can now make clear the original distinction between simple, imitative and mixed narrative styles (394c). He explicitly tells Adeimantus that this distinction is found in tragedies, dithyrambs, epic poetry, and "many other places too, if you understand me." (394c). Adeimantus responds affirmatively, "Now, I grasp what you wanted to say then" (394c).

Once Adeimantus grasps these distinctions with respect to narrative style, they discuss whether they should allow this imitative narrative style into their city. Socrates argues for the regulation of the imitative arts because of their strong influence in character formation: "Or haven't you observed that imitations, if they are practiced continually from youth onwards, becomes established as habits and nature, in body and sounds and in thoughts?" (395d). With this observation as a backdrop, Socrates lists several examples of improper models of human behavior: women, slaves, slavish men, people who are mad, people who work in bronze or other forms of manual labor, animals, and sounds of nature (395e–396b). Any imitative mode that encourages a guardian to imitate these forms must be banished. Indeed, people with these imitative skills would be banished from the city, "nor is it lawful for such a man to be born there" (398b). Socrates concludes his exploration of this topic with the following pronouncement: "we ourselves would use a more austere and less pleasing poet and teller of tales for the sake of benefit, one who would imitate the style of the decent man and would say what he says in those models that we set down as laws at the beginning, when we undertook to educate the soldiers" (398b). This pronouncement no doubt appeals to the austere dimensions of Adeimantus' character.[5] He readily agrees, "Indeed, that is what we should do, if it were up to us" (398b).

After this pronouncement, Socrates turns to a consideration of "song and melody." Socrates observes, "Couldn't everyone by now discover what we have to say about how they must be if we're going to remain in accord with what has already been said" (398c). At this point, Glaucon interjects. Socrates again calls the auditor's attention to this moment by saying, "Glaucon laughed out." Glaucon goes on to say, "I run the risk of not being included in everyone. At least I'm not at present capable of suggesting what sort of things we must say" (398c). Just as Adeimantus found it difficult to analyze the stylistic and structural aspects of narrative, Glaucon is hesitant to analyze the musical modes in which these tales are told. Glaucon may not be as puzzled as he pretends for he admits he has a "suspicion" (398c) of what he would prescribe. However, when the topic turns to a consideration of rhythm, he reaches the limits of his ability to analyze formal structure. He admits, "By Zeus, I can't say." More tellingly, he admits that he cannot tell which harmonic modes imitate which sort of life (400a). In other words, when asked to analyze the relationship between a formal structure, like a particular rhythm or a harmonic mode and its relationship to life, Glaucon has no answer for Socrates. His knowledge of Homer cannot lead him toward more reflective modes of thought about how he might cultivate self-knowledge or pursue a more virtuous mode of life. He remains mired in an aporetic state and his knowledge of Homer cannot lead him out of it.

In her book *Exiling the Poets*, Ramona Naddaff argues that the persuasiveness of Socrates' attack on Homer depends upon his extreme familiarity with Homer's poetry.[6] The persuasiveness of his attack also depends on his audience's familiarity with the poetry as well. However, in Adeimantus' case, his familiarity with Homer does not give him the ability to analyze the structure of Homeric discourse or to develop the capacity to be critical about the effects of that discourse on either himself or his culture more broadly. The fact that familiarity with Homer does not engender this reflective stance about him is precisely what Socrates aims to correct in his direct exchanges with Glaucon and Adeimantus about Homer's poetry and in his use of narrative on the dramatic level.

If we assume Socrates is a sympathetic advocate for the self-mastery model, we can understand his critique of Homer one way. If we allow that perhaps Socrates has good reasons to hesitate to embrace unconditionally this model, we can read and understand the critique of Homer differently. To explain, Socrates models a reflective mode of engagement with Homeric poetry during his dialogue with Glaucon and Adeimantus. For example, when reconsidering whether the poets should be allowed back in the city, Socrates enacts an imagined dialogue with Homer:

> Dear Homer, if you are not third from the truth about virtue, a craftsman of a phantom, just the one we defined as an imitator, but are also second and able to recognize what sorts of practices make human beings better or worse in private and in public, tell us which of the cities was better governed thanks to you? (599d–e)

Socrates asks challenging questions of Homer. He asks Homer what effect his poetry has in both the private and the public domains. By interrogating Homer, Socrates models the questioning attitude that he wants Glaucon and Adeimantus, and indeed all Athenian citizens, to adopt with respect to the influence of Homer on their individual lives and their broader communal ideals and practices. Here lies the crux of the matter. While Socrates is no doubt concerned about Adeimantus' inability to analyze the formal structure of Homeric discourse, he is much more concerned about these larger cultural issues.[7] Socrates wants Glaucon and Adeimantus to see Homer's limitations as the educator of Hellas. Once they recognize Homer's inadequacy in this regard, they will be in a better position to embrace a philosophical model for education.

Much like the former prisoner that returns to the cave, Socrates forces Glaucon and Adeimantus into examining the largest shadow on their own cave wall, the shadow of Homer. Socrates turns his enacted interrogation of Homer into a direct questioning of Glaucon about Homer and his legacy. He ask Glaucon if Homer would be able to name a city that set him up as its lawgiver (599e). Glaucon responds, "No I don't suppose so. At least, the Homeridae themselves do not tell of any" (599e). He asks Glaucon if there is any record of Homer leading a city to victory in war. Glaucon responds, "None" (600a). Socrates asks Glaucon if contributions in various human technical arts are attributed to Homer. Glaucon responds, "Not at all; there's nothing of the sort" (600a). Socrates then asks Glaucon about Homer's effect on the private lives of individuals, inquiring if there is a Homeric "way of life" just as there is a Pythagorean one. Again, Glaucon answers, "Nothing of the sort is said" (600b). Socrates then inquires why Homer did not acquire disciples like Protagoras and Prodicus if he were actually able to teach people to become better. Socrates forces Glaucon to admit that Homer does not have the ability to lead others to the good. Relentless in his attempt to get Glaucon to recognize the limitations of Homer's poetry, Socrates presents Glaucon with a final series of challenging questions. First, he asks, "If

Homer were really able to educate human beings and make them better because he is in these things capable not of imitating but of knowing, do you suppose that he wouldn't have made many comrades and been honored and cherished by them?" (600c). He asks Glaucon, "Do you suppose that if he were able to help human beings toward virtue, the men in Homer's time would have let him or Hesiod go around being rhapsodes and wouldn't have clung to them rather than to their gold?" (600d). Socrates' challenging queries to Glaucon reach a crescendo, "And wouldn't they have compelled these teachers to stay with them at home or, if they weren't persuaded, wouldn't they themselves have attended them wherever they went, until they had gained an adequate education?" (600d–e). Glaucon responds, "In my opinion, what you say is entirely true" (600e).

After this devastating attack, one might assume that Socrates sees no place for poetry in the well-ordered city or the well-ordered soul. However, I share the view of many scholars who argue that Plato, and his character Socrates, are not as unfavorably disposed toward the role of poetry as it appears on a surface reading of the *Republic*. Throughout this section, I have argued that the critique of poetry arises within the self-mastery model. Even within that model, however, there are indications that Socrates sees some positive value to poetry. In Book III, for instance, he reminds Adeimantus and Glaucon that there is "much to admire about Homer" (383b). In Book X, even as Socrates enumerates the potent harms of poetry, a careful reading of his words suggests that he has a more nuanced understanding of its value. Socrates allows that some poetry like hymns of praise or celebrations of good men should be admitted into a city, but still cautions against "the sweetened muse in lyrics or epics" (607a). If that muse resides in the city, "pleasure and pain will jointly be kings" (607a).

Socrates then explains that the attack on poetry was provisional in nature. He suggests "that it was then fitting for us to send it away from the city on account of its character. The argument determined us" (607b). Socrates envisions how poetry might respond to its forced exile. He suggests that poetry might "convict us for a certain harshness and rusticity" (607b). Socrates further contextualizes his attack by referring to "an old quarrel between philosophy and poetry" (607b). After this admission of his harshness with respect to poetry, Socrates suggests that other forms of poetry, not just hymns to the gods and celebrations of good men, but also those "directed to pleasure and imitation" might be allowed in the city (607c). He invites such poets to make a compelling argument to be allowed back into the city. Indeed, "we should be delighted to receive them back from exile, since we are aware that we ourselves are charmed by them" (607c). Socrates says "we shall listen benevolently to such arguments" (607c). With this admission, Socrates allows a place for poetry to be both pleasant and beneficial to the soul (607c). This return to poetry is another indication of where Socrates moves away from the self-mastery model and toward the harmony model where the emotions play a role in the cultivation of human flourishing.

Socrates' own narratives, those he tells in the *Republic* and indeed the recounting of the *Republic* itself, should be seen as just this sort of beneficial and pleasant discourse. He tells narratives about his own philosophical activity to cultivate critical awareness and self-reflection in his interlocutors, but he also uses narrative in a way that will please the emotions of the auditor. This pedagogical dimension of Socratic narrative help makes sense of Plato's seemingly incongruous rhetorical decision to cast Socrates as a narrator of the *Republic* given all of the negative assessment of narrative that occurs throughout Books II and III. Just as Socrates offers correctives to Homeric discourse, Plato does so as well by presenting us with the figure of Socrates himself. Plato offers us a new philosophic hero, Socrates the narrator, as a philosophical corrective to the Homeric heroes and the narratives told about them. In doing so, Plato attempts to set philosophy up as the new ruler of a regime formerly governed by Homer's army.

IV. NARRATING THE SOCRATIC STATE OF MIND

This section is divided into two parts. First, I analyze the narrative comments that Socrates makes about his own experience. Socrates' narrative self-description presents his philosophical practice as more in keeping with the harmony model than with the self-mastery model. This affinity appears in Socrates' willingness to disclose his emotional states to the auditor, his willingness to adapt his philosophic practice to the appetitive demands of his interlocutors, and his willingness to characterize his responses to the arguments and aporiai of the dramatic events in emotional terms. I then turn to the two narratives that Socrates tells in the dramatic context of the *Republic*, the Allegory of the Cave and the Myth of Er. I explore how Socrates uses narrative pedagogically on the dramatic level much as he uses it on the narrative level. These embedded narratives are mirrors that reflect outward to the narrative practice of philosophy that Socrates exhibits as he relates the *Republic* to us. They recapitulate many of the underlying themes of the *Republic* itself. As such, these embedded narratives suggest how Socratic narrative functions both pedagogically and therapeutically to heal the ills of our own cities and our own souls.

A. Socrates' Narrative Self-Disclosure

The *Republic* begins with Socrates narrating to an unknown person at an unknown place and time. Though the narrative conveys little about the context in which Socrates narrates, it reveals much about Socrates' internal experience:

> I went down to the Piraeus yesterday with Glaucon, son of Ariston, to pray to the goddess; and, at the same time, I wanted to observe how they would put on the festival, since they were now holding it for the first time. Now, in my opinion, the process of the native inhabitants was fine; but the one the Thracians conducted was no less fitting a show. After we had prayed and looked on, we went off toward town. (327a)

In these opening lines, Socrates presents himself as someone engaged in a wide range of human activities, not just those associated with the intellectual domain. Even the setting of Piraeus itself conveys an orientation toward the desiring part of the soul. Piraeus was the port city of Athens. Like many port cities, it offered numerous outlets for satisfying various appetites. Socrates further conveys his interest in matters that exist outside the intellectual domain when he expresses curiosity about the new religious festival, which offered numerous enticements for sensual experience. Indeed, this festival occasions his trip to Piraeus. Socrates also mentions his own activity of praying twice, which adds additional nuance to the holistic portrait he is painting of himself in his narrative comments to the auditor.[8]

Socrates continues his narrative and reports that Polemarchus' slave boy waylays them (327b). Here, Socrates illustrates his adaptability to circumstance. As in the *Lysis*, Socrates changes his plans because he encounters a group of people with plans that differ from his own. However, Socrates seems hesitant about this particular change in plans. He conveys this hesitancy to the auditor in two ways. First, Socrates draws attention to his physical body. The slave boy takes hold of Socrates' cloak and restrains him. Socrates emphasizes his physicality again by remarking that he "turned around and asked him where his master was" (327c). The external constraint on Socrates' physical body symbolizes the social constraint that turns him away from his journey homeward. By including this detail about the constraint of his physical body, Socrates conveys something about his inner state of mind to the auditor. He would rather return to Athens.

Socrates' hesitancy to stay in Piraeus also reveals itself in contrast with Glaucon's eagerness to stay. In fact, Glaucon, Adeimantus, and Polemarchus all attempt to keep Socrates there. In one sense, their attempts to lure Socrates into participating in the all-night festival represent the distracting pull of the appetites. Under this interpretive point of view, one could read Socrates as representing the intellectual path of reason that the philosopher should travel while eschewing the emotionally oriented pursuit of pleasure. However, the situation is a bit more complicated than one of strict juxtaposition between the demands of *epithumetikon* and the *logistikon*. Though Socrates would prefer to return to Athens, he expresses interest in the evening events. When Adeimantus asks, "is it possible you don't know that at sunset there will be a torch race on horseback for the goddess?" (328a), Socrates responds with enthusiasm. He asks Adeimantus for more details about the race (328a). Polemarchus senses Socrates' receptivity to Adeimantus' enticements and offers one more of his own: young boys in conversation (328a). Though it may well be the opportunity for philosophical conversation, more than the other activities, that sways Socrates' decision, Socrates willingly engages in this emotionally charged environment. Socrates does not tell Adeimantus and Polemarchus that he has little interest in these activities. He does not implore Glaucon to return to Athens and turn his back on them. Rather, Socrates agrees to stay. He accedes to the group demand, "Well if it is so resolved, that's how we must act" (328b).

Socrates' willingness to stay, even if it arises due to social constraint as in the *Lysis*, illustrates how his philosophical practice accommodates the appetitive demands of his interlocutors and perhaps his own as well, given that he enjoys both young men and conversation. While it is possible that Socrates simply "meets the interlocutors where they are" in order to move them toward a position where they can master these appetites and desires, it is striking that Socrates shares these details about the enjoyable dimension of this encounter with the auditor. In doing so, Socrates presents himself as participating in a full range of human experience, not exclusively those strictly intellectual endeavors we have come to associate with Socratic philosophic inquiry. Socrates takes pleasure in the sensual dimension of the scene as well as the intellectual delights of conversation. Furthermore, on the narrative level, Socrates appropriates this "descent" into the pleasures of Piraeus for his own pedagogical purposes. Socrates chooses to tell the story to the auditor. On the level of the retelling, Socrates reclaims these events as part of his own philosophical practice on both the internal and the external level. On the internal level, Socrates illustrates how much his self-knowledge includes knowledge of these emotional states by including these details in the narrative. On the external level, they are part of his attempt to engage the auditor in the philosophy. While Socrates' use of these emotional dimensions of human experience could merely be a rhetorical ploy to lure the auditor toward the philosophical life, it is more charitable to regard them as an integral part of Socrates' philosophical engagement with others. Taken together, the internal and the external dimensions of Socrates' practice serve as Plato's provocation to us, a provocation to view the practice of philosophy in more holistic terms.

As Socrates' narrative continues in Book I, he includes references to his inner experience. For example, he observes that Cephalus "seemed very old to me, for I had not seen him for some time" (328b). He is "really delighted to discuss [the matter of aging] with the very old" (328e). Socrates uses emotionally infused language to describe his response to Cephalus' description of his newfound self-mastery. He tells the auditor, "I was full of wonder at what he said and want[ed] him to say still more" (329e). The fact that

Socrates characterizes his response to Cephalus' attempt to master his emotions in emotional terms suggests the futility of Cephalus' endeavor. As the analysis of Cephalus in the preceding section makes clear, Cephalus cannot escape the emotional dimensions of life any more than he can escape the vicissitudes of age and the reality of death.

Socrates does not offer any narrative description about his state of mind during his subsequent conversation with Polemarchus. On the dramatic level, he tells Polemarchus that he does not understand Simonides' meaning of justice as giving each what is owed (331e–332a). Socrates expresses his view that "justice wouldn't be anything very serious, if it is useful for useless things" (333e) and that the just man will harm neither friend nor foe (335d). He aligns himself with Polemarchus by suggesting that they "do battle as partners" against those who say it is just to harm others (335e). However, Socrates does not provide any additional insight into his state of mind until he describes their shared emotional response to Thrasymachus' outburst. Socrates tells the auditor, "Then both Polemarchus and I got all in a flutter from fright" (336c). After Thrasymachus' outburst, Socrates again reveals his emotional state to the auditor, "I was astounded when I heard him, and looking at him, I was frightened. I think that if I had not seen him before he saw me, I would have been speechless" (336e).

Scholars frequently suggest that Socrates is being ironic in these remarks; I will address the larger implications of this possibility in the conclusion. However, even if Socrates is being ironic, irony does not provide a full explanation of why Socrates refers to his own emotional states. It remains the case that he mentions his fear twice. It is worth considering why he includes this dimension of his experience when he retells the story to the auditor. On the narrative level, the inclusion of his fear alerts the auditor to the importance of the challenge Thrasymachus raises. Socrates fears that he will not be able to provide a satisfactory defense of justice in the face of the view that justice is merely the interest of the stronger. Socrates is right to feel this fear because Glaucon takes up Thrasymachus' position again in Book II when he asks Socrates to "truly persuade" them that the just life is valuable for its own sake. Glaucon's renewed request indicates that Socrates was not altogether successful in challenging Thrasymachus' position. The rest of the *Republic* is Socrates' attempt to truly persuade Glaucon. The retelling of the *Republic* is Socrates' attempt to harmonize his fears about Glaucon's inability to understand with his hopes for the future of philosophy.

It is important to see that as narrator Socrates includes this description of his fear. He does not remove it from the tale. Even if Socrates is overstating the depth of his fear for rhetorical effect, he still presents himself in these emotional terms to the auditor. Indeed, Socrates points out the beneficial effects that his fear has on the progress of the philosophical conversation. For example, Socrates' awareness of Thrasymachus' emotional state helps him continue on with the argument. After describing how Thrasymachus "hunched up like a wild beast" and how "he flung himself at us as if to tear us to pieces" (336c), Socrates makes clear that he had been observing Thrasymachus' emotional state for some time. Socrates remarks, "just when he began to be exasperated by the argument, I had looked at him first, so that I was able to answer him" (336e). Since Socrates notices Thrasymachus' emotions and behaviors, he is prepared to answer Thrasymachus calmly. Thrasymachus, by contrast, is so angered by the argument that he cannot be restrained. After lurching out toward Socrates and Polemarchus, he "laughs scornfully" at Socrates' attempts to placate his concerns (336b).

One might easily take this point of contrast between them to support the standard view that the emotions are dangerous distractions that keep us from the philosophical path. Certainly, the uncontrolled emotionality of Thrasymachus threatens the sustained discussion that Socrates seeks. However, to take the threat of uncontrolled emotionality as a reason for excising the emotions entirely from philosophical experience would be a mistake. Socrates does not present himself as having a strictly rational response to Thrasymachus. He responds in emotional terms. He does not suppress his emotions completely. A trace of a tremor remains in his voice (336e). This remaining trace of emotion is important because it shows that Socrates' control of his emotions does not come from ignoring the presence of the emotional dimensions of his experience. Rather, Socrates manages his emotions by carefully observing them in both Thrasymachus and in himself. He acknowledges their presence and does not seek to dismiss his emotions from his philosophical experience either in the present moment or in the retelling of the experience.

Socrates does not try to hide his emotionality from the auditor. He could have told the narrative without including these aspects of the story. When he chooses to include them, Socrates validates the role the emotions play in his self-understanding and in his philosophical practice. The inclusion of the emotions on the narrative level also makes it more difficult to see Socrates' remarks about his emotional state as instances of irony, where he means the opposite of what he says. When Thrasymachus accuses Socrates of practicing irony with him, Thrasymachus himself is not privy to these self-disclosing remarks. The auditor is aware of this situational irony that arises between Socrates and Thrasymachus. On the narrative level, Socrates' self-disclosure seems genuine and it shows us how he integrates his emotions into his philosophical experience. In this way, Socrates models an alternative model of how to manage the emotions and their place in philosophy. This alternative model is what I refer to as the harmony model. It presents a different way of understanding the emotions. They are not something to master and control, but a complex range of phenomena that we must balance and incorporate into experience as Socrates incorporates his emotions into the narrative he tells.

The fact that Socrates integrates his emotions into his narrative self-presentation does not mean that we should regard the emotions as wholly positive. Indeed, the last image of Book I refers to the dangers of unregulated desire. Socrates laments that he has failed to learn what justice is, whether it is a virtue or not, and whether "the one who has it is unhappy or happy" (354c). By moving back into the unfolding of the dramatic events, Socrates draws the auditor into the *aporia* that he experiences with respect to the question about what justice is. Socrates explains that his inability to come to this definition occurs because he has been led astray by his unregulated desire for conversation about a variety of questions concerning justice without getting clear about what justice actually is. He compares himself to gluttons, "who grab at whatever is set before them to get a taste of it" (354b). Socrates' comparison is striking because it ends with a negative image of his experience of unregulated desire. Socrates recognizes that he has become like Thrasymachus, someone who cannot achieve his true desire because of an unbalanced response to his desires. By employing this image of the negative effects of unregulated desire, Socrates reinforces the necessity of finding a way to manage our appetites and emotions effectively. However, as the inclusion of these remarks in the narrative frame makes clear, Socrates advocates a form of self-regulation that includes the emotions in philosophical experience rather than a form of self-regulation that includes banishing the emotions from the philosophical domain, as the self-mastery model would advocate.

Book II begins with Socrates giving the auditor insight into his state of mind, and he does so again at several junctures throughout the book. What is striking about Socrates' narrative commentary in Book II is that he does not focus on his emotional states so much as his aporetic state of mind. Socrates reveals his willingness to be at a loss and his willingness to reassess his opinions. These aporetic qualities also involve an awareness of his emotional state. For example, Socrates acknowledges the fear he might feel at not knowing how to proceed as well as the frustration that might arise from having an inaccurate understanding. Nonetheless, Socrates willingly revises his opinions about the events and conveys this willingness to reassess his situation to the auditor. Consider in this regard the opening passage of Book II. Socrates remarks: "Now when I had said this, I thought I was freed from argument. But after all, as it seems, it was only a prelude" (357a). Another example of Socrates' willingness to reassess his situation occurs after Glaucon presents the Ring of Gyges story. Socrates reports, "I had it in mind to say something in response to it, but his brother Adeimantus said in his turn, 'You surely don't believe, Socrates, that the argument has been adequately stated?'" (362d). After Adeimantus reasserts the force of Glaucon's account, Socrates remarks, "I listened and although I had always been full of wonder at the nature of Glaucon and Adeimantus, at this time I was particularly delighted and said, 'that wasn't a bad beginning'" (368a). Another example of his narrative commentary underscoring his willingness to reassess the argument that occurs after the discussion of the seemingly incongruous nature of the guardian class. Socrates, Adeimantus, and Glaucon provisionally conclude that the guardians must be both gentle and spirited. Socrates conveys his dissatisfaction with their conclusion to the auditor. He laments, "I too was at a loss, and looking back over what had gone before I said, 'It is just, my friend, that we are at a loss for we've abandoned the image we proposed'" (375d).

Though Socrates does not disclose much about his emotions on the narrative level, he employs emotional language to describe his state of mind on the dramatic level. For example, he expresses his aporia about how to proceed in emotional terms:

> Now you truly don't seem to me to be persuaded. I infer it from the rest of your character, since, on the basis of the arguments themselves, I would distrust you. And the more I trust you, the more I'm at a loss as to what I should do. On the one hand, I can't help out. For in my opinion, I'm not capable of it; my proof is that when I thought I showed in what I said to Thrasymachus that justice is better than injustice, you didn't accept it from me. On the other hand, I can't not help out. For I'm afraid it might be impious to be here when justice is being spoken badly of and give up and not bring help while I am still breathing and able to make a sound. So the best thing is to succor here as I am able. (368b–c)

Socrates draws attention to this moment of emotional self-disclosure by telling the auditor, "Glaucon and the others begged me in every way to help out and not give up the argument, but rather to seek out what each is and the truth about the benefit of both so I spoke my opinion" (368c). At this point, Socrates presents the famous city and soul analogy. He explains that since they are having difficulty finding justice in the individual soul, they should enlarge the scope of their investigation to the level of the city. In doing so, they will hope to see the nature of justice as it emerges there, "bigger and in a bigger place" (368d). Then, Socrates describes his view of the purpose of this investigation, i.e., to return to an inquiry into the nature of justice in the soul: "I supposed it would look like a godsend to be able to consider the littler ones after having read these first." However, he immediately qualifies his belief in their ability to return from the consideration of justice in the city to justice in the soul, by remarking, "if, of course, they do happen to be the same" (368e).

Socrates does not offer any additional insight into his state of mind until Book IV. Socrates offers a brief narrative comment when he implores Glaucon to look very carefully to see if they can catch sight of justice. He tells the auditor, "And I caught sight of it and said, 'Here! Here! Glaucon, Maybe we've come upon a track; and in my opinion, it will hardly get away from us'" (432d). As he does in Book II, Socrates provides insight into his state of mind within the dramatic events of Book IV. He expresses hesitancy about finding justice within the parameters set by the current mode of investigation. He tells Glaucon that "we'll never get a precise grasp of it on the basis of procedures such as we're now using in the argument" (435d). Another example occurs after they discuss the three parts of the soul. Socrates returns to this definition of justice as minding one's internal business and gives an eloquent formulation of what I take to be the harmony model. Here, Socrates offers a different way of looking at how the parts of the soul should relate. They should function as three harmonious notes on a scale, each playing a vital role in the cultivation of internal justice (443d–e). He does not describe the *epithumetikon* as something to control or master but something that needs a context in which to sing properly. Perhaps describing himself here, Socrates refers to this harmonized man as someone who "becomes his own friend, and harmonizes the three parts, exactly like three notes in a harmonic scale, lowest, highest, and middle" (443d).

The last narrative reference Socrates makes to his internal state occurs at the beginning of Book V. Here, Socrates again emphasizes his willingness to adapt to circumstances that include the emotional domain. Socrates is ready to talk about the four forms of badness in the individual soul and their corresponding corruptive regimes. However, Polemarchus and Adeimantus demand to know about the sharing of women and children in common (449a–b). At this point, Socrates' narrative voice intervenes. Socrates' narrative commentary here draws attention to how he responds to the argument in emotional terms. For example, Socrates mentions he "was delighted" to think that those present would accept the formulation of the education of the guardians as he presented it previously (450a). Socrates tells them that anything else he says "admits of many doubts." In fact, Socrates tells them, "It could be doubted that the things said are even possible." He admits his fear that "the argument might seem to be a prayer" (450c–d). Glaucon responds to Socrates' emotional disclosure about the fate of the argument in emotional terms, assuring him, "your audience won't be hard-hearted or distrustful or ill-willed" (450d). Socrates uses emotional language as he responds to Glaucon. He warns Glaucon and the others about the tenuous status of the truth of what he will soon convey. He explicitly tells them "he is in doubt and seeking" (450e). He reveals that continuing with the argument "is a thing both frightening and slippery" (451a). Socrates makes clear that what he fears is not being laughed at, but rather dragging himself and his friends into error. Notice, however, that he is not fearful of his emotions as such. He does not express concern that the emotions will lead him into error. Rather, he discloses his emotions to convey the importance of finding the truth of the matter. He uses his emotions in the service of philosophy. By following

Socrates' model, the auditor has an opportunity to find the truth of the matter as well.

B. Looking at Socrates as Narrator on the Dramatic Level

In this section, I explore two philosophical narratives that Socrates tells as a character within the dialogue: the Allegory of the Cave and the Myth of Er. I argue that his pedagogical use of narrative on the dramatic level mirrors his use of narrative as a means to evoke philosophical reflection in the auditor. The fact that his interlocutors respond to the narrative on the dramatic level gives us some indication of how the auditor and by extension the reader should respond to his narrative retelling of the events of the *Republic*.

1. The Allegory of the Cave

The details of the Allegory of the Cave are well known and I will not recount them in detail. Instead, I focus on how Socrates elicits a philosophical response from Glaucon by using an interrogative narrative style.[9] I also examine the various responses that Glaucon has to Socrates' narrative interrogation. As the narrative begins, Socrates tells Glaucon:

> Make an image of our nature in its education and want of education, likening it to a condition of the following kind. See human beings as though they were in an underground cave-like dwelling with its entrance, a long one, open to the light across the whole width of the cave. They are in it from childhood with their legs and necks in bonds so that they are fixed, seeing only in front of them, unable because of the bond to turn their heads all the way around. Their light is from a fire burning far above and behind them. Between the fire and the prisoners there is a road above, along which see a wall, built like the partitions puppet handlers set in front of the human beings and over which they show the puppets. (514a)

Glaucon's first response to this image is simply, "I see" (514b). After Socrates describes the people who carry artifacts along the wall, Glaucon elaborates on his initial response. In doing so, he conveys his awareness that Socrates is telling a narrative, "It's a strange image and strange prisoners you're telling of" (515a). After Glaucon expresses his perplexity, Socrates immediately tells him, "They're like us." (515a). Socrates seems unwilling to continue until Glaucon understands the initial image and its applicability to his situation. To this end, Socrates asks Glaucon a series of questions that force him to reflect on precisely how the shadows define the parameters of reality inside the cave. He asks if "the prisoners would have seen anything more of themselves and of one other than shadows cast by the fire on the wall of the cave in front of them?" (514a). Glaucon answers, "How could they, if they had been prevented from moving their heads all their lives?" (514a).

Socrates also asks about the shadows of the objects carried (515b) and if the shadows were the source of any voices or sounds they hear in the cave (515b). Glaucon answers each of Socrates' questions with simple affirmative statements. He responds to Socrates' question about whether "truth would be nothing more than the shadows of the manufactured objects" with an emphatic "Most necessarily" (515c). At this point, Socrates seems satisfied with Glaucon's understanding and he continues the narrative.

Socrates allows the narrative of the cave to unfold gradually. As he did with his original description of the cave, Socrates intersperses his narrative with direct questions to Glaucon. After Socrates tells about the prisoner leaving the cave, he asks three questions of Glaucon. First, he asks, "What do you suppose he'd say if someone were to tell him that before he saw silly nothings while now, because he is somewhat nearer to what *is* and more turned toward beings, he sees more correctly?"(515d). Then, Socrates directs Glaucon to imagine further what would happen if someone "compelled the man to answer his questions about what they are?" (515d). In other words, Socrates' narrative describes the interrogative process that he is using on Glaucon. Socrates underscores this interrogative process by asking Glaucon "Don't you suppose he'd be at a loss and believe what was seen before is truer than what is now shown?" (515d). Glaucon answers, "Yes, by far!" (515d).

Socrates conveys the next part of the narrative by means of a series of questions. First, he asks, "And, if he compelled him to look at the light itself, would his eyes hurt and would he flee, turning away to those things that he is able to make out and hold them to be really clearer than what is being shown?" (515e). Glaucon responds, "So he would" (515e). Socrates continues in this interrogative narrative mode, "And if someone dragged him away from there by force along the rough, steep, upward way and didn't let him go before he had dragged him out into the light of the sun, wouldn't he be distressed and annoyed at being so dragged?" (516a). Socrates inquires further, "And when he came to the light, wouldn't he have his eyes full of its beam and be unable to see even one of the things now said to be true?" (516a). With this series of questions, Socrates outlines the various responses Glaucon is likely to have as Socrates' interrogative narrative forces him to engage the image of the cave. In other words, Socrates' narrative questioning forces Glaucon to take on the perspective of the cave dweller who leaves the cave.

The next section of the story where the former prisoner gradually acclimates to these higher realms occurs without Socrates asking direct questions of Glaucon. Instead, Socrates offers a series of suppositions about what the prisoner sees. Glaucon seems to have internalized the interrogative mode. He responds affirmatively at regular intervals just as if Socrates were asking him a question.[10] After Socrates describes the prisoner being reminded of the place where he lived originally, he returns to his direct interrogative mode. He asks Glaucon, "What then? When he recalled his first home and the wisdom there, and his fellow prisoners in that time, don't you suppose he would consider himself happy for the change and pity the others?" (516c). Socrates then describes the rewards, praises and prizes for the person who was quickest at identifying the passing shapes. He asks Glaucon for his own opinion; "Would he be desirous of them and envy those who are honored and hold power among these men? Or, rather would he be affected as Homer says and want very much 'to be on the soil, a serf to another man, to a portionless man,' and to undergo anything whatsoever rather than to opine those things and live that way?" (516d). Socrates' questions are strikingly direct. He forces Glaucon to engage the image of the cave, the results of seeing the realm of true justice, Homer's poetry, and the importance of how to live well.

In answer to these questions, Glaucon responds, "Yes. I suppose he would prefer to undergo everything rather than live that way" (516e). Socrates presses Glaucon further, "Now reflect on this too. If such a man were to come down again and sit in the same seat, on coming suddenly from the sun wouldn't his eyes get infected with darkness?" (516e). Glaucon responds, "Very much so." Socrates ends the narration of the return to the cave with a final series of questions about how the returned cave dweller would appear to those who never left the cave. He asks, "Wouldn't he be the source of laughter?" Then he asks another question: "Wouldn't it be said of him that he went up and came back with his eyes corrupted, and that it's not even worth trying to go up?" He inquires further, "And if they were somehow able to get their hands on and kill the man who attempts to release and lead up, wouldn't they kill him?" (517a). Glaucon responds, "No doubt about it" (517a).

Socrates ends his narration of the cave at this point and explicitly links the image of the cave with the image of the sun and the divided line (517b–c). Socrates' observation should cause Glaucon to reassess those images in light of this new understanding he has gained from interrogating the image of the cave. The narrative form of the Allegory of the Cave also links the story to the narrative structure of the entire *Republic*, as do the images of ascent and descent.[11] The narrative of the Allegory of the Cave offers a microcosm of Socratic narrative pedagogy more globally. When Socrates narrates the *Republic*, he goes back down into the cave of Piraeus, where he has just been with Glaucon, in order to bring the auditor out of his own cave. The interrogative mode of the cave narrative should stimulate the auditor to ask questions of Socrates and the narrative he tells. Socrates' narrative puts the auditor in the role of Glaucon. In this retelling of the cave story, Socrates makes clear that Glaucon must respond to the story. Socrates forces Glaucon to answer his questions. Unfortunately, we do not see any of these questions or answers that the auditor may or may not have. All we have is the force of Socrates' narrative retelling of the events at Cephalus' house. We do not see the effect of Socrates' narrative forcefulness and if it was an effective means of persuasion. We do not know if the auditor learns to ask questions. The most important questions are those that the auditor must learn to ask himself. The auditor should ask himself if he is like the cave dweller who would seek to kill the one who tries to lead him out. Or is he like the one who is dragged out to a new realm of existence? Simply put, in Socrates' telling of the cave story in his own narrative of the events of the *Republic*, we come to see the entirety of the *Republic* as the very same story, as the story of the descent into, ascent out of, and return to the cave. This self-referential narrative mechanism arises in the Myth of Er as well, where the tale that is "saved and not lost" is Socrates' own (621c).

2. The Narrative Dimensions of the Myth of Er

The Myth of Er concludes Plato's *Republic*. Most scholars agree that it is Socrates' final attempt to convince Glaucon of the intrinsic value of the philosophical life. By extension, we should regard it as Socrates' final attempt to convince the auditor as well. In the Myth of Er, Socrates recounts Er's journey to the afterworld where he sees the fate that awaits the human soul after death. The myth is saturated with narrative elements. I argue that these narrative elements cause us to reflect on the process that Socrates engages in as he narrates the *Republic*. By reflecting on Socrates' role as narrator of the *Republic*, we come to see his narrative as an extended act of self-reflection about his own philosophical practice. This narrative self-reflection provides a model for the auditor and, by extension, the broader Platonic audience about how we comport ourselves in the world as we face the cosmic journey of our souls.

Socrates underscores the narrative dimensions of the Myth of Er in numerous ways.[12] Socrates announces that he is narrating an account to Glaucon and the others: "I will not, however, tell you a story of Alcinous, but rather of a strong man, Er, son of Armenius, by race a Pamphylian" (614b). In characterizing his story in this way, Socrates distances himself from the Homeric narratives that he critiques in Books II and III and offers an alternative to them, just as he did in the Allegory of the Cave. As narrator of this account, Socrates gives Glaucon and the others background information about Er, who "died in war." Normally, death is regarded as the end of our life journey. Here, Socrates speaks of it as a beginning of a new journey: "on the tenth day when the corpses, already decayed, were picked up, he was picked up in a good state of preservation. Having been brought home, he was about to be buried on the twelfth day; as he was lying on the pyre, he came back to life, and come back to life, he told what he saw in the other world" (614b). Socrates will report that Er sees the fate of these souls, that he crosses over the River Lethe, that he returns to his body, and that he wakes up with the memory of what he saw. These memories stimulate Er himself to become narrator. He tells others what he learned. The *Republic* ends with Socrates commenting on Er's narrative. He addresses Glaucon directly: "And thus, Glaucon, a tale was saved and not lost; and it could save us, if we were persuaded by it, and we shall make a good crossing of the River of Lethe and not defile our soul" (621c). In these ways, Socrates emphasizes the narrative structure of the tale. Socrates' emphasis on the narrative form of this concluding myth draws attention to the potentially transformative power of narrative itself. By telling the myth of Er, Socrates links narrative activity with the activity of the souls in the afterlife. Just as Socrates narrates an account of his activities in his current embodied state, Socrates suggests that this narrative activity of soul will continue as the soul moves beyond its current bodily configuration. The fact that the souls gather as if at some festival (614e) is another link to the opening of the *Republic* which takes place after a festival (327a) and suggests that one reconfiguration of soul occurs through the telling of narratives about the fate of the soul.

Socrates emphasizes the narrative dimensions of this account in several ways. First, he notes that Er himself becomes a narrator: "he told what he saw in the other world. He said that when his soul departed, it made a journey in the company of many" (614c). Er's narrative activity is a textual reminder of Socrates' narrative activity both as narrator of this myth and as narrator of the whole of the *Republic*. Er's own account contains numerous references to narrative activity. For example, "the judges told the just to continue their journey to the right and upward" (614c); the unjust they told to continue their journey "to the left and downward" (614d). The judges give Er a special narrative role. Socrates explains how Er comes to receive this narrative role, "When he himself came forward, they said that he had to become a messenger to human beings of the things there, and they told him to listen and to look at everything in the place" (614d).

There are other narrative elements in the story that Socrates recounts as well. For example, Er mentions one instance of a nameless person reporting the fate of Ardiaeus the Great (615c–616a), the reporting of the journey of the souls from the plain to the extremities of the Heavens and their encounter with the spindle of Necessity (616c), the activity of the Sirens and the three daughters of Necessity (616d–617d). When the souls approach one of the daughters, Lachesis, Er reports the speech of "a certain spokesman, [who] first marshaled them at regular distances from each other; then, he took lots and patterns of lives from Lachesis' lap, and went up to a high platform" (617d). Er reports the spokesman's words within his speech:

> This is the speech of Necessity's maiden daughter, Lachesis, Souls that live a day; this is the beginning of another death-bringing cycle for the mortal race. A demon will not select you, but you will choose a demon. Let him who gets

the first lot make the first choice of a life to which he will be bound by necessity. Virtue is without a master; as he honors or dishonors her, each will have more or less of her. The blame belongs to him who chooses; god is blameless. (617e)

Er underscores the importance of this choice by emphasizing what the marshal said: "When he had said this, he cast the lots among them all and each picked up the one that fell next to him" (617e).

At this point, Socrates stops recounting Er's narrative as Er himself told it. Socrates takes over as narrator of the rest of the tale. He makes Er's account his own account. He tells Glaucon that he will omit some of Er's account: "Now, to go through the many things would take a long time, Glaucon. But the sum, he said, was this" (615a). Socrates emphasizes his narrative omissions again, noting that Er "said other things not worth mentioning" (615c). Despite this distancing of himself from Er, Socrates continues to link his retelling of the story to what Er himself said. Socrates mentions that Er himself said these things five times at the beginning of the narrative that Socrates reports.[13] But just after 617e, where Er reports how each soul chooses a lot, Socrates' own narrative voice breaks in. He stops telling the story from Er's narrative perspective and replaces Er's perspective with his own. Instead, Socrates refers to Er in the third person and reports that Er was not allowed to pick up the lot that fell before him (617e). Throughout this part of the story (616a–619e), Socrates does not emphasize Er's narrative activity. However, once the souls begin choosing their own fates, Socrates again refers to Er as narrator: "And the messenger from that place then also reported that the spokesman said the following, 'Even for the man who comes forward last, if he chooses intelligently and lives earnestly, a life to content him is laid up, not a bad one. Let the one who begins not be careless about his choice. Let not the one who is last be disheartened'" (619b).

By shifting in and out of his own narrative voice, Socrates reinforces both Er's role as narrator and his own role as narrator. Throughout the remainder of his account, Socrates uses these narrative markers to emphasize the importance of the choices that the soul makes and particularly to emphasize what fate befalls the soul who chose without the benefit of having practiced a philosophical life.[14] For example: "He [Er] said that when the spokesman had said this the man who had drawn the first lot came forward and immediately chose the greatest tyranny" (619d). Other examples include: "And it may be said," (619d); "he said that this was a sight surely worth seeing: how each of the several souls chose a life," (620a); "He said he saw a soul," (620a); "It is said when" (620d). However, after all of these references to Er's narrative activity, Socrates ends the account of Er's journey without reference to Er's narrative activity. He simply describes how the daimons lead the souls to Lachesis, Clotho and Atropos, through Necessity's throne, and then to the plain of Lethe. He also reports that each soul drinks from the river of Carelessness. Socrates concludes his account:

> Those who were not saved by prudence drank more than the measure. As he drank, each forgot everything. And when they had gone to sleep and it was midnight, there came thunder and an earthquake; and they were suddenly carried from there, each in a different way, up to their birth, shooting like stars. But he himself was prevented from drinking the water. However, in what way and how he came into his body, he did not know; but, all of a sudden, he recovered his sight and saw that it was morning and he was lying on the pyre. (621c)

In this last section of the myth, Socrates reports what happened to Er. Socrates reports that Er was prevented from drinking the water. Socrates' narrative does not tell us what prevents Er from drinking. We do not know if an external source prevented him or if some inner force guided his actions. As a result, we, along with the auditor, are left to wonder about the source of Er's timely temperance. Is he, like Socrates, unaffected by the desire to drink?[15] All of a sudden, Socrates tells us, Er returns to his body. Er catches sight of something, to borrow words from Diotima's speech in the *Symposium*, "something wonderfully beautiful in its nature."[16] Er sees the morning sun and the world of embodied existence unfold before him. Er goes forward to narrate what has happened to him. In doing so, he chooses his new life, the life as narrator of his own experience. This last narrative of the *Republic* takes us on the ultimate journey from death to afterlife to a return to physical life. It places what we may think of as our ultimate journey—from birth to death—within a larger context, which encourages us to rethink how we understand birth and death and life itself. This cosmic narrative leads us to consider Socrates' self-narrative in similar terms. In the *Phaedo*, Socrates refers to philosophy as a practice for death and dying (64a). Socrates' narrative commentary is part of this preparation. Through the activity of narrating, Socrates creates a new fate for the activities of his life. The narrative act opens a space where he can reconsider himself and his place in the world. Like Er, Socrates returns from his long journey to tell stories about his journey. He returns from Piraeus to tell the story of all that he has seen and done to all those who will listen. However, the *Republic* ends without a direct return to the temporality of the relationship between Socrates and the auditor. It ends with Socrates' exhortation to Glaucon. Through his narrative, Socrates has transported the auditor to a different state. By ending the dialogue in this way, Plato symbolically leaves the reader on the shores of Lethe. We, like the auditor, must decide how much of Socrates' narrative to drink and how to find our own way back. We, like Glaucon, would do well to listen to

Socrates' own tales and thereby fare well as we go forward to become our own philosophical muses, to sing the songs of our own immortality.

NOTES

1. On Plato's casting of Socrates as a new Homer, see E. Havelock, *Preface to Plato* (Cambridge: Belknap, 1982); J. Howland, *The* Republic: *The* Odyssey *of Philosophy* (Philadelphia: Paul Dry Books, 2004); T. Gould, *The Ancient Quarrel between Poetry and Philosophy* (Princeton: Princeton University Press, 1990); R. Klonoski, "The Preservation of Homeric Tradition: Heroic Re-Performance in the *Republic* and the *Odyssey*," *CLIO* 22 (1993): 251–271; R. C. Madhu, "Plato's Homer," *Ancient Philosophy* 19 (1999): 87–95; B. Rosenstock, "Rereading the *Republic*," *Arethusa* 16 (1983): 219–46; C. Segal, "The Myth Was Saved," *Hermes* 106 (1978): 315–337; D. O'Connor, "Rewriting the Poets in Plato's Characters," in *Cambridge Companion to Plato's Republic*, ed. G. R. F. Ferrari (Cambridge: Cambridge University Press, 2007), 55–89; Eva Brann, *The Music of the* Republic (Philadelphia, Paul Dry Books, 2004); G. Ferrari, "Plato and Poetry," in *Cambridge History of Literary Criticism, vol. I. Classical Criticism*, ed. G. Kennedy (Cambridge: Cambridge University Press, 1989): 92–148.

2. Thanks to Dr. John Thorburn for drawing my attention to the details of this story.

3. These references occur at 398c and 451b.

4. D. Cohen, "The Poetics of Plato's *Republic*: A Modern Perspective," *Philosophy and Literature* 24 (2000): 34–48.

5. On this dimension of Adeimantus' character, see Rosen, "Plato's *Republic*."

6. Naddaff, "Exiling the Poets," 39–40. See also S. Benardete, "Some Misquotations of Homer in Plato," *Phronesis* 8 (1963): 173–178.

7. See K. Robb, *Literacy and Paideia in Ancient Greece* (Oxford: Oxford University Press, 1994) and J. Vernant, *Myth and Thought the Greeks*, trans. Janet Lloyd with Jeff Fort (New York: Zone 2006).

8. On Socrates' religious practice, see Mark McPherran, *The Religion of Socrates* (University Park: Penn State Press, 1999).

9. Victorino Tejera notices this dimension of Socrates' narrative style. See *Plato's Dialogues One by One* (Lanham: University Press of America, 1984), 264.

10. 516b3, 516b8, and 516c2.

11. For a good treatment of the themes of ascent and descent, see J. Seery, "Politics as Ironic Community: On Themes of Descent and Return in Plato's *Republic*," *Political Theory* 16 (1988): 229–256.

12. On this point, see C. Baracchi, *On Myth, Life, and War in Plato's* Republic (Bloomington and Indianapolis: Indiana University Press, 2002).

13. 615c, 615c, 615d, 615e, 616a.

14. The references to sight also increase at this point. Socrates emphasizes that Er saw these things throughout the passage. *Republic*, 620a–621c.

15. *Symposium*, 176c.

16. *Symposium*, 210e.

Conclusion

Composing a Vision of Philosophy from Plato's Socrates as Narrator

In this concluding chapter, I explore three ways of looking at the models of philosophical practice that arise out of Plato's narrative portrait of Socrates. First, I will discuss the ironic dimensions of Socrates' narrative commentary. I have avoided a discussion of the ironic aspects of Socrates' narrative remarks until now because I see the presence of irony in them as an opportunity to think more deeply about the practice of philosophy itself. Irony has much to teach us: irony points to our own philosophical need for certainty and illuminates the complex nature of the practice of philosophy. Second, I suggest that there are spiritual dimensions to Socrates' narrative practice of philosophy if one takes into account Pierre Hadot's view of philosophy as a way of life. Socrates' narrative philosophical practice also demonstrates Michel Foucault's emphasis on the care of the self rather than mere knowledge of the self, the latter of which is normally associated with the intellectualist view of Socrates. I argue that Socrates' fluid model of narrative self-care is a useful one for us to follow today. Third, I consider the metaphysical implications of Socrates' narrative commentary. I suggest that the relationships between Socrates and his various auditors can be understood as images of the metaphysical relationship between soul and form. Viewed in this broad light, the narrative dimensions of these dialogues provide a model of the interconnectedness between the human psyche and the underlying formal structure of reality.

I. NARRATIVE IRONY AS PHILOSOPHICAL PROVOCATION

Socratic irony has been masterfully discussed by a number of prominent scholars.[1] Drew Hyland defines Socratic irony as "those instances of irony where the words and intentions are attributable, dramatically if not historically, to Socrates."[2] Hyland's insistence that Socratic irony hinges upon what is dramatically attributable to Socrates extends to the role of Socrates as narrator of these five dialogues as well. Scholars generally describe Socratic irony in six ways: (1) as simple irony where Socrates means the opposite of what he says; (2) as complex irony where Socrates' remarks are true in one sense and false in another; (3) as dramatic or tragic irony, where the irony depends upon the external audience having knowledge of events that the internal characters do not; (4) as conditional irony which appears in remarks such as "if you can give me proof, Euthyphro, I shall never stop praising your wisdom";[3] (5) as mocking irony which appears in the "compliments and flattery Socrates lavishes on others;" and (6) as distinguished from *eironeia*, which, at least as traditionally understood, involves sly dissembling and presenting a modest façade.[4]

Unfortunately, the presence of Socratic irony on the narrative level has not been sufficiently acknowledged as a distinct type of irony, much less fully explored. In this section, I focus primarily on the presence of irony in Socrates' self-disclosing remarks about his emotional states. In each of the narrated dialogues, Socrates describes himself as overcome by his emotions.[5] What are we to make of these perplexing passages? Are they ironic or not? Hyland offers many useful guideposts, though no hard-and-fast rules, for determining whether or not something is ironic. Initial plausibility is the first guidepost: "If something is completely so implausible as to be outlandish, we have good reason to suspect irony."[6] If one remains committed to a strongly intellectualist reading of Socrates as a philosopher who denigrates the role of the emotions in the philosophical life, it is tempting to read these moments of emotional self-disclosure as deeply implausible and hence ironic. With this ironic characterization in mind, it is easy to gloss over the importance of Socrates' emotional remarks. However, it is premature to dismiss Socrates' use of irony on the narrative level as lacking in philosophical importance. By way of elucidating this claim, I use Vlastos' distinction between simple and complex irony to illustrate the multi-faceted dimensions of Socratic narrative irony. I then argue that Socrates resembles an Aristotelian *eiron*, someone who presents a façade of excessive modesty.[7] This portrait of Socrates as *eiron* suggests that Plato prefigures Aristotle in seeing a positive value in the role of the *eiron*. Finally, I examine Socratic narrative irony as a manifestation of Platonic irony. Hyland defines Platonic irony as "irony that occurs in the action or structure of the dialogue which Socrates could not control."[8] I argue that Plato's ironic portrait of Socrates' narrative commentary asks us to reconsider the respective roles of reason and emotion in philosophical inquiry as well as the nature of philosophical inquiry itself.

A. Some Interpretations of Irony

Let us first reconsider a few examples of Socrates' narrative self-disclosure as forms of simple irony, where Socrates means the opposite of what he says. In the *Lysis*, Socrates mentions that he nearly "commit[s] a blunder" by almost revealing his presence to Lysis, but he "recovers himself and holds back from speech" (210e). If this remark is an instance of simple irony, then Socrates was in full control of his speech the whole time and did not almost reveal the subterfuge in which he and Hippothales engaged. Similarly, if his remarks are simple irony, he does not "rejoice greatly" at the apparently false conclusion about friendship he has reached with the young boys and no "strange suspicion comes over him" at all (218c). If Socrates' self-disclosing remarks in the *Charmides* are simple irony, then his brash confidence does not leave him. He is in no way overcome or even affected by his glimpse beneath Charmides' cloak and he has no difficulty composing himself in the presence of the beautiful young boy. Interpreting these remarks as simple irony would help avoid the problems that these emotional responses present for interpreting Socrates as a thoroughgoing rationalist. One could safely conclude that Socrates does not really experience these strong emotions and, in fact, remains entirely untouched by erotic desire throughout his encounter with Charmides thanks to his rational self-control.

I see two problems with viewing these narrative remarks as simple irony. First, there are so many examples of this narrative irony. In each narrated dialogue, Socrates presents himself as being overcome by some emotional response to a person's presence or emotional outburst or to a sophistic speech. Regarding these abundant textual examples as simple irony enables one to discount the importance of Socrates' emotional self-disclosure. However, such an interpretation does not adequately answer the question of why Socrates would so consistently present himself to his auditor in this way if he did not experience the events as he reports them. Is he simply being whimsical or perhaps forgetful? If we find persuasive Vlastos' view that Socrates does not cheat, lie, or intend to deceive, there is no satisfactory answer to this question.[9] While Socrates does, at times, make statements that can be interpreted as simple irony, his robust narrative descriptions of himself demand a more nuanced understanding of his irony than simple irony allows.

It seems more plausible to conclude that Socrates' remarks about how strongly his emotions affect him contain at least some level of truth. Perhaps, then, we should regard each of these instances as complex irony, where "what is said both is and isn't what is meant: its surface content is meant to be true in one sense, false in another."[10] If Socrates uses complex irony in

Vlastos' sense of the term, it is "conscious and non-deceptive," as Irwin emphasizes.[11] Furthermore according to Vlastos' view, Socrates intentionally evokes two different levels of meaning that the auditor would recognize and understand. How might we construe the two levels at work? It could be true that Socrates actually feels these strong emotional responses to people and events. The falsity may involve the degree to which Socrates feels these emotions—ranging from astonishment, fear, arousal, and confusion to outright bewilderment—but not as deeply and profoundly as he reports. Perhaps he is only a little aroused by the peek beneath Charmides' cloak, but not "outside himself," inflamed with passion.[12] Similarly, Socrates is really somewhat startled by Thrasymachus' outburst but hardly "in a flutter with fright."[13] Likewise, it seems unlikely that Protagoras' "virtuoso performance" so overwhelms Socrates that "everything goes black" or that Euthydemus' equivocations indeed send him reeling as if hit by a sucker punch, but perhaps Socrates is momentarily at a loss about the most productive philosophical course of action.[14] Furthermore, if Vlastos' view is that the careful interlocutor can detect complex irony, then the auditor should have the same ability given that the auditor has a similar, if not more familiar, relationship with Socrates. If these remarks are complex irony, Socrates makes these statements with the full anticipation that the auditor will see through the hyperbole and realize that Socrates was not quite so overcome as his descriptions may suggest.

I see three problems with viewing this narrative irony as complex irony. First, it reduces complex irony to mere hyperbole. Just as "taking his disavowals as complex ironies robs him of his strangeness and in fact eliminates his irony," as Alexander Nehamas suggests, the same is true of reading these narrative remarks as complex irony: much of their richness is lost.[15] Second, it is not at all clear that the auditor understands Socrates' irony. While there are indications that Crito understands Socrates' irony, there is no textual indication that the other auditors do. If the auditor remains oblivious to Socrates' irony, then it would be difficult to claim that Socratic narrative irony is non-deceptive. Given the likelihood that many auditors miss Socrates' irony, it is difficult to apply Vlastos' sense of complex irony to these cases without some qualification.[16] Third, viewing Socratic narrative irony as complex irony still leaves open the question of why Socrates would so consistently overstate his emotional responses to these events as he narrates them. One could argue that Socrates wants to engage the auditor in the practice of philosophy and he uses any means necessary to do so. Under this view, Socrates employs these hyperbolic statements to draw his auditors into the story and get them interested in philosophy through the more entertaining door of narrative rather than through the intellectual rigors of following an argument. In doing so, Socrates portrays himself as experiencing the same sorts of emotions, desires, and human motivations that the auditors themselves experience. While Socrates may also do his philosophical work on a higher intellectual plane than the average auditor, he never abandons the level of everyday discourse in which the auditor resides. Socrates remains there with the auditor even as he seeks to move the auditor beyond the confines of his normal experience.[17]

B. Narrative *Eironeia*

I suggest that many of these examples of narrative irony are, in fact, best understood as *eironeia*, as precisely the practice that Vlastos (and others) insist that Socrates transforms. In *Socrates, Ironist and Moral Philosopher*, Vlastos argues that even though most Attic Greek examples of *eironeia* included "sly, intentionally deceptive speech or conduct," Socrates did not use *eironeia* in this manner.[18] Indeed, Vlastos asserts that with Socrates' practice of irony, "*Eironeia* has metastasized into irony."[19] He admits that "exactly what made this happen we cannot say: we lack the massive linguistic data to track the upward mobility of the word."[20] However, Vlastos emphasizes Socrates' involvement in the process: "He changes the word not by theorizing about it but by creating something new for it to mean: a new form of life realized in himself which was the very incarnation of *eironeia*."[21] I suggest there is more to the story than Vlastos allows.

Ronna Burger's earlier work on Socratic irony prefigures many of Vlastos' conclusions. She examines the three instances in the dialogues where characters accuse Socrates of practicing *eironeia*.[22] Burger claims that Socrates effectively refutes each of these claims by revealing the contradictory motivations behind them: "In order to bring to light the contradictory attitude of those who accuse him of *eironeia*, Socrates must disclose its root. What he discovers in all three cases is the desire to be master of the demos."[23] She ultimately concludes that "The charges against Socrates' self-concealing speeches and deeds can be ascribed to Plato, then, not as judgments of Socrates but of the speakers who express them, whose words mean more than they realize; the accusations against Socratic *eironeia* are themselves represented in the Platonic dialogues ironically."[24] Unfortunately, neither Burger's nor Vlastos' exoneration of Socrates' habitual practice of *eironeia* takes into account the presence of *eironeia* on the narrative level. On this level, no one charges Socrates with *eironeia*; he engages in it willingly. Indeed, his practice of ironic self-disclosure looks habitual. It occurs in each of the five dialogues Socrates narrates. If Socrates the narrator does practice *eironeia*, what does his use of this form of dissembling tell us about his relationship with his various auditors? In my discussion of these dialogues, I have suggested that the relationship Socrates has with his auditors is friendlier than the relationships that obtain between Socrates and his usual interlocutors. The fact that Socrates narrates these accounts quite willingly and that his emotional self-disclosure occurs on the narrative level are two primary indications of this more cordial relationship. However, the presence of narrative irony—particularly if we read it as abusive, sly deception—makes it more difficult to see the relationships between Socrates and his various auditors as intimate. It is one thing to concede that Socrates might treat Thrasymachus or Callicles or Alcibiades ironically, but quite another to claim he would do so with Crito. A turn to Aristotle provides a solution to this ironic impasse.

Aristotle characterizes the *eiron* as "the mock-modest man [who] disclaims what he has or belittles it."[25] Aristotle explicitly associates this practice with Socrates. He writes, "Mock modest people, who understate things, seem more attractive in character; for they are thought to speak not for gain but to avoid a parade; and here too it is qualities which bring reputation that they disclaim, as Socrates used to do."[26] Aristotle does admit that one can understate too much, so much that it becomes a form of boastfulness. However, I suggest that Socrates falls into Aristotle's category of "those who use understatement with moderation and understate about matters that do not very much force themselves on our notice."[27] Such people, Aristotle concludes, "seem attractive."[28] In his perceptive exploration of Aristotle's treatment of the *eiron*, Paul Gooch suggests that "We cannot find in Plato's portrait any rehabilitation of the concept of the *eiron*."[29] Gooch claims further that Aristotle "disinfects *eironeia* of its customarily negative taint when nothing in Plato's usage or his own analysis required him to do so."[30] However, Gooch overlooks one aspect of the Platonic dialogues that may have required Aristotle to do so: Plato's narrative portrait of Socrates. If we view Socrates the narrator in these terms, i.e., as an *eiron*, Socrates has full control of his emotions but understates the level of control to "avoid a parade" of self-congratulatory pomposity. There does seem to be some truth to this insight. Indeed, Socrates would not be an effective symbol of *sophrosune* if he were to remark, "Now everyone recognizes that Charmides is indeed quite a beauty but I would be no different from the average man if I were affected by his charms. I entered into conversation with him prepared to show him the real value of temperance in short order." Similarly, Socrates would appear arrogant and obnoxious if he said, "Protagoras' performance was really of no intellectual value whatsoever and, after allowing the applause from his misguided throngs of admirers to die down, I reduced him to aporia in a few short argumentative moves." Socrates might draw a certain caliber of person to the practice of philosophy with such remarks, indeed someone like Thrasymachus, Callicles, or Alcibiades. However, their intellectual arrogance and disdain for others would ultimately impede their path toward the philosophical life. These auditors may not be the philosophical equals of Socrates, or even Thrasymachus, Callicles, or Alcibiades. Socrates senses their philosophical potential nonetheless. Further, he may recognize that they need to regard philosophy as a practice strongly connected to everyday human experience. If Socrates the narrator is an *eiron* after all, perhaps Plato, like Aristotle, did see pedagogical value in the good man acting with false modesty "to avoid pompousness."[31] In these five narrated dialogues, Plato places Socratic narrative *eironeia* in the service of philosophy and this makes all the difference in terms of how we interpret the aims of *eironeia*. *Eironeia* fosters philosophical inquiry: in Socrates, in his interlocutors, in his auditors, and in us. In this sense, Socrates' use of narrative irony brings the Socratic task of philosophy squarely into the communal plane of discourse. Philosophy is not merely Socrates' quest for self-understanding but a quest mediated by his desire to share his quest with others. He cares for himself as he cares for others.

Reading Socrates as an *eiron* calls for a reconsideration of a standard view of Socrates that occurs in the secondary literature, namely the view that Socrates does not engage in *eironeia*. If Socrates can properly be regarded as an *eiron*, we could hold onto another standard view of Socrates; namely, the intellectualist Socrates who sees little value in the emotional dimensions of human experience. Indeed, one could argue that this reading of Socratic *eironeia* undercuts the argument against a narrowly intellectualist portrait of Socrates that I have developed in the previous chapters. Regarding Socrates as an *eiron* supports the intellectualist view that Socrates uses these emotional displays as a rhetorical ploy to lure people toward the rational control over the emotions that the philosophical life of reason requires. However, this reading of Socratic *eironeia* reduces the nuanced levels of meaning in Socrates' emotional self-disclosure to simple irony. While such a reading may save the intellectualist Socrates, it comes at the cost of flattening out the complex portrait of Socrates that Plato gives us in these narrated dialogues. Indeed, it contradicts the textual evidence found throughout Socrates' narrative commentary, evidence that shows a careful and sustained regard for the emotional dimensions of human experience.

However, Socrates' narratives do not valorize reason at the expense of emotion any more than they valorize emotion at the expense of reason. Nowhere in his narrative remarks does Socrates say that reason will lead us astray. Likewise, nowhere in his narrative remarks does he say that his emotions are harmful for his practice of philosophy or detrimental to his understanding of self. Nowhere does he express shame at feeling overwhelming emotion. While Socrates does mention that he gains control of his excessive emotional responses, he does not excise these moments of intense passion from the narratives that he tells. He does not present these narratives of his philosophical practice as the inexorable march of rational argument toward truth. Indeed, his narratives convey encounters that lead to aporetic impasses of thought more often than they convey rational arguments that end in a settled understanding of truth. As he recounts his aporiai and his arguments, Socrates presents his emotions as an integral part of his philosophical encounters with others. He presents his emotions as a dimension of his human experience that he integrates into his philosophical inquiry. We see this integration of reason and emotion most clearly when he tells narratives about his philosophical practice. Indeed, Socrates' narrative activity itself models this integration of reason and emotion in philosophy. One way he does so is through the use of irony. We must use both reason and emotion to unpack his ironic self-presentation.

Interpreting Socratic narrative irony offers an opportunity to address the tension between Socrates' emotional self-disclosure and the standard view of Socrates as an intellectualist. We must ask ourselves what causes us to decide to read these dialogues in a certain way? What causes us to prioritize the parts of the dialogues where Socrates advocates reason and argument over the parts of the dialogues that illustrate the wide range of his experiences? Why do we fail to acknowledge that he includes accounts of his emotions in his narrative and that he tethers his narratives to the needs of his auditors just as he tethers his *elenchus* to the demands of his interlocutors? Surely, the weight of the scholarly tradition that regards Socrates as an intellectualist who is hostile to the emotions is partly to blame. The widespread definition of philosophy itself as the life of reason also makes it difficult to embrace a more emotional Socrates. But doesn't the model of Socrates as the relentless seeker of truth ask us to challenge traditional views and reassess the very definitions of truth and philosophy that we hold most dear? We would do better to embrace Pierre Hadot's notion of philosophy as a way of life than philosophy as the life of reason. Indeed, Hadot sees Socratic irony as a primary mechanism by which Socrates leads others to the philosophical life. He describes Socratic irony as "a kind of humor which refuses to take oneself or other people entirely seriously; for everything human and even everything philosophical, is highly uncertain, and we have no right to be proud of it. Socrates' mission, then, was to make people aware of their lack of knowledge."[32] Hadot's insight about Socratic irony provides a model for us to follow. We should seek to overcome our own need for philosophical certainty.

How we deal with irony also provides us with insight about how we might approach the respective roles of reason and emotion in philosophical inquiry. To explain, one response to the complexity of irony is to ignore it, to banish it from our philosophical considerations. Similarly, one response to the complexity of emotional experience is to banish it from our philosophical practices. Unfortunately, such a response distances philosophy from everyday experience, which is filled with emotional considerations about our personal situations. Socrates' emotional self-disclosure is not a call to disregard the necessity of reason and argument in the philosophical life; it does show that Socrates pursues truth in many ways and on many different levels. Reason is one of those levels. It is not the only one.

Similarly, irony demands that we engage it on many levels. When we detect the presence of irony, whether directed at us or at another, it often evokes a range of emotional responses: anger, laughter, scorn, and derision. As a result, understanding irony requires more than reason. Socratic irony is not an intellectual puzzle we must solve by shifting through the various levels of meaning that any particular utterance might plausibly have. Irony mires us in indecision. It creates a context that challenges our ability to interpret with certainty. We can despair over this situation or embrace it as a reflection of that dimension of our experience that pushes us onward to further reflection about the nature of our world and ourselves. Simply put, Socratic narrative irony symbolizes the irreducible complexity of life. Life, like irony, is irreducibly complex. The complexity involved in interpreting the irony in Socrates' narrative commentary has two main functions. First, as was the case in the *Lysis*, it forces the reader to confront a certain level of aporia, a certain level of not knowing, at the very outset of the dialogue. On this minimal level, we become like Socrates, whose self-knowledge depends upon a profound awareness of knowing that he does not know. Second, it illustrates the way in which narrative connects the present moment with the events of the past. The self-knowledge that Socrates exhibits on the narrative level connects past events with the present moment he finds himself in. We often do not know when the narrative is retold; this suggests that it could be at any time, that the story and the necessity of self-inquiry are relevant regardless of the context in which we, as readers, find ourselves immersed.

C. Platonic Irony

But where does this positive reading of Socratic narrative irony as a manifestation of Platonic irony leave us? Are we really better off seeing it in these terms? Given the largely negative interpretations of Platonic irony in the secondary literature, I think so. By means of elucidating this claim, I consider Alexander Nehamas' definition of Platonic irony. He regards Platonic irony as the pervasive way in which Plato "uses Socratic irony as a means for lulling the dialogues' readers into the very self-complacency it makes them denounce. It is deep, dark, and disdainful. It is at least as arrogant a challenge to Plato's readers as Socrates' irony was to his interlocutors and perhaps even more so."[33] Nehamas claims that we never overcome the traps of philosophical hubris on the one hand or philosophical complacency on the other. With respect to philosophical hubris, Nehamas is surely right to claim that once we think ourselves better than Euthyphro or any other interlocutor who claims to have the unassailable answer, we commit the very same mistake. With respect to philosophical complacency, Nehamas remarks, "Although we claim to agree with Socrates' uncompromising demand to devote our life to the pursuit of reason and virtue, we remain ultimately indifferent to it."[34]

While we must always guard against this possibility, I regard the presence of irony in these narrated dialogues more optimistically than Nehamas does for two reasons.

The first reason involves a view that some scholars hold regarding Socrates' narrative control. Consider, for example, the passage in the *Charmides* where Socrates describes himself as being outside himself with passion (155d). As I briefly discussed in the *Charmides* chapter, Seth Benardete notes, "the auditor learns that Socrates at this moment was no longer 'in himself.'" Benardete continues, "he learns this when Socrates is fully in control: as narrator he can say and not say what he wants about himself and everyone else. Self-control in the strict sense seems to be possible only if there is complete control of everyone else. Narration is the retrospective equivalent of what in the present would be universal tyranny."[35] This is a bold claim that Benardete makes about the nature of narrative and not one that I endorse. However, if Benardete is correct, surely this temptation exists in any narrative situation—particularly if the narrative is a monologue such as the lengthy narration of the *Republic*.

Plato anticipates Benardete's concerns because he portrays Socrates as both recognizing and resisting the temptation toward tyrannical discourse. Socrates' narratives contain dialogues. They contain other voices and other perspectives. Socrates' narrative is filled with voices that are other than his own. Beyond that, Socrates' narrative perspective typically diminishes over the course of the dialogues he narrates, the main exception being the *Euthydemus*. As his narratives progress, Socrates relinquishes this sort of totalizing narrative control. The fact that Socrates' narrative voice typically does not return at the end of the dialogues in any robust sense also mitigates the totalizing Socratic narrative perspective. In relinquishing narrative control, Socrates the narrator does two things. First, Socrates illustrates his own view that complete self-understanding escapes his grasp. Second, Socrates provides the auditor with the opportunity to search for self-understanding. The auditor must begin to look inward to find answers to the questions that remain unanswered by Socrates' narrative depiction of his philosophic practice.

Similarly, Socrates' narrative irony calls us to reassess and reintegrate the insights we gain into the insights we already have about Socrates and his interlocutors. The indeterminacy of irony reflects the ongoing nature of philosophical inquiry. The presence of irony calls us to see that philosophical inquiry is never finished. While this demand for ongoing reflection and reconsideration can be unsettling, it has positive dimensions as well. Irony can lead us to the practice of philosophy itself. Irony cultivates the intellectual adaptability necessary to work out these aporetic impasses of thought and to resolve seemingly intractable disagreements we have with others because the presence of irony demands that we see the other side of the matter. It motivates us to consider different interpretations of the same situation. When confronted with the competing interpretations that emerge when trying to make sense of irony, we are forced to make decisions about meaning for ourselves. As a result, we become more adept at challenging the limitations of traditional conceptions of truth, which is a deeply Socratic task.

II. NARRATIVE AS CARE OF THE SELF

At the beginning of *Technologies of the Self,* Michel Foucault observes, "When one is asked 'What is the most important moral principle in ancient philosophy?' the immediate answer is not, 'Take care of oneself' but the Delphic principle, gnothi sauton ('Know yourself')."[36] He then suggests, "Perhaps our philosophical tradition has overemphasized the latter and forgotten the former."[37] Foucault is right to point out this emphasis on self-knowledge over self-care. In fact, the intellectualist view of Socrates depends upon the privileging of knowledge of the self over care of the self. Throughout this book, I have shown that Plato's consistent portrayal of Socrates' narrative practice is a corrective to the intellectualist view that privileges self-knowledge over self-care. The sustained regard that Socrates shows for the emotions is an important part of how he cares for his own soul. While some might want a definite answer to what this Socratic self-care looks like, quite simply, there is no one answer to this question. But whatever answer we craft, one thing is certain. Throughout his narrative commentary, Socrates draws attention to his own emotions. If Socrates offers us a model of how to do philosophy, then we see a model that is quite comfortable with the emotional aspects of his experience and a model that uses those emotions in the service of philosophy. We come to care for ourselves through this acknowledgement of all these facets of our existence. By telling our own stories of our philosophical endeavors, we bring our souls closer to the Good.[38]

The ancient Pythagoreans engaged in a practice of ongoing self-reflection where they looked back over their day, analyzed their exchanges with others, the moral decisions they made, and the level of self-inquiry they achieved, and asked what they could do to improve their practices.[39] Plato's use of Socrates to narrate more than one dialogue suggests that Socrates may have habitually cared for himself by narratively reflecting on his own activities. If we regard his narrative practice in this Pythagorean light, Socrates' narrative practice becomes what Pierre Hadot terms, "spiritual practice." Hadot describes spiritual exercise as "practices which could be physical, as in dietary regimes, or discursive, as in dialogue and meditation, or intuitive, as in contemplation, but which were intended to effect a modification and a transformation in the subject who practiced them."[40] Hadot continues, "The philosopher teacher's discourse could also assume the form of a spiritual exercise, if the discourse were presented in such a way that the disciple, as auditor, reader, or interlocutor, could make spiritual progress and transform himself within."[41] This task of self-transformation involves an intimate awareness of the emotional dimensions of our experience. We must bring both emotion and reason to bear on the process of spiritual transformation.

Socrates' narratives illustrate the process of self-transformation. Furthermore, his narratives are an invitation to embark on Socrates' own careful process of self-examination. If we accept this invitation, a more expansive understanding of self-identity will unfold for us. The different levels of self-disclosure on narrative and dramatic levels suggest fluidity in Socrates' own sense of identity construction. Indeed, Socrates sees this very inquiry as the aim of his philosophical practice. In the *Phaedrus*, Socrates tells Phaedrus he is primarily interested in understanding himself. He describes his philosophical queries as centered around the question, "Am I a beast more complicated and savage than Typhon, or am I am tamer, simpler animal with a share in a divine and gentle nature?"[42] To answer this question fully is an ongoing process, a practice that takes place over a whole human life. As Hadot remarks, "Self-transformation is never definitive, but demands perpetual reconquest."[43]

The figure of Socrates seems to demand a similar reconquest, an ongoing attempt to grapple with the complexity of what he represents. We are inheritors of many visions of Socrates. As Christopher Taylor aptly observes, "Every age has to recreate its own Socrates."[44] The Stoics viewed him as a proto-Stoic; Christians regarded him as a Christlike martyr, willing to die for his beliefs. Neo-Platonists saw him as a representative of Plato's own metaphysical claims. The renewed interest in the ancients during the Renaissance led to a view of Socrates as a model of humanism. So too, the Enlightenment took him as a hero of liberation and Mill viewed him as sympathetic to his own views on individual human worth. Even Nietzsche who labels Socrates as "the cleverest of all self-deceivers," models himself after Socrates.[45] He titles the sections of his autobiography, *Ecce Homo*, with evocative reversals of Socratic maxims: "Why I Am So Wise," "Why I Am So Clever," and "Why I Write Such Good Books."[46] Even in contemporary times, there is the Socrates of the classicist, the Socrates of the historian, the Socrates of the political theorist, the Socrates of the analytic philosophers, the Socrates of the Straussians, the Socrates of the Tubingen school, the Socrates of the Postmodernist. And here, in this book, I have offered one more: the Narrative Socrates.

The narrative portrait of Socrates enables us to see Plato's Socrates as the first Socrates to recast Socrates in his own image. Plato shows us Socrates reforming and reshaping himself and his practice before the eyes and ears of his auditors. This reshaping of Socrates is an act of philosophical care on Plato's part to be sure. But it is also crucial to recognize that Plato depicts it as an ongoing act of self-care. Socrates forms and fashions versions of himself to better care for himself. Plato depicts Socrates as perpetuating his own immortality of soul, an immortality of word that captures his deeds. If we follow Socrates as a model, we should apply this practice of narrative self-care in our own interactions with those around us. If we follow Plato's model, we should create a public space for these narrative models to perpetuate themselves.

III. NARRATIVE, SOUL, AND FORM

Plato is perhaps most famous for his so-called "theory of forms" or "doctrine of ideas." However, Drew Hyland provocatively remarks "scholars know well that there is not a single mention in any Platonic dialogue of a 'theory' of ideas or forms. Nor does any character in any dialogue use the words 'epistemology,' 'metaphysics,' or 'ontology.'"[47] However, the idea of Plato's ideas maintains a tenacious grip on Platonic scholarship. Contemporary elaborations of this theory generally hold to some version of these three views: One: that for every particular thing that we experience in the physical world, there is a corresponding form or idea of that thing that exists in an eternal, immaterial, conceptual realm. Two, that there is some kind of causal relationship between the metaphysical form and the particular physical instantiation of it, though the exact nature of this relationship is the focus of many scholarly debates. To use Socrates' explanatory formulation, "what makes a thing beautiful is nothing other than the presence or communion of that beautiful itself."[48] Three, they are apprehended by the intellect, or somewhat differently put, they "are objects of knowledge for the soul."[49] For example, we experience a person or a painting as "beautiful" because our immortal soul remembers the idea of "the beautiful itself" in which the painting participates. We know a particular law or action is just because we retain a sense of "justice itself" which is reflected in that law or action.

In closing, I will offer a tentative suggestion about an alternative reading of the forms that I plan to explore in the sequel to this book. I believe that the narrative frame of these dialogues and the relationship between Socrates and the auditor in the frames contain an overlooked means of understanding what the forms might be and how souls interact with the formal structure of reality. To explain, Socrates reproduces an image of himself doing philosophy. The narrative image provides a model for the auditor to follow. Differently put, Socrates creates his own ladder of love as he retells stories of his philosophical activity to his auditors. Socrates' narrative takes his auditors, and by extension us, from the concrete details of what Socrates does to an awareness of the great sea of beauty of the forms themselves. The narrative retelling of the practice of philosophy, i.e., Socrates retelling his philosophical experience to others, mirrors the soul's contemplation of the forms.

One might regard Socrates' narratives as a descent into the cave, told in order to meet the auditors where they still reside, but his narratives are also part of the ascent out of the cave, which culminates in the vision of the Good itself. Socrates' narratives include both the ascending and descending structure of the entirety of philosophical practice. In this way, they are an expression of temporality itself, a movement into and out of the present moment. Socrates' narratives bring us out of the boundedness of our present experience but also return us to it. They bring us into and out of the cave. Listening to Socrates' narratives brings us into the light and back into the darkness to bring others into the light as we tell our own philosophical stories. In the section on the Myth of Er in the *Republic* chapter, I suggested that narrating is a mode of philosophizing that prepares the soul for death and dying. It creates a narrative immortality of soul that exists long after the soul has separated from itself bodily. So too Socrates' relationship with his auditors mirrors the soul's relationship with the forms. The auditors are like the soul, receiving information and nourishment and love from the form of Socrates and the form of the stories that he tells. As such, they model how the soul comes to understand true justice. Socrates' narrative reproduction of himself shows him feeding on his own activity, his philosophical activity gives birth to more philosophical activity through narrative reproduction. Socrates' narratives provide an image of immortality, one that he creates himself. Much like Er's account is saved and not lost, Socrates saves his practice of philosophy by telling stories about it. Plato presents Socrates as saving his own tales, so they are not lost. Socrates was his own philosophical muse. Plato's dialogues continue that salvific act.

NOTES

1. For good discussions of irony in the Platonic dialogues, see P. Plass, "Philosophic Anonymity and Irony in the Platonic Dialogues," *American Journal of Philology* 85 (1964): 254–278; R. Burger, "Socratic *Eironeia*," *Interpretation* 13 (1985): 143–149; C. Rowe, "Platonic Irony," in *Nova Tellus: Anuario del Centro de Estudios Classicos* 5 (1987): 83–101; Paul Gooch, "Socratic Irony and Aristotle's *Eiron*: Some Puzzles," *Phoenix* 41 (1987): 95–104; J. Seery, "Politics as Ironic Community. On the Themes of Descent and Return in the *Republic*," *Political Theory* 16 (1988): 229–256; G. Vlastos, *Socrates: Ironist and Moral Philosopher* (Ithaca: Cornell University Press, 1991); D. Hyland, *Finitude and Transcendence*; R. Rutherford, *Art of Plato*; D. Roochnik, "Irony and Accessibility," *Political Theory* 25 (1997): 869–886; A. Nehamas, *The Art of Living: Socratic Reflections from Plato to Foucault* (Berkeley: University of California Press, 1998); I. Vasiliou, "Conditional Irony in the Socratic Dialogues," *Classical Quarterly* 49 (1999): 456–472; M. Gifford, "Dramatic Dialectic in *Republic* Book 1," in *Oxford Studies in Ancient Philosophy* 20, ed. D. Sedley (Oxford: Oxford University Press, 2001): 34–106; C. Griswold, "Irony in the Platonic Dialogues," *Philosophy and Literature* 26 (2002): 84–106; S. Rubarth, "Plato, McLuhan, and the Technology of Irony," *International Studies in Philosophy* 34 (2002): 95–114; S. Scolnicov, "Plato's Ethics of Irony,"

in *Plato Ethicus: Philosophy Is Life*, ed. Maurizio Migliori (Sankt Augustin: Academia Verlag, 2003):289–300; M. Lane, "The Evolution of *Eironeia*," in *Oxford Studies in Ancient Philosophy* 31, ed. David Sedley (Oxford: Clarendon Press, 2006): 49–83; M. Lane, "Reconsidering Socratic Irony" in *The Cambridge Companion to Socrates*, ed. Donald Morrison (Cambridge: Cambridge University Press, 2010): 237–259.

2. Hyland, *Finitude and Transcendence*, 91.
3. *Euthyphro*, 9b2–3. Vasiliou explains conditional irony in these terms: "This irony is expressed in a conditional, with the antecedent frequently explicit, but sometimes implicit although clear from the context. The irony lies in the fact that if the antecedent were true, then Socrates would really believe the consequent; however it is clear to the reader, though not always to the interlocutor, that Socrates believes that the antecedent is false, which therefore suggests that he believes the negation of the consequent." Vasiliou, "Conditional Irony," 462.
4. T. Brickhouse and N. Smith, *The Philosophy of Socrates* (Boulder: Westview, 2000), 63.
5. See *Lysis*, 210e–211a and 218c; *Charmides*, 154c and 155d; *Protagoras*, 328d and 339e; *Euthydemus*, 295d and 303a–c; and *Republic*, 336c and 336d.
6. Hyland, *Finitude and Transcendence*, 105.
7. Aristotle, *Nicomachean Ethics*, 1128a.
8. Hyland, *Finitude and Transcendence*, 91.
9. Vlastos, *Ironist, Moral Philosopher*, 38–44.
10. Vlastos, *Ironist, Moral Philosopher*, 31. For critiques of Vlastos' view, see J. Gordon, "Against Vlastos on Complex Irony," *The Classical Quarterly* 46 (1991): 131–137; P. Gottlieb, "The Complexity of Socratic Irony: A Note on Professor Vlastos' Account," *The Classical Quarterly* 42 (1992): 278–79; C. D. C. Reeve, "Vlastos's Socrates: Ironist and Moral Philosopher," *PSA Study Group in Greek Political Thought* 11 (1992): 72–82; and Brickhouse and Smith, *Philosophy of Socrates*.
11. T. Irwin, "Socratic Puzzles," *Oxford Studies in Ancient Philosophy* 10 (1992): 241–66.
12. *Charmides*, 155d.
13. *Republic*, 336c.
14. *Euthydemus*, 303a.
15. A. Nehamas, "Voices of Silence: On Gregory Vlastos' Socrates," *Arion* 2 (1992): 181.
16. Plax suggests that "Crito is not unaware of Socratic irony." "Lover of Family," 42. Strauss, in contrast, sees Crito as "impervious to it." "*Euthydemus*," 1.
17. Pierre Hadot remarks, "Socrates is simultaneously in the world and outside it. He transcends both people and things by his moral demands and the engagement they require; yet he is involved with people and with things because the only true philosophy lies in the every day." *What Is Ancient Philosophy*, trans. Michael Chase (Cambridge: Belknap of Harvard University Press, 2004), 38.
18. Vlastos, *Ironist, Moral Philosopher*, 25.
19. Vlastos, *Ironist, Moral Philosopher*, 28.
20. Vlastos, *Ironist, Moral Philosopher*, 29.
21. Vlastos, *Ironist, Moral Philosopher*, 29.
22. She discusses Thrasymachus in the *Republic*, Callicles in the *Gorgias*, and Alcibiades in the *Symposium*.
23. Burger, "Socratic *Eironeia*," 147.
24. Burger, "Socratic *Eironeia*," 149.
25. Aristotle, *Nicomachean Ethics*, 1128a.
26. Aristotle, *Nicomachean Ethics*, 1128a.
27. Aristotle, *Nicomachean Ethics*, 1128a.
28. Aristotle, *Nicomachean Ethics*, 1128a.
29. Gooch, "Socratic Irony," 103.
30. Gooch, "Socratic Irony," 103.
31. Aristotle, *Nicomachean Ethics*, 1127b23–6.
32. Hadot, *What Is Ancient Philosophy*, 26.
33. Nehamas, *Art of Living*, 44.
34. Nehamas, *Art of Living*, 46.

35. Benardete, "Plato's *Charmides*," 15.

36. M. Foucault, *Technologies of the Self*: A Seminar with Michel Foucault, ed. L. H. Martin, H. Gutman, P. Hutton (London: Tavistock, 1988), 19.

37. Foucault, *Technologies*, 19.

38. I offer an extended example of this practice in "On the Advantages and Disadvantages of Philosophy for Life," in *Politics and Religion: A New Synthesis*, ed. Alstair Welchmann (New York: Springer Press, forthcoming).

39. On Pythagorean practices, see Walter Burkert, *Lore and Science in Ancient Pythagoreanism* (Cambridge: Harvard University Press, 1972).

40. Hadot, *What Is Ancient Philosophy*, 6.

41. Hadot, *What Is Ancient Philosophy*, 6.

42. *Phaedrus*, 230a.

43. Hadot, *What Is Ancient Philosophy*, 36.

44. Taylor, *Socrates*, 100.

45. F. Nietzsche, *Twilight of the Idols*, in *The Anti-Christ, Ecce Homo, Twilight of the Idols and Other Writings*, trans. Judith Norman, ed. Aaron Ridley and Judith Norman (Cambridge: Cambridge University Press, 2005), 166.

46. F. Nietzsche, *Ecce Homo*, in *The Anti-Christ, Ecce Homo, Twilight of the Idols and Other Writings*, trans. Judith Norman, ed. Aaron Ridley and Judith Norman (Cambridge: Cambridge University Press, 2005).

47. Hyland, *Finitude and Transcendence*, 168.

48. *Phaedo*, 100d.

49. Mark McPherran, *The Religion of Socrates*, 293.

Selected Bibliography

Adkins, A. W. H. "Arete, Techne, Democracy and Sophists: *Protagoras* 316b–328d." *The Journal of Hellenic Studies* 93 (1973): 3–12.
Adkins, A. W. H. *Merit and Responsibility*. Oxford, UK: Oxford University Press, 1960.
Annas, J., and Christopher Rowe, eds. *New Perspectives on Plato, Modern and Ancient*. Washington, D.C.: Center for Hellenic Studies, 2002.
Annas, J. "Plato and Aristotle on Friendship and Altruism." *Mind* 86 (1997): 32–554.
Arieti, J. *Interpreting the Dialogues: The Dialogues as Drama*. Savage: Rowman and Littlefield, 1991.
Aristotle. *Nicomachean Ethics*. Translated by W. D. Ross. Oxford, UK: Oxford University Press, 1980.
Balaban, O. *Plato and Protagoras*. Lanham, MD: Lexington Books, 1999.
Baracchi, C. *On Myth, Life, and War in Plato's* Republic. Bloomington and Indianapolis: Indiana University Press, 2002.
Beaty, M. and A. M. Bowery. "Cultivating Christian Citizenship: Martha Nussbaum's Socrates, Augustine's *Confessions*, and the Modern University." *Christian Scholars Review XXXI* (2003): 21–50.
Benardete, S. "On Interpreting Plato's *Charmides*." *Graduate Faculty Philosophy Journal* 11 (1986): 9–36.
Benardete, S. "Some Misquotations of Homer in Plato." *Phronesis* 8 (1963): 173–178.
Bentley, R. "On Reading Plato's Methods, Controversies and Interpretations." *Polis* 15 (1998): 122–137.
Berger, H. "Facing Sophists: Socrates' Charismatic Bondage in *Protagoras*." *Representations* 5 (1984): 66–91.
Blondell, R. *The Play of Character in Plato's Dialogues*. Cambridge, UK: Cambridge University Press, 2002.
Bloom, A. *Love and Friendship*. New York: Simon and Schuster, 1993.
Bolotin, D. *Plato's Dialogue on Friendship*. Ithaca, NY: Cornell University Press, 1979.
Booth, W. *The Rhetoric of Fiction*. Chicago: University of Chicago Press, 1983.
Booth, W. *The Rhetoric of Irony*. Chicago: University of Chicago Press, 1974.
Bowery, A. M. "Know Thyself: Socrates as Storyteller." In *Philosophy in Dialogue Form: Plato's Many Devices*, edited by Gary Scott, 82–109. Evanston, IL: Northwestern University Press, 2007.
Bowery, A. M. "Recovering and Recollecting the Soul." In *Plato's Forms. Varieties in Interpretation*, edited by Bill Welton, 111–136. Lanham, MD: Lexington Books, 2003.

Bowery, A. M. "Socratic Reason and Emotion: Revisiting the Intellectualist Socrates in Plato's *Protagoras*." In *Socrates: Reason or Unreason as the Foundation of European Identity*, edited by Ann Ward, 1–29. Cambridge: Cambridge Scholars Press, 2007.

Brann, E. "The Tyrant's Temperance." In *Music of the Republic*, 66–87. New York: Paul Dry Books, 2004.

Bremer, J. *Plato and the Founding of the Academy*. Washington, D.C.: University Press of America, 2002.

Brickhouse, T., and N. Smith. "Socrates and the Unity of the Virtues." *Journal of Ethics* 1 (1997): 311–324.

Brickhouse, T., and N. Smith. *The Philosophy of Socrates*. Boulder: Westview, 2000.

Bruell, C. "Socratic Politics and Self-Knowledge: An Interpretation of Plato's *Charmides*." *Interpretation* 6 (1977): 141–203.

Burger, R. "Plato's Non-Socratic Narrations of Socratic Conversations." In *Plato's Dialogues—The Dialogical Approach*, edited by Richard Hart and Victorino Tejera, 121–142. Lewiston: The Edwin Mellen Press, 1997.

Burger, R. "Socratic *Eironeia*." *Interpretation* 13 (1985): 143–149.

Burkert, W. *Ancient Mystery Cults*. Cambridge, MA: Harvard University Press, 1987.

Burkert, W. *Lore and Science in Ancient Pythagoreanism*. Cambridge, MA: Harvard University Press, 1972.

Byrd, M. "The Summoner Approach. A New Method for Plato Interpretation." *Journal of the History of Philosophy* 45 (2007): 365–381.

Carson, A. "How Not to Read a Poem. Unmixing Simonides from Protagoras." *Classical Philosophy* 82 (1992): 110–130.

Chance, T. *Plato's* Euthydemus. Berkeley: University of California Press, 1992.

Clay, D. *Platonic Questions: Dialogues with the Silent Philosopher*. University Park, PA: Penn State Press, 2000.

Coby, P. "Minding Your Own Business: The Trouble with Justice in Plato's *Republic*." *Interpretation* 31 (2004): 37–58.

Coby, P. *Socrates and the Sophistic Enlightenment. A Commentary on Plato's* Protagoras. Lewisburg, PA: Bucknell University Press, 1987.

Cohen, D. "The Poetics of Plato's *Republic*: A Modern Perspective." *Philosophy and Literature* 24 (2000): 34–48.

Coolidge, F. "On the Grounds for Aristocracy and the Rejection of Philosophy: A Reflection on Plato's *Charmides*." *Journal of Speculative Philosophy* 9 (1995): 208–228.

Cooper, J. M. "Plato's Theory of Human Motivation." In *Essays on Plato's Psychology*, edited by Ellen Wagner, 91–114. Lanham, MD: Lexington Books, 2001.

Cooper, J. M. *Reason and Emotion. Essays on Ancient Moral Psychology and Ethical Theory*. Princeton: Princeton University Press, 1999.

Cooper, J. "The Unity of Virtue." *Social Philosophy and Policy* 15 (1998): 233–274.

Craig, L. *The War Lover: A Study of Plato's Republic*. Toronto: University of Toronto Press, 1994.

Cropsey, J. "Virtue and Knowledge: On Plato's *Protagoras*." *Interpretation* 19 (1991): 137–155.

DeJong, I. *Narrative in Drama: The Art of the Euripidean Messenger-Speech*. Leiden, Neth.: Brill, 1991.

Damasio, A. *Descartes' Error: Emotion, Reason, and the Human Brain*. New York: Avon Books, 1994.

Devereux, D. "The Unity of the Virtues in Plato's *Protagoras* and *Laches*." *Philosophical Review* 101 (1977): 129–141.

Dewald. C. "Narrative Surface and Authorial Voice in Herodotus' *Histories*." *Arethusa* 20 (1987): 147–150.

Dickey, E. *Greek Forms of Address from Herodotus to Lucian*. Oxford, UK: Clarendon, 1996.

Dorter, K. *Plato's* Phaedo: *An Interpretation*. Toronto: University of Toronto Press, 1982.

Dover, K. J. *Greek Homosexuality*. London: Duckworth, 1978.

Dover, K. J. *Greek Popular Morality in the Time of Plato and Aristotle*. Indianapolis: Hackett, 1974.

Drake, R. "Extraneous Voices: Orphaned and Adopted Texts in the *Protagoras*." *Epoché* 10 (2005): 5–20.
Ebert, T. "The Role of the Frame Dialogue in Plato's *Protagoras*." In *Plato's Protagoras. Proceedings of the Third Symposium Platonicum Pragense*, edited by Ales Havlicek and Filip Karfik, 9–20. Prague: OIKOYMENH, 2003.
Edmonds R. G. *Myths of the Underworld Journey: Plato, Aristophanes and the Orphic Gold Tablets*. Cambridge, UK: Cambridge University Press, 2004.
Ellis, W. M. *Alcibiades*. New York: Routledge, 1989.
Ferejohn, M. "Socratic Thought-Experiments and the Unity of Virtue Paradox." *Phronesis* 29 (1984): 105–122.
Ferejohn, M. "The Unity of Virtue and the Objects of Socratic Inquiry." *Journal of the History of Philosophy* 20 (1982): 1–12.
Ferrari, G. "Plato and Poetry." In *Cambridge History of Literary Criticism*. Vol. I, *Classical Criticism*, edited by G. Kennedy, 92–148. Cambridge, UK: Cambridge University Press, 1989.
Ferrari, G. R. F. *City and Soul in Plato's* Republic. Chicago: University of Chicago Press, 1999.
Foucault, M. *Technologies of the Self: A Seminar with Michel Foucault*. Edited by L. H. Martin, H. Gutman, and P. Hutton. London: Tavistock, 1988.
Foucault, M. *The Hermeneutic of the Subject Lectures at the Collège de France 1981—1982*. Translated by Michael Chase. New York: MacMillan, 2006.
Freyburg, B. *Philosophy and Comedy: Aristophanes, Logos, and Eros*. Indianapolis: Indiana University Press, 2008.
Friedländer, F. *Plato*. Translated by Hans Meyerhoff. Princeton: Princeton University Press, 1964–69.
Gadamer, H. G. "Logos and Ergon in Plato's *Lysis*." In *Dialogue and Dialectic: Eight Hermeneutical Studies on Plato*, translated by P. Christopher Smith, 1–20. New Haven, CT: Yale University Press, 1980.
Gagarin, M. "The Purpose of Plato's *Protagoras*." *Transactions and Proceedings of the American Philological Association* 100 (1969): 133–164.
Gallop, D. "Justice and Holiness in *Protagoras* 330–331." *Phronesis* 6 (1961): 86–93.
Geier, A. *Plato's Erotic Thought: The Tree of the Unknown*. Rochester, NY: University of Rochester Press, 2002.
Gerson, L. *Knowing Persons*. Oxford, UK: Oxford University Press, 2003.
Gifford, M. "Dramatic Dialectic in *Republic* Book 1." In *Oxford Studies in Ancient Philosophy*, vol. 20, edited by David Sedley, 34–106. Oxford, UK: Oxford University Press, 2001.
Goldberg, L. *A Commentary on Plato's* Protagoras. New York: Peter Lang, 1983.
González-Castán, O. "The Erotic Soul and its Movement towards the Beautiful and the Good." *Revista de Filosofía* 21 (2000): 75–86.
Gonzalez, F. "A Short History of Platonic Interpretation and the 'Third Way.'" In *The Third Way: New Directions in Platonic Studies*, edited by Francisco Gonzalez, 1–22. Lanham, MD: Rowman and Littlefield, 1995.
Gonzalez, F. *Dialectic and Dialogue: Plato's Practice of Philosophical Inquiry*. Evanston, IL: Northwestern University Press, 1999.
Gonzalez, F. "Giving Thought to the Good Together." In *Retracing the Platonic Text*, edited by John Russon and John Sallis, 113–154. Evanston, IL: Northwestern University Press, 2000.
Gonzalez, F. "How to Read a Platonic Prologue: *Lysis* 203a–207d." In *Plato as Author: The Rhetoric of Philosophy,* edited by Ann Michelini, 15–44. Leiden, Neth.: Brill, 2003.
Gonzalez, F. "Plato's *Lysis*: An Enactment of Philosophical Kinship." *Ancient Philosophy* 15 (1995): 69–90.
Gooch, P. "Plato on Philosophy and Money." *Philosophy in the Contemporary World* 4 (2000): 13–20.
Gooch, P. "Socratic Irony and Aristotle's *Eiron*: Some Puzzles." *Phoenix* 41 (1987): 95–104.
Gordon, J. "Against Vlastos on Complex Irony." *The Classical Quarterly* 46 (1996): 131–137.
Gordon, J. *Plato's Erotic World: From Cosmic Origins to Human Death*. Cambridge, UK: Cambridge University Press, 2012.

Gordon, J. *Turning Toward Philosophy*. University Park, PA: Pennsylvania State University Press, 1999.
Gottlieb, P. "The Complexity of Socratic Irony: A Note on Professor Vlastos' Account." *The Classical Quarterly* 42 (1992): 278–79.
Gould, J. *The Development of Plato's Ethics*. New York: Russell and Russell, 1972.
Gould, T. *The Ancient Quarrel between Poetry and Philosophy*. Princeton: Princeton University Press, 1990.
Griswold, C. "Irony in the Platonic Dialogues." *Philosophy and Literature* 26 (2002): 84–106.
Griswold, C. "Relying on Your Own Voice, An Unsettled Rivalry of Moral Ideals in Plato's *Protagoras*." *Review of Metaphysics* 53 (1999): 283–307.
Griswold, C. *Self-Knowledge in Plato's* Phaedrus. New Haven, CT: Yale University Press, 1986.
Guthrie, W. K. C. *A History of Greek Philosophy*. Cambridge, UK: Cambridge University Press, 1975.
Haden, J. "Friendship in Plato's *Lysis*." *Review of Metaphysics* 37 (1983): 327–356.
Hadot, P. *What Is Ancient Philosophy?* Cambridge, MA: Belknap Press, 2004.
Halliwell, S. "Between Public and Private: Tragedy and Athenian Experience of Rhetoric." In *Greek Tragedy and the Historian*, edited by Christopher Pelling, 121–141. Oxford, UK: Clarendon, 1997.
Halliwell, S. *The Aesthetics of Mimesis*. Princeton: Princeton University Press, 2002.
Halperin, D. "Plato and the Erotics of Narrativity." In *Oxford Studies in Ancient Philosophy: Methods of Interpreting Plato and His Dialogues*, edited by Julia Annas, J. C. Klagge, and Nicholas D. Smith, 93–129. Oxford, UK: Clarendon Press, 1992.
Harris, W. *Ancient Literacy*. Cambridge, UK: Cambridge University Press, 1989.
Hart, R. and Victorino Tejera, eds. *Plato's Dialogues: The Dialogical Approach*. Lewiston, NY: Mellen Press, 1997.
Hartman, M. "How the Inadequate Models for Virtue in the *Protagoras* Illuminate Socrates' View of the Unity of Virtues." *Apeiron* 18 (1984): 110–117.
Havelock, E. *Preface to Plato*. Cambridge, MA: Belknap, 1982.
Hesiod. *Theogony*. Translated by Richmond Lattimore. Ann Arbor: University of Michigan Press, 1988.
Hitchcock, D. "The Origin of Professional Eristic." In *Plato: Euthydemus, Charmides. Proceedings of the V Symposium Platonicum. Selected Papers*, vol. 13, edited by Tom Robinson and Luc Brisson, 59–67. Sankt Augustin: Academia Verlag, 2000.
Homer. *Iliad*. Translated by Stanley Lombardo. Indianapolis: Hackett, 1997.
Homer. *Odyssey*. Translated by Stanley Lombardo. Indianapolis: Hackett, 2000.
Howland, J. "Re-Reading Plato: The Problem of Platonic Chronology." *Phoenix* 45 (1991): 189–214.
Howland, J. *The Republic: The* Odyssey *of Philosophy*. Philadelphia: Paul Dry Books, 2004.
Hyland, D. "Eros, Epithumia, and Philia in Plato." *Phronesis* 13 (1968): 32–46.
Hyland, D. *Finitude and Transcendence in the Platonic Dialogues*. Albany: State University of New York Press, 1995.
Hyland, D. *The Virtue of Philosophy: An Interpretation of Plato's* Charmides. Athens: Ohio University Press, 1981.
Irwin, T. *Plato's Ethics*. Oxford, UK: Oxford University Press, 1995.
Irwin, T. *Plato's Moral Theory*. Oxford, UK: Oxford University Press, 1977.
Irwin, T. "Socratic Puzzles." *Oxford Studies in Ancient Philosophy* 10 (1992): 241–66.
Jackson, R. "Socrates' Iolaos: Myth and Eristic in Plato's *Euthydemus*." *Classical Quarterly* 40 (1990): 378–395.
Jaeger, W. *Paideia*. Translated by G. Hightet. Vol. 1. Oxford, UK: Oxford University Press, 1986.
Kahn, C. *Plato and the Socratic Dialogue: The Philosophical Use of a Literary Form*. Cambridge, UK: Cambridge University Press 1996.
Kato, S. "The Crito-Socrates Scenes in the *Euthydemus*: A Point of View for a Reading of the Dialogue." In *Plato:* Euthydemus, Charmides. *Proceedings of the V Symposium Platonicum.*

Selected Papers, vol. 13, edited by Tom Robinson and Luc Brisson, 123–132. Sankt Augustin: Academia Verlag, 2000.

Kingsley, P. *Ancient Philosophy, Mystery, and Magic: Empedocles and the Pythagorean Tradition*. Cambridge, UK: Cambridge University Press, 1995.

Klein, J. *A Commentary on Plato's Meno*. Chapel Hill: University of North Carolina Press, 1965.

Klonoski, R. "The Preservation of Homeric Tradition: Heroic Re-Performance in the *Republic* and the *Odyssey*." *CLIO* 22 (1993): 251–271.

Konstan, D. *The Emotions of the Ancient Greeks*. Toronto: University of Toronto Press, 2006.

Krentz, P. *The Thirty at Athens*. Ithaca, NY: Cornell University Press, 1982.

Lada, I. "'Empathic Understanding': Emotion and Cognition in Classical Dramatic Audience-Response." *Proceedings of the Cambridge Philological Society* 39 (1993): 94–140.

Laertius, D. *Lives of Eminent Philosophers I–II*. Translated by R. D. Hicks. Cambridge, MA: Harvard University Press, 1979–80.

Lampert, L. *How Philosophy Became Socratic*. Chicago: University of Chicago Press, 2010.

Landy, T. "Limitations of Political Philosophy: An Interpretation of Plato's *Charmides*." *Interpretation* 26 (1998): 183–199.

Landy, T. "Philosophy, Statesmanship, and Pragmatism in Plato's *Euthydemus*." *Interpretation* 25 (1998): 181–200.

Landy, T. "Virtue, Art, and the Good Life in Plato's *Protagoras*." *Interpretation* 21 (1994): 287–308.

Lane, M. "Reconsidering Socratic Irony." In *The Cambridge Companion to Socrates*. Edited by Donald Morrison, 237–259. Cambridge, UK: Cambridge University Press, 2010.

Lane, M. "The Evolution of Eironeia." In *Oxford Studies in Ancient Philosophy,* 31, edited by David Sedley, 49–83. Oxford, UK: Oxford University Press, 2006.

Lear, J. *A Case for Irony*. Cambridge, MA: Harvard University Press, 2011.

Lear, J. "Inside and Outside the *Republic*." In *Plato's Republic. Critical Essays*, edited by Richard Kraut, 61–94. Lanham, MD: Rowman and Littlefield, 1997.

Liddell, H. G., R. Scott, H. S. Jones, and Roderick McKenzie. *A Greek-English Lexicon*. 9th ed. Oxford, UK: Clarendon Press, 1986.

Linforth, M. "The Corybantic Rites in Plato." *University of California Publications in Classical Philology* 13 (1998): 121–162.

Lloyd, G. *Man of Reason: Male and Female in Western Philosophy*. Minneapolis: University of Minnesota Press, 1984.

Long, C. "Crisis of Community: The Topology of Socratic Politics in the *Protagoras*." *Epoché* 15 (2011): 361–377.

Lorenz, H. "The Analysis of the Soul in Plato's *Republic*." In *The Blackwell Guide to Plato's Republic*, edited by Gerasmios Santas, 146–165. Malden: Blackwell, 2006.

Lorenz, H. *The Brute Within: Appetitive Desire in Plato and Aristotle*. Oxford, UK: Clarendon Press, 2006.

Lotter, H. P. P. "The Significance of Poverty and Wealth in Plato's *Republic*." *South African Journal of Philosophy* 22 (2003): 189–206.

Madhu, R. C. "Plato's Homer." *Ancient Philosophy* 19 (1999): 87–95.

Madigan, A. "*Laches* and *Charmides* v. the Craft Analogy." *New Scholasticism* 59 (1985): 377–87.

Marrou, H. *A History of Education in Antiquity*. Translated by G. Lamb. Madison: University of Wisconsin Press, 1956.

McAvoy, Martin. "Carnal Knowledge in the *Charmides*." In *Dialogues with Plato*, edited by Eugenio Benitez, 62–102. Edmonton, Canada: Academic Printing and Publishing, 1996.

McCabe-Smith, M. "Silencing the Sophists: The Drama of the *Euthydemus*." *Proceedings of the Boston Area Colloquium in Ancient Philosophy* 15 (1999): 139–168.

McCoy, M. *Plato on the Rhetoric of Philosophers and Sophists*. Cambridge, UK: Cambridge University Press, 2011.

McGuirk, J. "Eros in Platonic Friendship and the *Lysis* Failure." *Yearbook of the Irish Philosophical Society* 11 (1991): 127–37.

McKee, P. "Surprise Endings: Cephalus and the Indispensable Teacher of *Republic* X." *Philosophical Investigations* 31 (2008): 68–82.
McKim, R. "Socratic Self-Knowledge and 'Knowledge of Knowledge' in Plato's *Charmides*." *Transactions of the American Philological Association* 115 (1985): 59–77.
McKirahan, R. "Socrates and Protagoras on Holiness and Justice (*Protagoras* 330c–332a)." *Phoenix* 39 (1985): 342–354.
McKirahan, R. "Socrates and Protagoras on Sophrosune and Justice: *Protagoras* 333–334." *Apeiron* 18 (1984): 19–25.
McPherran Mark. *The Religion of Socrates*. University Park: Pennsylvania State University Press, 1996.
Merlan, P. "Form and Content in Plato's Philosophy." *Journal of the History of Ideas* 8 (1947): 406–430.
Michelini, Ann, ed. *Plato as Author: The Rhetoric of Philosophy*. Leiden, Neth.: Brill, 2003.
Migliori, M. ed. *Plato Ethicus: Philosophy Is Life*. Sankt Augustin: Academia Verlag, 2003.
Miller, M. *Plato's* Parmenides: *The Conversion of the Soul*. University Park: The Pennsylvania State University Press, 1991.
Miller, M. *The Philosopher in Plato's* Statesman. The Hague: Nijhoff, 1980.
Mooney, B. "Plato's Theory of Love in the *Lysis*." *Irish Journal of Philosophy* 7 (1990): 131–159.
Morris, T. F. "Knowledge of Knowledge and of Lack of Knowledge in the *Charmides*." *International Studies in Philosophy* 21 (1989): 49–61.
Morris, T. F. "Plato's *Lysis*." *Philosophy Research Archives* 11 (1985): 269–279.
Morrison, D., ed. *The Cambridge Companion to Socrates*. Cambridge, UK: Cambridge University Press, 2011.
Morrison, J. S. "The Place of Protagoras in Athenian Public Life (360–415 B.C.)." *Classical Quarterly* 35 (1941): 1–16.
Mortley, R. J. "Plato and the Sophistic Heritage of Protagoras." *Eranos* 67 (1969): 24–32.
Naddaff, R. *Exiling the Poets*. Chicago: University of Chicago Press, 2003.
Nails, D. *Agora, Academy and the Conduct of Philosophy*. Dordrecht, Neth.: Kluwer, 1995.
Nails, D. "The Dramatic Date of Plato's *Republic*." *Classical Journal* 93 (1998): 383–396.
Nails, D. *The People of Plato*. Indianapolis: Hackett, 2002.
Nehamas, A. "Plato and the Mass Media in Aesthetics and the Histories of Art." *The Monist* 71 (1988): 214–234.
Nehamas, A. "Socratic Intellectualism." *Proceedings of the Boston Area Colloquium in Ancient Philosophy* 2 (1986): 275–316.
Nehamas, A. "What Did Socrates Teach and to Whom Did He Teach It?" *Review of Metaphysics* 46 (1992): 279-306.
Nehamas, A. *The Art of Living: Socratic Reflections from Plato to Foucault.* Berkeley: University of California Press, 1998.
Nehamas, A. "Voices of Silence: On Gregory Vlastos' Socrates." *Arion* 2 (1992): 156–186.
Nichols, M. *Socrates on Friendship and Community: Reflections on Plato's* Symposium, Phaedrus, *and* Lysis. Cambridge, UK: Cambridge University Press, 2009.
Nietzsche. F. *The Anti-Christ, Ecce Homo, and Twilight of the Idols*. Translated by Aaron Ridley and Judith Norman. Cambridge, UK: Cambridge University Press, 2005.
Nightengale, A. *Genres in Dialogue: Plato and the Construct of Philosophy*. Cambridge, UK: Cambridge University Press, 1985.
Nightengale, A. *Spectacles of Truth in Classical Greek Philosophy*. Cambridge, UK: Cambridge University Press. 2004.
North, H. *Sophrosyne: Self-Knowledge and Self-Restraint in Greek Literature*. Ithaca, NY: Cornell University Press, 1966.
Notomi, N. "Critias and the Origins of Political Philosophy." In *Plato:* Euthydemus, Charmides. *Proceedings of the V Symposium Platonicum. Selected Papers vol.13*. Edited by Tom Robinson and Luc Brisson, 237–249. Sankt Augustin: Academia Verlag, 2000.
Nussbaum, M. *Cultivating Humanity*. Cambridge, MA: Harvard University Press, 1997.
Nussbaum, M. *Fragility of Goodness: Luck and Ethics in Greek Tragedy and Philosophy*. Cambridge, MA: Harvard University Press, 1986.

Nussbaum, M. *Love's Knowledge: Essay on Philosophy and Literature*. New York: Oxford University Press, 1990.
Nussbaum, M. "Upheavals of Thought: The Intelligence of Emotions." *Graduate Faculty Philosophy Journal* 23 (2002): 235–238.
O'Brien, D. "Socrates and Protagoras on Virtue." In *Oxford Studies in Ancient Philosophy* 34, edited by D. Sedley, 59–131. Oxford, UK: Oxford University Press, 2003.
O'Connor, D. "Rewriting the Poets in Plato's Characters." In *Cambridge Companion to Plato's Republic*, edited by G. R. F. Ferrari, 55–89. Cambridge, UK: Cambridge University Press, 2007.
O'Connor, D. "Socrates and Political Ambition: The Dangerous Game." *Proceedings of the Boston Area Colloquium in Ancient Philosophy* 15 (1999): 31–51.
Pangle, L. "Friendship and Human Neediness in Plato's *Lysis*." *Ancient Philosophy* 21 (2001): 305–323.
Parke, H. D. *Festivals of Athens*. Ithaca: Cornell University Press, 1977.
Parry, R. "The Craft of Ruling in Plato's *Euthydemus* and *Republic*." *Phronesis* 48 (2003): 1–28.
Pearson, L. "Force and Persuasion in Plato's *Republic*." PhD diss., Waco, TX: Baylor University, 2009.
Pelling, C., ed. *Greek Tragedy and the Historian*. Oxford, UK: Clarendon, 1997.
Penner T., and C. Rowe. *Plato's* Lysis. Cambridge, UK: Cambridge University Press, 2005.
Penner T. "The Unity of Virtue." *Philosophical Review* 82 (1973): 35–68.
Penner, T. "What Laches and Nicias Miss—And Whether Socrates Thinks Courage Is Merely a Part of Virtue." *Ancient Philosophy* 12 (1992): 1–27.
Planeaux, C. "Socrates, Alcibiades, and Plato's *Ta Poteideia*: Does the *Charmides* Have an Historical Setting?" *Mnemosyne* 52 (1998): 72–77.
Planeaux, C. "Socrates, an Unreliable Narrator? The Dramatic Setting of the *Lysis*." *Classical Philology* 96 (2001): 60–68.
Plass, P. "Philosophic Anonymity and Irony in the Platonic Dialogues." *American Journal of Philology* 85 (1964): 254–278.
Plato. *Charmides*. Translated by Rosamond Kent Sprague. In *Plato. Complete Works*, edited by J. Cooper, 630–663. Indianapolis: Hackett 1997.
Plato. *Charmides*. Translated by Thomas West and Grace Starry West. Indianapolis: Hackett 1986.
Plato. *Euthydemus*. Translated by Rosamond Kent Sprague. In *Plato. Complete Works*, edited by J. Cooper, 708–745. Indianapolis: Hackett 1997.
Plato. *Plato. Complete Works*. Edited by John Cooper. Indianapolis: Hackett, 1997.
Plato. *Platonis Opera*. Edited by Johannes Burnet. Oxford, UK: Oxford University Press, 1903.
Plato. *Plato's* Protagoras *and* Meno. Translated by Robert Bartlett. Ithaca, NY: Cornell University Press, 2004.
Plato. *Plato's* Protagoras. Translated by B. A. F. Hubbard and E. F. Karnofsky. Chicago: University of Chicago Press, 1982.
Plato. *Protagoras*. Translated by Stanley Lombardo and Karen Bell. Indianapolis: Hackett, 1992.
Plato. *The* Republic *of Plato*. Translated by Allan Bloom. New York: Basic Books, 1991.
Plax, M. "Crito in Plato's *Euthydemus*: The Lover of Family and of Money." *Polis* 17 (2000): 35–59.
Press, G., ed. *Plato's Dialogues: New Studies and Interpretations*. Lanham, MD: Rowman and Littlefield, 1993.
Press, G. *Plato : A Guide for the Perplexed*. New York: Continuum, 2007.
Press, G. "The State of the Question in the Study of Plato." *Southern Journal of Philosophy* 34 (1996): 507–32.
Reece, R. "Drama, Narrative, and Socratic Erōs in Plato's *Charmides*." *Interpretation* 26 (1998): 65–76.
Renault, M. *The Last of the Wine*. New York: Vintage, 1984.
Reeve, C. D. C. "Vlastos's Socrates: Ironist and Moral Philosopher." *PSA Study Group in Greek Political Thought* 11 (1992): 72–82.

Rice, D. "Plato on Force: The Conflict Between His Psychology and Political Sociology and His Definition of Temperance in the *Republic*." *History of Political Thought* 10 (1989): 565–576.
Rickless, S. "Socrates' Moral Intellectualism." *Pacific Philosophical Quarterly* 79 (1998): 355–367.
Robb, K. *Literacy and Paideia in Ancient Greece*. Oxford, UK: Oxford University Press, 1994.
Robb, K. "Orality, Literacy and the Dialogue Form." In *Plato's Dialogues—The Dialogical Approach*, edited by Richard Hart and Victorino Tejera, 29–64. Lewiston: The Edwin Mellen Press, 1997.
Roberts, R. *Emotions. An Essay in Aid of Moral Psychology*. Cambridge, UK: Cambridge University Press, 2003.
Roberts, R. *The Schooled Heart*. Cambridge, UK: Cambridge University Press, 2003.
Robinson T. and Luc Brisson, eds. *Plato: Euthydemus, Charmides. Proceedings of the V Symposium Platonicum. Selected Papers*, vol. 13. Sankt Augustin: Academia Verlag, 2000.
Roochnik, D. *Beautiful City*. Ithaca: Cornell University Press, 2003.
Roochnik, D. "Irony and Accessibility." *Political Theory* 25 (1997): 869–886.
Roochnik, D. "The Serious Play of Plato's *Euthydemus*." *Interpretation* 18 (1990): 211–232.
Rorty, A. "Commentary on Nehamas: The Limits of Socratic Intellectualism: Did Socrates Teach Arete?" *Proceedings of the Boston Area Colloquium in Ancient Philosophy* 2 (1986): 317–330.
Rosen, S. "Is Metaphysics Possible?" *Review of Metaphysics* 45 (1991): 235–257.
Rosen, S. *Plato's Republic. A Study*. New Haven, CT: Yale University Press, 2008.
Rosen, S. *Plato's Sophist: The Drama of the Original and Image*. New Haven, CT: Yale University Press, 1983.
Rosen, S. *Plato's Statesman: The Web of Politics*. New Haven, CT: Yale University Press, 1995.
Rosen, S. *Plato's Symposium*. New Haven, CT: Yale University Press, 1968.
Rosen, S. "The Role of Eros in Plato's *Republic*." *Review of Metaphysics* 18 (1965): 452–475.
Rosenstock, B. "Rereading the *Republic*." *Arethusa* 16 (1983): 219–246.
Roth, M. "Did Plato Nod? Some Conjectures on Egoism and Friendship in the *Lysis*." *Archiv für Geschichte der Philosophie* 77 (1995): 1–20.
Rowe, C. *Plato and the Art of Philosophical Writing*. Cambridge, UK: Cambridge University Press, 2007.
Rowe, C. "Platonic Irony." *Nova Tellus: Anuario del Centro de Estudios Classicos* 5 (1987): 83–101.
Rowe, C. "The *Lysis* and the *Symposium*: Aporia and Euporia?" In *Plato:* Euthydemus, Charmides. *Proceedings of the V Symposium Platonicum. Selected Papers*, vol. 13, edited by Tom Robinson and Luc Brisson, 205–215. Sankt Augustin: Academia Verlag, 2000.
Rubarth, S. "Plato, McLuhan, and the Technology of Irony. *International Studies in Philosophy* 34 (2002): 95–114.
Russon, J., and John Sallis, eds. *Retracing the Platonic Text*. Evanston, IL: Northwestern University Press, 2000.
Rutherford, R. *The Art of Plato: Ten Essays in Platonic Interpretation*. Cambridge, UK: Cambridge University Press, 1995.
Rutherford, R. "Unifying the *Protagoras*." *Apeiron* 25 (1992): 135–156.
Ryle, G. *Plato's Progress*. Cambridge, UK: Cambridge University Press, 1966.
Savan, D. "Self-Predication in *Protagoras* 330–331." *Phronesis* 9 (1964): 130-135.
Sayre, K. *Plato's Literary Garden: How to Read a Platonic Dialogue*. South Bend, IN: Notre Dame Press, 1995.
Scheier, C. "The Unity of the *Protagoras*: On the Structure and Position of a Platonic Dialogue." *Graduate Faculty Philosophy Journal* 17 (1994): 59–81.
Schmid, T. *Plato's Charmides and the Socratic Ideal of Rationality*. Albany: State University of New York Press, 1998.
Scolnicov, S. "Plato's Ethics of Irony." In *Plato Ethicus: Philosophy Is Life*. Edited by Maurizio Migliori, 289–300. Sankt Augustin: Academia Verlag, 2003.

Scott, G., ed. *Philosophy in Dialogue Form: Plato's Many Devices*. Evanston, IL: Northwestern University Press, 2007.
Scott, G. A., ed. *Does Socrates Have a Method? Rethinking the Elenchus in Plato's Dialogues and Beyond*. University Park: Pennsylvania State University Press, 2002.
Scott, G. *Plato's Socrates as Educator*. Albany: SUNY Press, 2000.
Sedley, D. "Socratic Irony in the Platonist Commentators." In *New Directions in Platonic Interpretation*, edited by Julia Annas and C. J. Rowe, 37–57. Washington, D.C.: Center for Hellenic Studies, 2002.
Seery, J. "Politics as Ironic Community: On Themes of Descent and Return in Plato's *Republic*." *Political Theory* 16 (1988): 229–256.
Segal, C. "The Myth Was Saved." *Hermes* 106 (1978): 315–337.
Segal C. "Tragic Beginnings: Narration, Voice, and Authority in the Prologues of Greek Drama." *Yale Classical Studies* 29 (1992): 85–110.
Smith, N., and Paul B. Woodruff, eds. *Reason and Religion in Socratic Philosophy*. Oxford, UK: Oxford University Press, 2000.
Solomon, R. "Reasons for Love." *Journal for the Theory of Social Behavior* 32 (2002): 115–144.
Solomon, R. "The Joy of Philosophy: Thinking Thin Versus the Passionate Life." *Review of Metaphysics* 55 (2002): 876–878.
Sprague, R. "Plato's Sophistry." *Proceedings of the Aristotelian Society* 51 (1997): 21–61.
Strauss, L. *City and Man*. Chicago: Rand McNally, 1964.
Strauss, L. *On Plato's* Symposium. Edited by Seth Benardete. Chicago: University of Chicago Press, 2001.
Strauss, L. "On the *Euthydemus*." *Interpretation* 1 (1970): 1–20.
Strauss, L. "Plato." In *History of Political Philosophy*. 3rd edition. Edited by Leo Strauss and J. Cropsey. Chicago: University of Chicago Press, 1987.
Stalley, R. "Sophrosune in the *Charmides*." In *Plato:* Euthydemus *and* Charmides. *Proceedings of the V Symposium Platonicum. Selected Papers*, vol. 13, edited by Tom Robinson and Luc Brisson, 265–277. Sankt Augustin: Academia Verlag, 2000.
Stern, P. "Tyranny and Self-Knowledge: Critias and Charmides in Plato's *Charmides*." *American Political Science Review* 93 (1999): 399–412.
Stokes, M. *Plato's Socratic Conversations*. Cambridge, UK: Cambridge University Press, 1986.
Stroud, R. "The Gravestone of Socrates' Friend, Lysis." *Hesperia* 53 (1984): 355–60.
Svenbro, Jesper. "The Interior Voice: On the Invention of Silent Reading." In *Nothing to Do with Dionysos. Athenian Drama in its Social Context*, edited by J. Winkler and F. Zeitlin, 366–384. Princeton: Princeton University Press, 1990.
Szlezák, T. *Reading Plato*. New York: Routledge, 1999.
Tarrant, D. "Plato as Dramatist." *The Journal of Hellenic Studies* 75 (1955): 82–89.
Tarrant, H. "Chronology and Narrative Apparatus in Plato's Dialogues." *Electronic Antiquity* I, no. 8 (1994): scholar.lib.vt.edu/ejournals/ElAnt/V1N8/tarrant.html (accessed 9/17/12).
Tarrant, H. "Orality and Plato's Narrative Dialogues." In *Voice into Text*, edited by Ian Worthington, 129–147. Leiden: Brill, 1996.
Tarrant, H. "Plato, Prejudice, and the Mature-Age Student in Antiquity." *Dialogues with Plato*. Edited by E. Benetiz. *Apeiron* 29 (1996): 105–20.
Tarrant, H. "Plato's *Euthydemus* and a Platonist Education Program." *Dionysius* 21 (2003): 7–22.
Taylor, C. C. W. *Plato's* Protagoras. Oxford, UK: Oxford University Press, 2002.
Taylor, C. C. W. *Socrates*. Oxford, UK: Oxford University Press, 1998.
Tejera, B. *Rewriting the History of Ancient Greek Philosophy*. Westport, CT: Greenwood Press, 1997.
Tejera, V. "On the Form and Authenticity of the *Lysis*." *Ancient Philosophy* 10 (1990): 173–191.
Tejera, V. *Plato's Dialogues One by One*. Lanham, MD: University Press of America, 1999.
Tessitore, A. "Plato's *Lysis:* An Introduction to Philosophic Friendship." *Southern Journal of Philosophy* 28 (1990): 115–132.

Thayer, H. "Plato's Style: Temporal, Dramatic and Semantic Levels in the Dialogues." In *Plato's Dialogues—The Dialogical Approach*, edited by Richard Hart and Victorino Tejera, 85–129. Lewiston: The Edwin Mellen Press, 1997.
Thesleff, H. "Looking for Clues. An Interpretation of Some Literary Aspects of Plato's Two-Level Model." In *Plato's Dialogues: New Studies and Interpretations*, edited by G. Press, 17–45. Lanham, MD: Rowman and Littlefield, 1993.
Thesleff, H. "Plato and His Public." In *Noctes Atticae*, edited by B. Amden, 289–301. Copenhagen: Museum Tusculanum Press, 2002.
Thesleff, H. "Platonic Chronology." *Phronesis* 34 (1989): 1–26.
Thesleff, H. *Studies in Platonic Chronology.* Helsinki: Societas Scientiarum Fennica, 1982.
Thesleff, H. "Studies in Plato's Two-Level Model." *Commentationes Humanarum Litterarum* 113. Helsinki: Societas Scientiarum Fennica, 1999.
Thesleff, H. "The Early Version of Plato's *Republic*." *Arctos* 31 (1997): 149–174.
Thesleff, H. *The Philosopher Conducting Dialectic.* In *Plato's Dialogues: New Studies and Interpretations*, edited by G. Press, 53–66. Lanham, MD: Rowman and Littlefield, 1993.
Thornton, B. S. "Cultivating Sophistry." *Arion* 6 (1998): 180–204.
Tindale, G. "Plato's *Lysis*: A Reconsideration." *Apeiron* 18 (1984): 102–109.
Toulmin, S. *Return to Reason.* Cambridge, MA: Harvard University Press, 2001.
Tsouna, V. "Socrates' Attack on Intellectualism in the *Charmides*." *Apeiron* 30 (1997): 63–78.
Tuckey, G. *Plato's Charmides.* Cambridge, UK: Cambridge University Press, 1951.
Tuozzo, T. *Plato's Charmides.* Cambridge, UK: Cambridge University Press, 2011.
Tuozzo, T. "What's Wrong with These Cities? The Social Dimension of *Sophrosune* in Plato's *Charmides*." *Journal of the History of Philosophy* 39 (2001): 321–350.
Van Der Ben, N. *The Charmides of Plato: Problems and Interpretations.* Amsterdam: B. R. Grüner, 1985.
Vander Waerdt, P. *The Socratic Movement.* Ithaca: Cornell University Press, 1994.
Vasiliou, I. "Conditional Irony in the Socratic Dialogues." *Classical Quarterly* 49 (1999): 456–472.
Vernant, J. P. and M. Detienne. "Cunning Intelligence in Greek Culture and Society." Translated by J. Lloyd. Chicago: University of Chicago Press, 1991.
Versenyi, L. "Plato's *Lysis*." *Phronesis* 20 (1975): 185–198.
Vlastos, G. *Socrates: Ironist and Moral Philosopher.* Ithaca: Cornell University Press, 1991.
Vlastos, G. *Socratic Studies.* Cambridge, UK: Cambridge University Press, 1994.
Vlastos, G. "The Individual as the Object of Love in Plato." In *Platonic Studies*, 3–11. Princeton: Princeton University Press, 1973.
Vlastos, G. "The Unity of the Virtues in the *Protagoras*." In *Platonic Studies*, 221–267. Princeton: Princeton University Press, 1981.
Wakefield, J. "Why Justice and Holiness are Similar: *Protagoras* 330–331." *Phronesis* 32 (1987): 267–276.
Walsh, J. "The Dramatic Dates of Plato's *Protagoras* and the Lesson of *Arete*." *Classical Quarterly* 34 (1984): 101–106.
Ward, A., ed. *Socrates: Reason or Unreason as the Foundation of European Identity*, edited by Ann Ward. Cambridge, UK: Cambridge Scholars Press, 2007.
Ward, A. "Statesmanship and Citizenship in Plato's *Protagoras*." *The Journal of Value Inquiry* 25 (1991): 319–333.
Waugh, J. "Neither Published nor Perished: The Dialogues as Speech, not Text." In *The Third Way: New Directions in Platonic Studies*, edited by Francisco Gonzalez, 61–80. Lanham, MD: Rowman and Littlefield, 1995.
Weiss, R. "Courage, Confidence, and Wisdom in the *Protagoras*." *Ancient Philosophy* V (1985): 11–24.
Weiss, R. *The Socratic Paradox and Its Enemies.* Chicago: University of Chicago Press, 2006.
West, E. "Plato's Audiences or How Plato Replies to the Fifth-Century Intellectual Mistrust of Letters." In *The Third Way: New Directions in Platonic Studies*, edited by Francisco Gonzalez, 41–60. Lanham, MD: Rowman and Littlefield, 1995.

Wilson, P. "Leading the Tragic Khoros: Tragic Prestige in the Democratic City." In *Greek Tragedy and the Historian*, edited by Christopher Pelling, 81–108. Oxford, UK: Clarendon Press, 1997.
Winkler, J., and F. Zeitlin, eds. *Nothing To Do with Dionysos. Athenian Drama in its Social Context*. Princeton: Princeton University Press, 1990.
Woodbury, L. "Simonides on Arete." *Transactions of the American Philological Association* 84 (1953): 135–163.
Woodruff, P. "Socrates on the Parts of Virtue." *Canadian Journal of Philosophy* (1976): 101–116. Suppl. vol. 2.
Woolf, R. "The Written Word in Plato's *Protagoras*." *Ancient Philosophy* 19 (1999): 21–30.
Worthington, I., ed. *Voice into Text*. Leiden, Neth.: Brill, 1996.
Yong, P. "Intellectualism and Moral Habituation in Plato's Earlier Dialogues." *Apeiron* 29 (1996): 49–61.
Yunis, H. "Writing for Reading. Thucydides, Plato, and the Emergence of the Critical Reader." In *Written Texts and the Rise of Literate Culture in Ancient Greece*, edited by Harvey Yunis, 189–212. Cambridge, UK: Cambridge University Press, 2003.
Zuckert, C. *Plato's Philosophers*. Chicago: University of Chicago Press, 2009.

Index

Adeimantus, 8, 12, 13, 141, 146, 148, 154, 155, 159, 160, 175, 179, 181; familiarity with Homer, 167, 169–171; opening of the *Republic*, 175; and the regulation of emotion, 161–163, 165n30, 165n32; Socrates' effect on, 171, 172–173
Agathon, 85, 86, 155
Alcibiades, 82, 85, 109, 111, 196; role in the *Protagoras*, 87–90, 92; role in the *Symposium*, 59, 155; Socrates' interest in, 75–77, 90
Allegory of the Cave, 7, 9, 13, 150, 161, 167, 172; narrative elements of, 182–185; rhetorical effect of, 174, 185, 204
Apollodorus, 69n49, 79, 82, 92
aporia, 29, 30, 33, 44, 49, 52, 196, 197, 199; auditors' experience of, 18; in the *Charmides*, 44, 49, 52; in the *Euthydemus*, 122, 124, 133; in the *Lysis*, 17; in the *Republic*, 179; interlocutors' experience of ; in the *Charmides*, 49, 56; in the *Euthydemus*, 123, 128; in the *Lysis*, 18, 22, 24, 25, 26, 29, 30; in the *Protagoras*, 81, 90, 120; in the *Republic*, 174; relationship to narrative and friendship, 33–35; Socrates' own, 8, 13; in the *Charmides*, 54, 56; in the *Euthydemus*, 124, 136; in the *Lysis*, 18, 26, 27, 34; in the *Protagoras*, 81, 93; in the *Republic*, 159, 167, 180
Aristophanes, 98n28, 155
Aristophanic allusions, 79, 139n11
Aristotle, 13, 15n12, 94, 164n13, 192, 195–196
auditor, 1, 2, 4, 10, 11; of the *Charmides*, 10, 40, 41, 42–44, 45, 46, 49, 50; of the *Euthydemus*, 101–104, 129–133; of the *Lysis*, 18, 19, 23, 25, 26, 27, 30, 33–35; narrative training of, 5–9; Plato as auditor of, 65–42; possible autonomy of, 53–55, 56, 60, 62–63; of the *Protagoras*, 74; opening frame, 74–78; pedagogical effect on, 96; similarity with Hippocrates, 78–80; of the *Republic*, 151, 174, 176, 177, 178–179, 181, 184, 185, 188

Bartlett, Robert, 75
Benardete, Seth, 40–41, 63, 68n35, 200
Bentley, Robert, 77
Berger, Harry, 92, 93
Beversluis, J., 53
Bolotin, David, 24
Brann, Eva, 40, 52
Bruell, Christopher, 40, 55, 68n28
Burger, Ronna, 195
Byrd, Miriam, 135

Callias, 81, 84–85, 87, 88–89, 89; house of, 75, 77, 79–80, 83, 84, 90, 91, 93
Cephalus, 12, 141, 154, 154, 155, 159, 176, 184; and self-mastery, 151–153
Chaerephon, 5, 10, 42, 58, 75, 78; model of intemperance, 44–46
Chance, Thomas, 128, 140n31
Charmides, 4, 6, 10, 40; blush, 81; headache, 41, 47, 51; model of intemperance, 46–51
Charmides, 1, 2, 4, 5, 10, 39; narrative setting, 40–41; opening scene, 42–44; Socratic state of mind in, 58–61
Clinias, 11, 101, 102; blush, 112; exchange with the brothers, 109–115; exchanges with Socrates, 115–117, 120
Coby, Patrick, 77, 78, 82, 94
Cooper, John, 94
cooperation, 39, 45, 57, 93, 99n59, 102, 107, 112, 116, 120, 138
Cratylus, 2
Critias, 10, 40–41, 42, 44, 45, 58, 62, 138; with Charmides against Socrates, 55–57; in *Protagoras*, 84, 85, 87, 89; as symbol of intemperance, 51–55
Crito, 4, 9, 11, 101–103; and aporia, 124; ending exchange, 129–133; opening frame of *Euthydemus*, 103–108; narrative about speechwriter, 129–131
Critobulus, 106, 107, 109, 113, 131, 133, 138
Ctesippus, 11; in the *Euthydemus*, 101, 102, 109, 110–111, 117–120; in the *Lysis*, 18, 19–22, 24; attitude toward Hippothales, 19–20; compared to Hippothales, 21; compared to Menexenus, 22–24; Socrates' preference for, 29

daimon, 31, 109, 122, 134, 187
Dionysodorus, 11, 101, 102, 103, 104, 105, 106, 109; blush, 126; exchanges with Clinias, 109–115, 116–117; exchanges with Ctesippus, 117–120, 124, 125; Socrates' desire to study with, 133, 134; Socrates' response to, 128–129

Echecrates, 106, 121
Eco, Umberto, 4

eiron, 13, 192, 196; Aristotle's view of, 196; Socrates as, 197
eironeia, 192; narrative, 195–199
elenchus, 30, 31, 58, 80, 90, 132, 158, 198
emotions: of the auditors: in *Charmides*, 54; in *Euthydemus*, 104; in *Protagoras*, 76–78, 79; and harmony, 12, 149–151; and Homer, 77; and irony, 192, 193–194, 195, 196–197; of the interlocutors; in *Charmides*, 44–45; in *Euthydemus*, 112, 120, 125, 128; in *Lysis*, 19, 20, 23, 28; in *Protagoras*, 78, 79–81, 82, 90; in *Republic*, 151, 152–153, 156, 157, 160, 161–162; in narrative commentary, 5, 6, 10, 12; in *Charmides*, 41, 58–59; in *Euthydemus*, 102, 126, 135, 136, 137; in *Lysis*, 26, 30, 31, 32; in *Protagoras*, 74, 91, 92, 94–96; in *Republic*, 167, 176, 177–178, 192; role in philosophy, 2–3, 13; in *Charmides*, 59–61; in *Euthydemus*, 134, 137; in *Lysis*, 23, 28, 30, 31, 32; in *Protagoras*, 73, 74, 94–96; in *Republic*, 145, 148, 149, 158, 161, 173, 178–179, 198–199; and self-mastery, 6, 29, 141–145, 148; Socrates' attention to in others; in *Lysis*, 24, 26, 28; in *Euthydemus*, 102, 112, 113, 126; in *Charmides*, 50–51, 52; in *Protagoras*, 78, 79–81, 82, 90; in *Republic*, 151, 152–153, 156, 157, 160, 161–162; Socrates' emotional self-awareness, 2, 3, 5, 10, 13; in *Charmides*, 39, 41, 58, 60; in *Euthydemus*, 134, 136; in *Lysis*, 17, 28, 29–30, 34; in *Protagoras*, 73, 74, 91, 92, 94–96; in *Republic*, 167, 175, 180, 181, 201
enslavement, 78, 136, 147
epithumetikon, 6, 141–145, 148, 150, 153, 155, 161, 163, 174, 180
eros, 3, 27, 28, 45, 76, 95, 161, 163
Eryximachus, 76, 84, 155
Euclides, 1
Euthydemus, 11, 101, 102, 103, 104, 105, 106, 109; exchanges with Clinias, 109–115, 116–117; exchanges with Ctesippus, 117–120, 124, 125; Socrates' desire to study with, 133, 134; Socrates' response to, 128–129

Euthydemus, 1, 2, 4, 9, 10, 11, 13; Crito's role in, 103–108, 121–124, 129–133; ending exchange, 129–133; opening frame, 103–108; Socrates' self-disclosure in, 134–138
Euthyphro, 5
Euthyphro, 5, 192, 199

Ferrari, Giovanni, 159
forms, 203–204
Foucault, Michel, 191, 201
friendship, 2, 7, 10, 56, 106, 137, 150, 156, 193; in the *Lysis*, 17, 18, 19, 22, 23, 25, 25–26, 27, 28; relationship to narrative and aporia, 33–35

Gadamer, Hans-Georg, 33, 35
Gagarin, Michael, 82
Glaucon, 7, 8, 12, 13, 138, 141, 144–146, 151–152, 154, 157; and Allegory of the Cave, 182–184; and harmony model, 149, 150–151; and limits of self-mastery, 159; and the Myth of Er, 183–187, 185; response to Socrates, 171, 180
Glaucus, 145, 149
Gonzalez, Francisco, 26, 33, 62, 99n59
Gooch, Paul, 196
Gorgias, 3, 5, 14n2

harmony model, 6, 7, 12, 13, 141, 167, 173, 178, 180; definition of, 149–151
Hadot, Pierre, 191, 198, 201–202, 205n17
Hesiod, 2, 13, 168, 172
Hippias, 4, 82, 85, 86, 87, 89, 90; and his students, 84–85
Hippocrates, 74, 75, 77–78, 105; blush, 80–81, 90; morning encounter with Socrates, 78–82, 86, 87, 88, 90; Socrates' attitude toward, 90, 92, 95, 96
Hippothales, 19–21, 23, 25, 27, 28, 29, 30, 32, 34, 193; blush, 19, 25, 26
Homer: references to in *Protagoras*, 77, 84, 85, 92, 96; Socrates' critique of, 13, 167, 168–174, 183, 185; Socrates as corrective to, 13, 167, 174
Hyland, Drew, 42, 52, 62, 64, 192, 203

intellectualist/intellectualism, 2, 11, 28, 61, 73, 74, 134, 145, 191, 192, 197, 198, 201; revisiting Socrates as intellectualist, 94–96
irony, 4, 5, 11, 13; in *Charmides*, 40; in *Euthydemus*, 107, 135; as philosophical provocation, 192–199; Platonic irony, 199–200; in *Protagoras*, 77, 86, 87; in *Republic*, 156, 157, 168, 169, 178; Socratic irony, 5, 13, 169, 192, 195, 198, 199
Irwin, Terrence, 73, 193

justice, 2, 6–7, 8, 12, 52; Cephalus' definition, 153; in the city, 7, 143, 146, 150–151, 180; Glaucon's view of, 161, 162; as harmony, 12, 141, 150–151; in *Protagoras*, 92, 95–96; in the soul, 6, 144, 145, 146, 150, 163, 180; Polemarchus' definition, 154, 156; Thraysmachus' definition, 157–158

Kahn, Charles, 94
Kalliope, 2
Krenz, Peter, 57, 65

Lada, Ismene, 28
Laches, 3
Lampert, Lawrence, 15n9, 40, 42, 68n30, 81, 98n31, 99n53, 165n27
Landy, Tucker, 60, 64
Latcherman, David, vii
logisitkon, 6, 7, 141, 143–145, 147, 148, 149, 149–150, 161, 168, 175
Long, Christopher, 75, 77
Lorenz, H., 143
Lysis, 1, 2, 4, 6, 10, 13, 17, 35, 193, 199; comparison with *Charmides*, 40, 41, 43, 51, 56, 58; comparison with *Euthydemus*, 130, 134; comparison with *Protagoras*, 74–75; comparison with *Republic*, 175, 176; Socrates' state of mind in, 26–32; structure of, 18
Lysis, 6, 17, 18, 21, 21–26, 27, 28, 29, 30, 31, 34; aptitude for philosophy, 20, 22, 25–27; attitude toward Hippothales, 21; compared to Menexenus, 22, 23–24; Socrates attitude toward, 20, 21, 28

McAvoy, Martin, 41, 60
McCoy, Marina, viii, 61, 75, 97n8
McKim, Richard, 62
Menexenus, 18, 22, 23–25, 24–27, 26, 31
Mill, John Stuart, 202
Minotaur, 123
muse, 2, 12, 13, 15n9, 16n21, 77, 78, 96, 111, 135, 148, 173, 188
Myth of Er, 13, 145, 167, 174, 182, 184; narrative dimensions of, 185–188

Naddaff, Ramona, 171
Nails, Debra, 76, 138n4
narrative: abandonment of, 1, 14n1; audience, 3, 43, 74, 106, 151; *eironeia*, 195–199; frame, 12, 18, 61, 62, 101, 179, 203; Homeric, 13, 167, 185; irony, 13, 192–194, 200; mediation, 3, 9; pedagogy, 11, 106, 184; Plato's use of, 1, 2, 4, 167, 195, 196; practice of philosophy, 7, 10, 133, 168, 191; self-care, 13, 58, 60, 61, 62, 191; self-reflection in, 4, 8, 10, 13, 17, 51, 62, 65, 144, 167, 174, 185, 201; setting, 10–11, 17, 40–41, 44, 74, 79, 103
Nehamas, Alexander, 15n12, 73, 194, 199
Nietzsche, Friedrich, 15n12, 202
Notomi, N., 54
Nussbaum, Martha, 28, 73, 94

Odysseus, 68n30, 85

Pangle, Lorraine, 35
Pausanias, 76, 85, 86
pedagogy, 5, 11; dramatic level, 11, 80, 81, 174, 182; narrative level, 45, 74, 80, 87, 95, 96, 106, 107, 113, 167, 174, 184; Socrates' motivation, 45, 68n33, 90, 101–102, 106, 176; Socratic model, 73, 75, 80, 131; Sophistic, 83–86, 106, 109–114, 117–120, 125–129
Phaedo, 104, 121
Phaedo, 104, 106, 121, 124, 188
Phaedrus, 4, 33, 60, 202
Phaedrus, 76, 84, 202
Philebus, 5
Philoctetes, 61
Plato, 1, 2, 9, 12; pedagogical motivation in *Charmides*, 42, 43, 61, 62, 66; pedagogical motivation in *Euthydemus*, 101, 129, 134, 138; pedagogical motivation in *Lysis*, 28, 33, 35; pedagogical motivation in *Protagoras*, 73, 82, 87, 93, 95, 96; pedagogical motivation in *Republic*, 167, 173, 174, 176, 185, 188; use of irony, 199–200; view of philosophy, 192, 195–197, 201–202
Plax, Max, 106, 109
poetry, 13, 28, 34, 59, 70n63, 77, 135, 143, 161, 163, 167, 183; Socratic critique of, 168–174
Polemarchus, 8, 12, 99n52, 141, 152, 153, 156–157, 159, 160, 165n24, 175, 177, 181; and self-mastery, 154–156
political, 10, 39, 57, 63–66, 76, 101, 105, 108, 144, 145, 147, 151, 202
Potidaea, 40, 55, 58, 75
Prodicus, 77, 82, 85–86, 87, 89, 109, 132, 172
Protagoras, 1, 2, 4, 5, 10, 11; comparison with *Charmides*, 134, 138; comparison with *Euthydemus*, 101, 103, 104, 105, 109, 109, 129, 130; narrative frame of, 74–78; reassessing intellectualism in, 94–96; Socrates' narrative description in, 78–90; Socrates' state of mind in, 90–92
Protagoras, 4, 5, 81–82, 172; auditor's interest in, 75, 77; Hippocrates' interest in, 78–81, 82; intellectualism of, 95–96; preference for long speech, 4, 88–89, 92, 93, 186; Socrates' attitude toward, 75–77, 78–81, 90–93, 196

rationalist, 10, 73, 94, 193
rationality, 65, 73, 149
reader, 4, 8, 9; possible effect on in *Euthydemus*, 103, 124, 129, 135; possible effect on in *Charmides*, 40, 45, 50, 55, 62, 66; possible effect on in *Protagoras*, 75, 78, 87, 96; possible effect on in the *Republic*, 182, 188
reason, 2–3, 6, 15n11, 28, 31–32, 54, 58, 59, 60, 73, 94, 106, 144, 145, 175, 193, 197–199, 201
the *Republic*, 1, 2, 3, 4, 5, 7, 8, 10, 12, 13, 141–187; treatment of poetry in, 59, 77,

135
Roochnik, David, 160
Rosen, Stanley, vii, 147–148, 160, 163, 165n24
Rutherford, Richard, 59, 96

satyr, 58
Satyrus, 78–79
Schmid, Thomas, 31, 42, 52, 69n54
Scott, Gary, 16n19, 35n1, 36n16
self-mastery model, 6–7, 12–13, 29, 171, 179; and Adeimantus, 161–163; and Cephalus, 151–153, 176; and Glaucon, 159–161; limitations of, 146–149, 149–150; and Polemarchus, 154–156; and Thrasymachus, 156–157; in the *Republic*, 141–145; relationship with poetry, 173; Socrates' attitude toward, 171, 174
Simmias, 121
Simonides, 85, 86, 89, 177
slave, 1, 8, 78–79, 154, 159, 170, 175
Socrates : as *eiron*, 195–199; as intellectualist, 2, 70n63, 73, 74, 94–96, 134, 191, 192, 197, 198, 201; interest in eros, 3, 25, 28, 45, 76; as model of *sophrosune*, 10, 58–62; as muse, 2, 13, 77–78, 188; self-description, 26–32, 58–61, 90–93, 134–138, 174–181; qualities of narrative pedagogy, 5–9, 106, 184; use of irony, 34, 45, 77, 86, 105, 107–108, 135, 138, 156, 157, 169, 177, 178
Socratic method, 31, 58; method of self-care, 58; question and answer, 89
sophrosune, 10, 39, 42, 44, 45, 48, 49, 52, 53–55, 55–56, 57, 62, 196; Socratic *sophrosune*, 58–61, 65

Sophists, 4, 11, 13, 49, 74, 75, 77, 193; Hippocrates' desire to learn from, 79–81; Socrates' description of in *Euthydemus*, 106–107, 109–115, 117–120, 124–129; Socrates' description of in *Protagoras*, 83–90; Socrates' desire to study with, 105, 107–108, 131
Smith, Nicholas, 36n29, 100n68, 100n74, 205n4, 205n10
Stern, Paul, 65
Strauss, Leo, 103, 139n10
Straussians, 202
Symposium, 3, 15n15, 33, 59, 65, 79, 82, 155, 188

Taylor, Christopher, 202
Tejera, Victorino, 4
Terpsion, 1
Theaetetus, 1
Theaetetus, 1
Theodorus, 1, 40
Thesleff, Holger, 14n2, 16n16
Theseus, 123
Thirty Tyrants, 40, 57, 63–64, 65
Thrasymachus, 5, 7, 8, 12, 69n49, 150, 156, 157–158, 165n27, 177, 193; blush, 8, 158
thumetikon, 6, 141, 144, 149, 150
tyranny, 10, 39, 45, 53, 57, 62, 63–64, 65–66, 87, 165n24, 187, 200

Vasiliou, I., 205n3
Vlastos, Gregory, 33, 192, 193–194, 195

Weiss, Roslyn, 15n12, 94

Zalmoxis, 47
Zuckert, Catherine, 15n9